LACAN—THE UNCONSCIOUS REINVENTED

THE CENTRE FOR FREUDIAN ANALYSIS AND RESEARCH LIBRARY

Series Editors:
Anouchka Grose, Darian Leader, Alan Rowan

CFAR was founded in 1985 with the aim of developing Freudian and Lacanian psychoanalysis in the UK. Lacan's rereading and rethinking of Freud had been neglected in the Anglophone world, despite its important implications for the theory and practice of psychoanalysis. Today, this situation is changing, with a lively culture of training groups, seminars, conferences, and publications.

CFAR offers both introductory and advanced courses in psychoanalysis, as well as a clinical training programme in Lacanian psychoanalysis. It can provide access to Lacanian psychoanalysts working in the UK, and has links with Lacanian groups across the world. The CFAR Library aims to make classic Lacanian texts available in English for the first time, as well as publishing original research in the Lacanian field.

OTHER TITLES IN THE SERIES

- *Lacan and Lévi-Strauss or The Return to Freud (1951–1957)*
  by Markos Zafiropoulos

- *The Trainings of the Psychoanalyst*
  by Annie Tardits

- *Sexual Ambiguities*
  by Geneviève Morel

- *Freud and the Desire of the Psychoanalyst*
  by Serge Cottet

www.cfar.org.uk

LACAN—THE UNCONSCIOUS REINVENTED

Colette Soler

Translated by
Esther Faye and Susan Schwartz

KARNAC

First published in 2014 by
Karnac Books Ltd
118 Finchley Road
London NW3 5HT

Originally published as *Lacan, L'inconscient Réinventé*
Presses Universitaires de France 2009

British Library Cataloguing in Publication Data

A C.I.P. for this book is available from the British Library

ISBN-13: 978-1-78049-099-1

Typeset by V Publishing Solutions Pvt Ltd., Chennai, India

www.karnacbooks.com

CONTENTS

ACKNOWLEDGEMENTS

This volume takes up, orders, and problematises some of my contributions from over the last ten years. They are all linked to my seminars held during this time in the School of Psychoanalysis of the Forums of the Lacanian Field. When it seemed necessary, I have provided endnotes to give details of the date and place of publication.

Colette Soler

The translators gratefully acknowledge the invaluable assistance of Claire Dumans, Leonardo Rodríguez, and Chantal Degril.

Esther Faye and Susan Schwartz

ABOUT THE AUTHOR

Colette Soler, holder of the University Agrégation and a psychoanalyst trained by Jacques Lacan, practises and teaches psychoanalysis in Paris. She is a founder member of the School of Psychoanalysis of the Forums of the Lacanian Field, and the author of *What Lacan Said about Women* (Other Press, 2003), *Lacanian Affects* (Routledge, forthcoming), as well as numerous other publications.

INTRODUCTION

I am going to question the foundations of the trajectory of Lacan's teaching. After the excitement of his staggering intervention at Rome in 1953 with "Function and field of speech and language"—which renewed Freudian vocabulary for the first time in France—his continual advances have always made students and readers uneasy. In this teaching that extends over twenty years, there is not a single halt, but additions, revisions, and indeed even reversals.

It is true that some sentences persist and endure over time—"the unconscious, it speaks", "the unconscious is structured like a language"—but, and there is a "but", these sentences no longer signify the same thing from one end of his teaching to the other. From the intersubjective speech of the 1950s to the "I speak with my body" of the 1970s, there is a world of difference that involves a redefinition of the unconscious itself.

Hence the rich and colourful texture of the small world of those who call themselves Lacanian. How can one situate oneself amongst the upholders of pure speech—who, indeed, are in competition with the psychotherapies that borrowed it from them long ago—or those who swear solely by object *a*, or by *jouissance*, or by the clinic and nothing but the clinic, or by topology, or by the Borromean knot, etc.?

It is a strange result. In fact, did not Freud himself advance in successive stages, contesting in 1916 his first theory of anxiety in its relation to the symptom, renewing in 1920 his definition of the unconscious by emphasising repetition and the death drive and revising his doctrine of the psychical apparatus? This did not produce the idea of a first, a second, or even a third Freud and the unity of his enunciation is not in doubt as it is with Lacan. Is it because the difficulties in reading Freud are not less but more masked by a style that is always systematically didactic? With Lacan, on the contrary, the difficulties are on the surface, while the logic of his successive steps remains implicit.

It is a fact that Lacan proceeded by assertion rather than by explanation, multiplying surprising formulas and apparent paradoxes over the years. Some saw this as the sign of a mischievous character seeking to impress. I see rather another form of didacticism: Lacan tried to wake up his audience. He had reasons for believing them asleep, he who had experienced, to his cost, the entropy of Post-Freudian analytic thought. Moreover, his success remains quite uncertain, for after the first burst of incredulity the most striking of his formulas became all the more prone to repetition, to being transformed into what he called "pretty fossils".

These surprises in transmission would not garner so much attention in other fields. Who would reproach the poet, the painter or artists in general for producing something new, like the conjurer who draws a rabbit out of the hat? Psychoanalysis, however, is not art, but a social bond governed by rules for which the analyst is responsible and the effects of which on the analysand are not independent of the manner in which the experience is formulated. There is no place here for whim or gratuitous invention.

Freud invented the procedure that allows what he named *the unconscious* to be explored. A strange thing, indeed, that only responds to the one who summons it. Certainly there are dreams, slips, bungled actions, and above all symptoms, all these formations that, since Freud, reveal the unconscious, but in such enigmatic forms that they do no more than pose the question of what it—the unconscious—says, what it wants. Moreover, these "formations of the unconscious" can be ignored. That's precisely what was done in previous centuries when dreams were already interpreted, but differently, as the voice of gods or of destiny. Since Freud, those who have received his message may think that in ignoring them one will suffer the consequences, that symptoms and repetition will be rife. But that's because they have already decided on the unconscious as cause. Here we touch on the extent to which the unconscious is not a thing like any other: its ex-sistence is only verified in a relatively convincing way in the practice that establishes it—thus, not without the act of the analyst. "Ontically, then, the unconscious is the elusive" (Lacan, 1981b, p. 32): it does not conclude, as if it were awaiting interpretation. Hence Lacan was quite justified in saying that the status of the unconscious was less ontological than ethical.

The position Lacan took in psychoanalysis is clear in his "return to Freud": it involved taking a fresh look at the new experience invented by Freud. He did this in a way that was closer to the scientific spirit, and also more comprehensive, having understood that the practical direction of this experience is a function of how it is formulated. The opposition theory/practice, clinic/concept has no value here, and despite the boastings of those who declare themselves to be pure clinicians in psychoanalysis, theory cannot dispense with the facts that emerge in practice—and it is not so sure that things are so very different in science. This is why the desire of the psychoanalyst, at work in each treatment, operates no less at the level of the "praxis of theory" (Lacan, 1990a, p. 99).

So I will be questioning the trajectory of Lacan as analysand of psychoanalysis itself, the logic of his contributions and their consequences for the direction of the treatment. I am not going to explore the possible affinities, sources or differences with his contemporaries for the delectation of the history of ideas. Neither is it a question of his desire: I do not aim to interpret Lacan. Rather, I will be questioning the mainspring of his successive developments. Indeed, I eventually saw that the constant revisions of his elaborations, however inventive they are, have nothing capricious about them and are at every step based on reason—analytic reason—for it is the unsolved problems of the previous step which orient his progress. Except that he only rarely explains the impasses to be resolved and it is up to the reader to sweat a bit in order to grasp them.

I'm not going to deal with the whole of Lacan's trajectory but only those steps that led him to assert an unprecedented formula, the formula that says against all expectation that the unconscious—until then always described as symbolic—is real. Once established, the thesis has immense practical and clinical consequences, which are far from always being recognised and which, because of this, struggle to pass to the act—the analytic act.

PART I

THE UNCONSCIOUS, REAL

CHAPTER ONE

Trajectory

L acan himself did not fail to question his own trajectory and to reappraise each one of his steps. The new formulas as well as the theses of this reappraisal are striking theoretical rectifications (Soler, 2008a). Ultimately, we have a Symbolic which is no longer language but *langue*, to be written *lalangue* (I will come back to this); an Imaginary which is not signification subordinated to the Symbolic but is essentially form and representation; finally, a Real outside of the Symbolic whereas its previous definition located it at the limit points of linguistic formalisation.

Why? The question is not intended to mark out a periodisation, to chart a first, second, and third Lacan. Chronology is in itself inert and presents a drawback that is not entirely innocent: indeed it elides the One that links all the textual variations. This One is not at the level of theses but at the level of what I call the choice that grounds a unique saying [*un dire unique*], beyond the variations of statements [*les dits*]. With chronological sequence, whether one knows it or not, One-saying [*l'Un-dire*] is surreptitiously divided up into successive textualities, and in the name of a methodical reading it becomes so multiple that in the end it is simply resorbed.

In fact, it is this One whose value Michel Foucault, to his credit, highlighted in 1969 in his lecture "What is an author?", at which Lacan was present. In it he emphasised how much this dimension of the One of the author was ineradicable. I say to his credit, for the moment belonged to a certain structuralism that announced the death of the author and its reduction within the supposed laws of textuality. Today, of course, this notion has misfired and we are instead in an era where there are more authors than real texts.

The trouble with chronology is, as we say, that the enunciation driven out through the door returns through the window and no less so than in the authorised argument. The oft-repeated "Lacan said that", followed by random quotations, then obscures times that were initially distinguished and ushers in the most confusing indistinctness. In this way, the splitting of the name from the saying that carried it takes place. From then on, this teaching is transformed into a vast pantry from which each one takes a sample as he pleases. The result is that the more that readers multiply, the more the coherence that animates the movement from one step to the next evaporates.

Lacan was in fact by no means adept at chronology, but the contrary is not the case either. In order to characterise what he was doing, he liked to use the notion of clearing a path, clearing a path by breaking through the barriers in a field resistant to thought or movement. Clearing can proceed in a discontinuous way, with its fertile moments and its times of stasis and assimilation, but the notion suggests the continuity of an effort which constitutes an oriented whole, creating furrows in the field in question.

I will therefore approach the logic of changes with the one enunciation that produces them together. They do not have the same status, for the enunciation is contingent and thus unpredictable. In this sense, despite the logic of the passages, a second time cannot be purely and simply deduced from a first, even if the former is not without deriving from the latter and—as is well-known—will shed light on it retroactively.

It will thus be a matter of grasping what of the analytic experience exceeded each thesis and hence what grounds each advance. This means that the mainspring of this *work in progress*, to which only death gave the word "end", owes nothing either to linguistics—even if revisited through poetry as Jakobson did—or to structural anthropology.

Structuralist?

Yet, effectively, the name of Lacan remains associated with the structuralist trend of the 1970s. It is true that he explored the structuralist path methodically, seeking to establish that the unconscious belongs to a rational order that has its own laws. But is it enough to acknowledge that a symbolic order simultaneously govens the social groups studied by anthropology, the language structures of linguistics, and the discourse of the unconscious, for the—*ism* of structuralism to be warranted in psychoanalysis? I do not believe that Lacan was ever a structuralist, even at the time of metaphor and metonymy. The subject of psychoanalysis is not structural man, if I may use this expression, and has never really been so at any moment in Lacan's elaboration.

This is seen at the level of the premise—as it is for the object of every discipline—a premise not necessarily made explicit.

By hypothesis, linguistics and structural anthropology, which take as their object the compositional laws of the structures that concern them, posit a subject who is no more than the pure subject of a combinatory. The analytic hypothesis is different. The fact that Lacan had strongly emphasised that psychoanalysis knows no other subject than that of science, and made of "this special mode of subject" what he calls "the crucially important mark of structuralism" (Lacan, [1966] 2006, p. 731), must not mislead us on this point. Psychoanalysis certainly knows no other subject than this non-incarnated subject, the subject that is only "the navel" in the pure combinatory of the mathematics of the signifier, a navel that even logic cannot manage to eliminate. But this subject is not the object of psychoanalysis. The subject that psychoanalysis receives and deals with is the one who suffers. And not from just anything, but from a suffering tied to truth, the truth that involves the object of his phantasy and even a bit more: the living being marked by language. Lacan found a word to designate it: "analysand". Without him, there is no psychoanalysis, whereas the study of myths can take place quite happily without the "mythand", as Lacan calls him by analogy with analysand. Likewise, the splitting of a mask is nothing other than symbolic and elides the bearer, just as the ritual assumed to be homologous with the economy of mythemes rejects "from the field of structure the agent of the ritual" (Lacan, [1966] 2006, p. 732). The difference is immediately recognisable.

One could certainly speak of a structuralist moment in Lacan to designate the time when his elaborations borrow from the linguistics of Saussure and Jakobson, or from the structural anthropology of Lévi-Strauss: the time when he emphasises what psychoanalysis may share with these disciplines—namely, the laws of composition of the unconscious that Freud taught us to decipher, which have the subject of science as a correlate and which, like the elementary structures of kinship, operate without the knowledge of the psychological subject.

However, considering the matter more closely, it is not difficult to confirm the constancy, from this moment, of what I call the objection to the structuralist reduction, the objection inherent to psychoanalysis as conceptualised by Lacan. Let us acknowledge this objection from the first step. The laws of speech, Lacan said, and a big deal was made of this. Yes, but Lacan could say at the same time that speech is an act, and this act is unthinkable with just the subject of science. And yet we have "The Purloined Letter", which in spite of its chronology Lacan wanted to place at the start of his *Écrits*, precisely to accentuate the structural element of our experience. "The programme traced out for us is hence to figure out how a formal language determines the subject" (Lacan, [1956a] 2006, p. 31). What apparently could be more structuralist than this expression? But the objection follows: the programme cannot be fulfilled, he says, other than by a subject "contributing willingly", and this implies "a subjective conversion" (Lacan, [1956a] 2006, p. 31) often connected to a dimension of drama. So we say farewell to structuralism. I will not multiply the examples here: they are to be found throughout Lacan's seminars and writings, consistent with the idea of a subject who, unlike the pure subject of science, is credited with a position and with a responsibility toward that position—in other words, a subject more ethical than "pathematic".

The structuralist moment

From the structural moment, we can extract a very precise definition of the Symbolic.

I won't dwell on the time needed by Lacan to disinvest the term "symbol", so popular then, and to substitute "signifier" for it, thus clarifying from the outset that the signifier in psychoanalytic usage is not necessarily verbal, and that it is only homologous with the linguistic signifier through its differential character and its laws of composition.

The Symbolic is thus not reducible to the signifier even though it presupposes it. That is why, at the start, there is a whole vocabulary of *access* to the Symbolic, more or less realised or not, achieved or not. And Lacan evokes, for example, access to a *genuine* symbolic relation, as if the Symbolic had its chosen ones and that if all speaking beings shared language, they didn't all share the Symbolic. This vocabulary of access is obviously suspect. It had initiatory implications which many people became mired in but which are unsatisfactory in terms of the requirements of rationality and the ideal of transmission. Over a whole decade, Lacan worked to reduce this idea and to provide a conceptually rigorous definition of the Symbolic.

This definition makes of the Symbolic a specific mode of organisation of the signifier via metaphor, the signifying chain's synchronicity. The thesis is well known but it requires precision. In fact, Lacan defines the Symbolic through the conjunction of three metaphors, which he introduced in the seminar *The Psychoses*: the metaphor of the subject and the metaphor of the symptom formalised in "The agency of the letter in the unconscious", and then the metaphor of the Father in "On a question prior to any possible treatment of psychosis". The first question to ask is if there is an interdependence between these three metaphors, or even an order of determination.

The metaphor of the symptom is the metaphor of the trauma of the first encounter with *jouissance*. It is one of the forms of the unconscious as signifying chain, and thus of the unconscious as language, which Lacan reformulates thanks to this linguistic tool, and that Freud called repression and the return of the repressed. This is a shorthand way of saying it, because it is necessary to distinguish, as Lacan did, the use of metaphor in repression and its poetic or rhetorical usage, but the basic thesis remains the same. With his two expressions, "repression" and "return of the repressed", Freud left in suspense the question of knowing where the repressed element subsists. How did it remain active in readiness to make a return in spite of its disappearance? Freud, who did not publish his "Project for a scientific psychology", knew there was a problem here. The metaphor of the symptom responds to this question: the signifier remains metonymically latent in the signified of current discourse and remains accessible, decipherable from the excess of signification it produces.

The metaphor of the symptom, identical to repression-return of the repressed, is not for everyone, and in particular, Lacan specifies, not for those subjects for whom the signifier returns in the real, outside the chain (the unconscious revealed, as Freud said), those very same ones for whom, we can hypothesise, the metaphor of the father has failed. The metaphor of the symptom must thus be seen as subordinate to that of the father and excluded in psychosis.

This metaphor of the father also formalises the synchrony of a chain of signifiers, but once these are taken as those of the Oedipus—father, mother—and thus inseparable from the significations of relationships, love, and procreation—beyond the relation to *jouissance*, it will engage and order the social link between the sexes (man/woman) and the generations (parents/children).

But what is to be said about the supposed subject of the unconscious chain who, if I may say, is in some way its real signified, irreducible as much to the signifiers of the chain as to the significations it engenders? Would it be elusive? Elusive, unless it is a specific metaphor that allows it to be pinned down and which Lacan clearly calls the metaphor of the subject, thanks to which "his ineffable and stupid existence" and the x of his being are inscribed, but not without a cost. Lacan illustrated it in his commentary on Victor Hugo's poem, "Boaz Asleep", where the fertility of his "sheaf" does not go without the sickle.

So we have three linked metaphors that allow the metonymic drift of discourse to be anchored, and thus the whole imaginary of signification to be shaped by "induction" from the signifier. From the Symbolic to the Imaginary an order of determination is thus established, from which another cliché is born, to be added to the one about access to the Symbolic. The same old cliché of the possible, even necessary, surpassing of the imaginary passions of the analysed subject. A cliché that is maintained in spite of the whole of analytic experience, as well as Lacan's explicit objections and in total disregard of his later elaborations.

I will leave aside the steps that follow so I can refer to the trajectory's endpoint, to the moment when Lacan uses the formalism of the Borromean knot. This knot where three rings of string, representing the three di(said)mensions [*dit-mensions*] of the Symbolic, the Imaginary, and the Real, are knotted as three in such a way that if any one of them is cut the knot is undone.

Re-evaluations

I'm noting the opposition between the new and the old formulas without justifying them for the time being. Knotting is substituted for the metaphoric function. What Lacan first of all divided up with the binary of the metaphor of the father functioning or foreclosed, with its corresponding signifiers—the signifier in the chain of the symptom versus the signifier in the real, and hence outside the chain—is then replaced in the Borromean knot with the opposition: knotted or not knotted in a Borromean way. This is so true that in 1975 he said that the Name-of-the-Father is the Borromean knot. With the addition of the operation of knotting, the symptom—which as a "sexual substitute" in Freud's terms knots together Symbolic and Real, signifier and *jouissance*—binds itself to the meaning of the phantasy, produced between the Imaginary and the Symbolic.

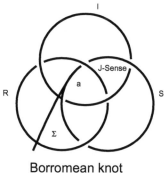

Borromean knot

That Lacan's first formulations can be resituated in the vocabulary of the Borromean knot shows us that with the knot Lacan was on the path to a more inclusive schematisation, one which allows a formulation of the facts of both neurosis and psychosis. This is already an advantage, but a generalised theory is only of interest due to the new aspects of the Real that it allows us to approach. And indeed it is really that which is in question.

As a supplementary function, the knot, which Lacan will later name "*sinthome*" and which he adds to the three consistencies of the Imaginary, the Symbolic, and the Real, requires at first that these latter be rethought in terms of their autonomy, their equivalence that Lacan would repeatedly assert, and even their knotting in twos.

The Symbolic that is written in the knot is therefore no longer a linguistic chain. Lacan himself made this explicit. I refer to two striking formulas from amongst many others: "Contrary to what I have said", he states, "the signifiers S_1 and S_2 do not make a chain". It's categorical. And again: "The unconscious does not have a grammar". In other words, the unconscious does not have a syntax that produces grammatical signification. The unconscious is certainly conditioned by language, by the fact that it speaks, but it is not language, making sentences, making "propositions". It is rather *langue*, that is, an inconsistent multiplicity of differential elements that do not fix meaning. We have thus arrived at a Symbolic without metaphor, which Lacan introduced at the same time as his considerations on *lalangue*, written as one word and which is not language. And indeed, we can see Lacan methodically challenging one by one the metaphors previously elaborated with so much care.

The definition of the symptom changes: it is no longer a function of metaphor (thus of the chain), but the function of the isolated one-letter [*la lettre-une*] that he writes as $f(x)$. His comments allow for no ambiguity: f is the function of *jouissance*, the *jouissance* of any element of the unconscious (x) that from now on he calls "letter". This is a return to a variant of the signifier in the Real, outside the chain, through which he at first defined the central phenomenon of psychosis.

Here, a digression. These new formulations certainly do not abolish the symbolic as language, but require it to be thought of as a superimposed structure, necessitating a supplementary condition added by discourse. This condition is that of linguistic science itself, but more essentially for us, it is that of psychoanalysis, as it operates in each treatment in order to extract from the analysand's speech his own unconscious language. In other words, the symbolic as language is already an effect of discourse. I will come back to this.

As for the function of the Name-of-the-Father, it is no longer a function of the signifier, nor even a function of the letter. It is a function of knotting, from a nominating saying [*dire de nomination*] that can certainly have symbolic effects, but which in itself is an existential and not a symbolic function. Clinical consequences follow from this.

Finally, the metaphor of the subject *exits* in favour of the proper name as the unforgeable signature of the living being that speaks.

From then on, what becomes of the category of the Imaginary that is not essentially knotted to the Symbolic? The Imaginary, governed and established by metaphor, was defined as signification. These significations went from narcissism and the relations with one's counterpart right up to phallic signification. Hence the idea, formulated at that time, that without the Other the subject could not even situate himself in the position of Narcissus.

Ultimately, Lacan says that the Imaginary is the body. To understand this it is necessary to add: the body without phallic signification, and thus the image, which has its own consistency, that of form: the adored, but also sometimes, abhorred image. In this way he returns to a primary mirror stage. This image will be colonised by the representations which *langue* conveys and which Lacan qualifies as idiotic to emphasise their existence outside-meaning.

As for the Real, it ex-sists. Ex-sistence outside. This is very different from knocking up against a limit to formalisation in the symbolic combinatory, against an impossible to write. This latter limit, according to Lacan's expression, is a "function of the real" in the Symbolic, and to be distinguished from the Real outside the Symbolic, which is rather on the side of the living being. This is a living being about which we have no idea, which cannot be imagined and about which the Symbolic knows nothing—despite the life sciences.

The re-evaluation is thus quite general. But what made it necessary? Or at least, because it is not a matter of necessity, what grounded it in the contingency of Lacan's saying? In what way was the theory of the Symbolic as metaphor insufficient?

"Real" subjects

I have never doubted the inadequacies of the thesis about the subject—as supposed, as split and as "want-to-be" [*manque à être*]. Though perfectly convincing at the level of the logic of the unconscious signifying chain, this thesis is perfectly incapable on its own of accounting for the whole of analytic experience, because the speaking being, the one affected by the unconscious, is not reducible to the barred subject of the unconscious. Hence my interest in the various supplements which Lacan brought to the notion of the subject over time, to return to what he calls in 1975 the "real subject", defined as not merely supposed.

I'll start with a well-known formula: "A subject supposes nothing, he is supposed". It is from 1967, where it was used to introduce the matheme of the transference. Indeed it can be said that once there is a signifier, a subject is supposed. If there are hieroglyphics on a stone, a subject is supposed. S/subject. There is nothing to add here. What is this subject? In the chain he can only be determined as a signified. But remaining distinct from the signified, the supposed subject—I would have to say: the sub-posed [*le sous-posé*] subject—instead makes a hole in the signified. This is why we can write it as (−1) in the matheme of the signifier and the signified:

$$\frac{S_1}{s \, // \, (-1)} \rightarrow S_2$$

Or, we can state, as Lacan does again in *Encore*, that "his being is always elsewhere". We can certainly already say of this subject that he is real, but in the sense that it is impossible to reduce this structure of supposition in the field of language.

Lacan undertook an extraordinary emptying out of the obvious facts of experience. First of all, that of the experience of the counterpart: far from being evanescent, human beings are well and truly there; they are noisy and they take up space, to say the least. A whole generation of Lacanians brought up on the mirror stage got into the habit of automatically referring this to the Imaginary, as if that sufficed to make the facts vanish into thin air.

It is not only true in the experience of the counterpart but equally at the level of interpretation: the subject of the text supposes nothing, but all the same there needs to be someone to make the supposition. Champollion in front of his hieroglyphics is not a supposed subject; it is he who supposes. And what? Not the subject, but first of all the signifier, since he supposes that the pattern of lines on the stone is writing.

I evoke Champollion, but I could take Freudian deciphering. Short-circuiting the subject of intentionality, it implies another subject, the one supposed to the deciphered chain and which, since Lacan, we call the "subject of the unconscious". Freud called this unconscious desire. But he is only supposed by a Freud who supposes, who treats the analysand's speech precisely as material: that is, as a text, in accordance with his tradition of writing. To treat the unconscious, to treat speech as a text, is to suppose that the unconscious is a knowledge. Such was the step taken by Freud. In this sense, Jean-Claude Milner (Milner, 2006) can say that Freud is in the field of what he calls "modern knowledge" ["*savoir moderne*"]. Opposed to speech, this knowledge does not speak, it says nothing to anybody: it excludes any message. It is constructed from little fragments, from "surplus knowledge" ["*plus de savoir*"] added to "surplus knowledge", according to the expression he uses. Freud's difference, however, which means that we cannot simply include him in the company of those Milner calls the "Jews of knowledge"—assuming that one agrees with his definition—is that this unconscious text is not reducible to absolute "surplus knowledge" since it is concerned with quite another thing: for Freud, the drives, conspicuously absent from Milner's book. Whether it is Champollion or Freud, what would the one who supposes the signifier be called if he were not called a subject? Not to mention the idea of that which "suffers" ["*pâtit*"] from the signifier, according to the expression in *The Ethics of Psychoanalysis*.

The one who speaks is divided between what he is as a supposed subject, a subject made of absence whose being is always elsewhere, and what he is as presence. I could say, presence of the speaking individual. The question is the following: what determines this subject, enough to convert this game of hunt the slipper into a *hic et nunc*, in the here and now? I said presence of the individual: it is Lacan's phrase. He uses it in *Encore* and then on the subject of Joyce whom he calls *the individual* [English in the original]. Indeed, it was necessary to wait for *Encore* for Lacan to put forward his hypothesis: this subject and this individual are the same. Did he ever doubt it? I do not believe so, but the question was not a philosophical one about the essence of man. It was a question about analytic practice: how could one catch this supposed subject who slides in the chain with a process reduced to speech? In other words, how could one access the referent, the Thing itself? And isn't this exactly what all interpretation aims at? To stop the sliding, to end deciphering, and to say what the ballast is, to aim at its heart? Lacan's line of thought on this point is instructive.

From the start he sought a principle for the mooring of the being that interpretation could target, but to this end he at first explored the resources of language. All his developments on the quilting points that stop the sliding of the chain, on the primordial signifier, and on the phantasy as absolute signification, are so many attempts at answers. The possible formulas of interpretation follow, because that is what is in question: interpretation as approximated signification, or interpretation that delivers the primordial signifier of a subject moored by the three metaphors I discussed earlier.

Could he have stopped there? Surely not, if one believes that the signifier and its order is not only causal but just as much caused. I could use the Freudian metaphor here which differentiates the work of the entrepreneur who handles the rules of manufacturing from the investor, the one who lays down the capital without which there would be nothing, not even the slightest dream, not to mention symptom. It is what Lacan seeks to return to and what he calls by different names over the course of time, designating at each moment what interpretation targets.

The first of these terms—and one which marks a moment of transition—is the Thing. The Thing is a fixed kernel of being, which no signifier represents but which may have a proper name; then the object as central cause, that he will write as the *a-thing* [*l'achose*]; then finally the *parlêtre*. These are so many names of a real subject that responds in the *hic and nunc*, let us say, in its libidinal or *jouissive* presence, and which the seminar *The Four Fundamental Concepts of Psychoanalysis* situated in their separation from the signifying chain.

However, this presence is not disconnected from speech for this thing speaks, it speaks the truth and cannot do otherwise even if it lies. But it cannot speak the truth of the real, of what it is as real, even though truth aims at the Real. Hence the formula in "L'étourdit" that marks another point of transition by inverting the first thesis of the dominance of the Symbolic. I quote: "The saying [*dire*] comes from where the Real commands truth". It is a reversal which substitutes a Real master who commands the subject for the hypothesis of the Symbolic master. Hence the title I used in 1997, "The commandments of *jouissance*" (Soler, 1998, pp. 15–25).

This re-evaluation displaces the conception of the Real itself in sanctioning the impotence of language to do anything other than make a fiction/fixing [*fi(x)ion*] of the real, if I may say this using Lacan's wordplay. From then on the Real is split, as I have said, between the Real belonging to the Symbolic and the Real outside the Symbolic which only the Borromean knot allows to be inscribed. The first of these is reducible to the impossibles over which the Symbolic presides. First, the core of the subject of science that is impossible to eliminate (-1), which I just mentioned. On this point I recommend Gabriel Lombardi's work on Cantor, Gödel, and Turing, *L'aventure mathématique. Liberté et rigueur psychotique* (Lombardi, 2005), which studies very closely this question of the real scar of the subject that cannot be eliminated from any order of language. Then, the impossible to write of sex, let us say it without playing on words, the at least two (*le moins deux*) of the partner who would make the sexual relation. Finally, with the knot, Lacan seeks a framework which allows the clinic of the "real subject" to be approached. He says it explicitly and I have had the opportunity on several occasions to insist on this. This subject who not only makes a hole in the chain, who is no longer solely mentality, but who has bodily substance—that is to say, the *parlêtre*, whatever his clinical structure, let us say, generic man, *the individual*, precisely according to the expression applied to Joyce (Lacan, [1975b] 1987, p. 28).

CHAPTER TWO

Towards the Real

I have jumped from the structure of language to the Borromean knot so as to situate the underlying framework of the Lacanian trajectory, but this is only intelligible and justified if it follows the development step by step.

It is in so far as psychoanalysis as a practice of speech mobilises the Imaginary and the Symbolic, namely the field of semblants, that the Real is brought into question, and one can wonder if it is not a *delire-à-deux*, as Lacan ultimately put it. This is obviously a major question.

The Real can emerge in speech and limit the infinite drift of both deciphering and meaning. Lacan put forward three successive elaborations of the Real that imply, moreover, three definitions of the final pass of analysis and not just one. What animates this quest?

On this question, the popular thesis according to which all these advances are so many efforts at thinking the relations between the signifier and *jouissance* is not adequate. No doubt these relations were reformulated over time, but the real questionis: why go beyond the first consistent construction on this theme, mainly elaborated in the 1960s, that of the object *a*? For this already allowed the whole of analytic experience to be rethought from the perspective of the economy of *jouissance*, since this object, to put it succinctly, is simultaneously

17

the main effect of language that mortifies *jouissance* and the remainder which conditions all our surplus *jouissance*. With this object, Lacan writes both the *jouissance* that is lacking—let us say, Freud's lost object—and that which remains condensed in the objects of surplus *jouissance*. And this sheds light on the "destitution" at the end of analysis and the procedure of the pass is established, set out in 1967 in the "Proposition on the psychoanalyst of the school" (Lacan, 1995).

What functions as Real?

Let's start with a sentence from "Radiophonie" which seems to me to be especially instructive for it evokes the relation of truth to the Real. The truth which speaks and which is articulated in each analysis, what is its aim? It is situated from "the supposition of what functions as real in knowledge, which is added to it (to the Real)" (Lacan, 1970b, p. 95). We see the splitting of the notion of the Real here: a Real internal to the Symbolic and a Real to which knowledge is added. In both cases, it is clear that it is not unconscious knowledge that is said to be real.

At the outset, unconscious knowledge is so barely thought of as Real that it is simply "supposed". It is the definition of the transference: the distress—let us say the symptom, whatever it is—which brings someone to analysis, and which can be written as a signifier that Lacan called the signifier of the transference, S. From the moment it is addressed to analysis, it supposes that there are other signifiers, unconscious signifiers that can give it meaning. And in fact the effects of deciphering prove the supposition, at least partially, but this does not allow us to conclude that the unconscious is real.

On the contrary, what functions as real in knowledge are, let us say, the "negativities" of structure. This term is a way of designating what the structure of language renders impossible. These limit points are hence trans-structural, setting out the inevitable limits to analytic elaboration, which correspond to what is Real within the Symbolic.

The first impossible situated by Lacan stems from the incompatibility of speech and desire. This may make desire an articulated signified, yet it is nonetheless inarticulable. The object that causes it, although incarnated in four "episodic substances" (Lacan, 2001b, p. 309)—oral, anal, scopic, and invocatory—is still impossible to say. It is in this sense that the object could be classed as Real, as Lacan did for a time. In other words, articulated truth is powerless to say the real that governs it: the truth never concludes but it persists. We repress it and it returns; we gag it and it speaks elsewhere; we ask it to say the last word, the final word, as I expressed it not long ago, and it only half-says. However, its repetitive insistence provides a glimpse of the real of the unnameable cause that animates it. In this way, Lacan first took phantasy to be that which functions as the real by virtue of the impossible to say of this "object that lacks", this object which one "no longer has", even though it provides the surplus *jouissances* through which desire is linked to *jouissance*. Appealing to logic, he made it homologous with an axiom, the irreducible constancy of which constitutes the nucleus of all that can be articulated of the unconscious, which analysis allows to be seen in a lightening flash.

This did not yet produce a knowledge of the impossible. On the contrary, a "vain knowledge of a being that slips away" was the verdict in 1967. "Vain knowledge of a being that slips away" marks a limit that may produce an unpleasant surprise in a practice where the transference, beyond therapeutic hopes, has made the prospect of knowledge seem enticing. But there is no knowledge of object *a*. It is inferred from what we decipher of desire, it is imagined corporeally, orally, excrementally—but psychoanalysis cannot be a science of the object (Lacan, [1966] 2006, p. 733).

In the next step, Lacan is searching for what functions as real in knowledge, following the model of logic and the impasses to formalisation. He now evokes not induction as with object *a*, but writing: more precisely, the impossible to write. This heralds a transition and a conclusion through a logical demonstration of the impossible, the premise being that via analytic saying something writes itself. Undoubtedly, with the question of knowledge comes the question of what "to write itself" means in a practice that has no other instrument than speech.

A joining of speech to the Real, and not simply to truth, is posited here. Through chatter, something of the real is reached, Lacan will say. The saying in analysis leaves traces of writing that are relative to the analytic discourse. Lacan now reformulates the classic definition of logical modalities—the possible, the contingent, the necessary and the impossible—to include time: the time of what stops for the contingent and the possible, or the time of what does not stop for the necessary and the impossible. What "stops not writing itself" is the definition of contingency. The expression indicates that analysis not only explores what we might believe to be already there, but produces something new that can now write itself. What "does not stop not writing itself" in a psychoanalysis is the impossible which occupies the place of the real.

What is it then that stops not writing itself via the race for the always half-said truth, through the inaccessible mirage, if not the traces of its powerlessness? In terms of structure, language only writes the one and even the one on its own. It is the One in all its forms: the Ones that the unconscious ciphers, the One of phallic *jouissance*: that is, the One fallen under the blow of castration "which makes a function of the subject" (Lacan, 1975d, p. 9), the one of saying of the One on its own. Hence the famous "there is the One" ["*y a d'l'Un*"], the One and none other, repeated by Lacan for a whole year. Analysis has no other product.

This insistent contingency of the one that does not stop writing itself demonstrates indirectly the real "specific" to the ciphering of the unconscious: that is, the impossible of writing the supposed two of sex, the two that is not, that "does not stop not writing itself". This is as "inaccessible" as the two of the series of whole numbers in the absence of which "there is no sexual relation", no relation between the *jouissance* of the One and the Other. Consequently, the phantasy and its object appear as an imaginary suppletion to the Real, to the foreclosure of the sexual relation.

Demonstrating this happens not on paper but in the treatment, case by case, and precisely by putting love life into question. It is a special demonstration, founded, says Lacan, on insistence (Lacan, 1975c, p. 17) and lasting until this reiterated One takes on the value of the demonstration of the impossibility of two. I could say that it is a pass to the One and nothing else, or also a pass "to the not [*pas*] two", with all the equivocation of this expression.

Until now, we see not the real unconscious but only what functions as real.

For a long time I wondered what made Lacan take the step in the seminar *Encore* of going beyond the emphasis he placed for years on the structure of language, its logic and its topology, to emphasise the effects of *lalangue* (written as one word), an unheard of thesis in relation to what had come before: the unconscious as "lucubration of knowledge" (Lacan, 1998, p. 139). This latter unconscious, he specifies, is "situated on the basis of its deciphering", the one which we try to grasp from the work of association in the transference, and which he had claimed was "structured like a language".

I note that this new chapter is strictly contemporary with his first use of the Borromean knot, and which is immediately followed with the emphasis from 1970 in "*Lituraterre*" on the function of writing as another mode of the speaking being. This conjunction is not an accident.

The navel

My hypothesis is that Lacan is led beyond his conception of the unconscious through his elaborations on the structure of language. A decisive formula in this progress, dating from the 1969 "Report on 'The Analytic Act'", states that the unconscious is "knowledge without a subject" (Lacan, 1984b, p. 19). It corresponds to the notion of the "subject supposed to know" which defines transferential belief. I take it as a kind of navel on which everything that is re-elaborated from then on is based.

The unconscious is certainly a knowledge since it is deciphered, but why without a subject? Because of linguistic structure: the signifier, which we write S_1, can only ever represent the subject for other signifiers, written S_2, which is knowledge. Where Lacan had for many years written the knotting of signifiers in the chain $S_1 \rightarrow S_2$—a knotting which seemed appropriate to explain the meaning produced between interpretation and free association—he now uncovers an impossible: the impossible copulation of the representative or representatives of the subject with knowledge. This impossible is attributable to the fundamentally differential structure of the signifier that is only isolated as one by its difference from others. Jakobson opened up this path with his phonology at the level of the a-semantic signifier. From then on the structure of the representation of the subject is recurrent: whatever the signifier that represents him might be, it leaves him irremediably separated from other signifiers. We could then say, although it might not please Freud, "There where knowledge without a subject was, I cannot come to be". Challenging his first formulations, what Lacan ultimately elaborates is that the signifiers of the unconscious do not form a chain with those of the subject.

An unconscious "knowledge without a subject". How could it be the subject's if not by the mediation of what, in structure, is not language: that is, the enjoying substance of the body, the body the subject has and which he needs in order to enjoy? This unconscious can be said to be the subject's since its signifiers are those extracted from his symptom through deciphering. If, before being deciphered, they do not represent him, they nevertheless affect his *jouissance* as an event of the body.

This is the Lacanian hypothesis emphasised in 1973 at the end of *Encore* (Lacan, 1998, pp. 141–142), but to me it seems consistent with the very notion of "knowledge without a subject" that Lacan formulated well before then. This implies that the signifier itself is at the level of *jouissance*, that it is "the apparatus of *jouissance*" (Lacan, 1998, p. 55). The living being is its "point of insertion", as he said from the start of the seminar *The Other Side of Psychoanalysis*. In other words, "knowledge without a subject", more than the object, is the apparatus of *jouissance* that presides over the *jouissance* that is as well as over the *jouissance* that is not.

From now on, there is a question. Where do they, these intrusive signifiers which are not the S_1s representing the subject, this subject whose "being is always elsewhere", come from (Lacan, 1998, p. 142)? The reference to *lalangue* provides the answer: from nowhere else than from *lalangue*, where the battery of signifiers in its differential structure is present but without yet constituting a language. "Knowledge without a subject" requires the emphasis on *lalangue*, written as one word, which is the place from which differential signifiers can pass over to language. For that to happen, the signifier One, and not just any old one, must be extracted and differentiated from some of the other ones of *lalangue*.

The two unconsciouses

From now on, the notion of unconscious knowledge is split. Lacan uses the pejorative term "lucubration" in order to say that the unconscious deciphered in terms of knowledge always remains limited—one only knows a bit of it—and secondly, that it is hypothetical in relation to the knowledge deposited in *lalangue*, which is itself impregnable. I quote: *lalangue* "articulates things by way of knowledge [*de savoir*] that go much further than what the speaking being sustains [*supporte*] by way of enunciated knowledge" (Lacan, 1998, p. 139). Lacan concludes more generally that language does not exist, that it is just what we try to know of *langue*. He even describes linguistics itself as a lucubration: in other words, as a "delusion" with a scientific goal.

We must understand that this disparity of two knowledges—the knowledge of *lalangue* and the knowledge deciphered in language—would not be conceivable without the differential structure of the signifier, or else the thesis would itself be lucubrated. The act of deciphering consists in extracting a signifier or a series of signifiers from the analysed material of the symptom. Lacan put it explicitly: by deciphering, an unknown signifier of knowledge that did not represent the subject but that governed his *jouissance* in the symptom, an S_2 therefore, call it sign or letter—in other words, a signifier as cause and object of *jouissance*—becomes S_1, a signifier acknowledged as master of his *jouissance*. A change of status of the master signifier thus occurs. This "incarnated" signifier, S_1, is differentiated from the S_1s borrowed from the Other of discourse which can range from the Ideals of the Other to the phallus, but is also differentiated from the other signifiers of *lalangue*, for the structure of representation of this new S_1 in relation to knowledge is recurrent and not reducible by deciphering.

It is what the following schema shows: $(S_1 (S_1 (S_1 \rightarrow (S_2))))$ (Lacan, 1998, p. 143). It is homologous at the level of the unconscious to the subject's division from knowledge.

$$
\begin{array}{cc}
\text{The subject} & \text{His unconscious} \\[4pt]
\dfrac{S_1}{\$} \quad \rightarrow & \underbrace{S_2 \text{ unconscious knowledge}} \\[10pt]
& \underbrace{(S_1 (S_1 (S_1}_{\text{deciphered } S_2} \quad \rightarrow \quad \underset{S_2 \text{ of lalangue}}{(S_2))))}
\end{array}
$$

From now on, *lalangue* appears as the vast reserve from which deciphering extracts only some fragments. This should be noted in relation to identification to the symptom: the *lalangue*-unconscious remains as an impregnable knowledge whose effects exceed us.

CHAPTER THREE

Lalangue, traumatic

Why write it as one word? The references are numerous, and Lacan explained it in this way: it is because of its homophony with "lallation". "Lallation" comes from the Latin *lallare*, which the dictionaries say designates the act of singing "la, la" to send infants to sleep.[1] The term also designates the babbling of the infant who does not yet speak but who already makes sounds. Lallation is sound separated from meaning, but nonetheless, as we know, not separated from the infant's state of satisfaction.

Here a small digression. An apparently enigmatic and hardly even serious remark in the lecture "Joyce, the symptom" is now clarified (Lacan, 1987, p. 35). Speaking of the symptom as an event of the body, he calls it "tied to that which: *l'on l'a, l'on l'a de l'air, l'on l'aire, de l'on l'a*". One can even sing it. The implication of this remark is the link of *lalangue* with the symptomatic body.

Lalangue evokes the speech that is transmitted before syntactically structured language. Lacan says that *lalangue*, as one word, means the mother tongue: in other words, the first things heard, to parallel the first forms of bodily care.

A second reason is that a single word in the singular designates a function that is not to be confused with the multiplicity of diverse *langues*

25

in the sense of idioms. They cannot be completely separated, and it is possible to speak of *lalangues* as one word, for in each *langue* in its difference from others we find a function of *lalangue* as translinguistic.

A-structural lalangue

What distinguishes *lalangue* from *langues* is that in *lalangue* there is no meaning. Lacan formulates this in *Television: langue* only provides the cipher of meaning, as each of its elements can take on any meaning whatsoever. This is why Lacan can say elsewhere that *lalangue* has nothing to do with the dictionary (Lacan, 1971–1972, 4th November, 1971, p. 4). Each *langue*, however, is guaranteed by the dictionary. The dictionary lists the elements one by one—let us say, the signifiers—and shows, via quotations, the meanings that usage has determined. That meaning is determined by use proves that each *langue* comes from discourse: that is, from what is said, from diction, in any given historicised social bond. The quotations of the dictionary can ground use, even authorised use. I won't dwell on the other uses defined by their not being authorised— the different slangs and other registers of *langue*—which correspond to the fact that social links are never homogeneous and that use varies as a function of class, social circle, education, etc. What is called a living *langue* is an evolving *langue*. The dictionary, in introducing words and new locutions, in abandoning obsolete words, etc., tries to fix at a given moment the way that words are tied to their meanings. To say that *lalangue* has nothing to do with the dictionary is precisely to say that what is lacking in *lalangue* is this tethering of words to any agreed meaning.

Unlike the Symbolic, *lalangue* is thus not a constituted body but a multiplicity of differences that have not taken shape. There is no (−1) of *lalangue* that would make it a set. There is no order in *lalangue*. It is not a structure of language or of discourse. For language, order is the ordered pair of the subject that inscribes it $S_1 \rightarrow S_2$. It is the basis of the transference as a link to the subject supposed to know and it also structures free association and all its effects of meaning. For discourse, order is the semblant, written at the top left of Lacan's mathemes, which orders the social bond. Every discourse is thus an order. This is not the case with *lalangue*, which is the a-structural level of the verbal apparatus. Could one say that *lalangue* is a pulverulent proliferation? No, for that would not designate *lalangue* itself but a usage of *lalangue* outside discourse. *Lalangue* is rather the "set of all equivocations" possible, which nonetheless does not make a whole.

Hence the problem Lacan raises of knowing how one moves from these ones of pure difference to the signifier One, written with a capital, S_1 or even to the swarm of S_1s that it may form, and that I invoked just now, like a new master signifier inscribed in the field of *jouissance*. Where are we to find the unit-element? Jakobson insisted that the phoneme is a differential unit that has no meaning. But neither does the word, Lacan remarked. Since *lalangue* comes from speech that has been spoken and heard, any word that is heard can take on any meaning. A famous example would be *"Nom-du-Père"* (Name-of-the-Father) and *"non dupe erre"* (non-dupe errs) that are only distinguished through writing. *Lalangue* is made up of ones that are signifiers but at a basic level of pure difference. It follows that the One incarnated in *lalangue*—I emphasise *incarnated*—the one that is fused with *jouissance* and is not simply one amongst others, this One, I quote, "is something that remains indistinct [*indécis*] between the phoneme, the word, the sentence, and even the whole of thought" (Lacan, 1998, p. 143). It is the whole problem of the uncertainty of deciphering. Lacan will certainly speak of the letter one of the symptom—I will come back to this—but "indeterminate" means that we cannot identify this One with certainty. In other words, we do not know it. The unconscious as *lalangue* has effects at the level of *jouissance*, but it remains essentially unknown.

Lalangue *cemetery*

Lalangue is nonetheless linked to discourse. I quote from "La troisième" (Lacan, 1975a): *lalangue* "is the deposit, the alluvium, the petrification in which is marked the way a group handles its unconscious experience". Unconscious experience implies the effect of speech and discourse on the substance of the body. It is what discourse, in a given social bond, has ordered and conveyed historically of the *jouissance* that is deposited in a *langue*. And when I say "discourse", this includes its most trivial and most banal productions as well as its most sublimated and original inventions in poetry and literature. Here we would pose the question, to which I will return later, of the private discourse from which the subject has been constituted.

We could say here that a *langue* is permanently impregnated by the *jouissance* that governs speech and its enjoyed signifiers. But a term such as "impregnated" which evokes life would be misleading. A *langue* is rather a cemetery. I translate in this way what Lacan notes: even when it is said to be living, even when it is in use, a *langue* is always a dead *langue* for it involves "the death of the sign" (Lacan, 1975a). What it gathers is the *jouissance* that has passed over to the sign, or to the letter, a mortified *jouissance* that "presents itself as dead wood". A cemetery, but a constantly updated one, just like a real cemetery. Some new signs are admitted, signs that I would be tempted to say are excorporated from lived experiences. These signs, passing over to the word, secrete new words, expressions, equivocations, which, though it might not please academics, wait for no dictionary in order to be in use, and "in use" here means "use of *jouissance*". Some other signs, in contrast, become obsolete, inappropriate for the *jouissances* of their time, and hence outside use. *Langue* is dead, but it comes from life and the whole problem is therefore to know how a dead *langue* can operate on the living being, traumatically.

The effects of lalangue

Lalangue is an impregnable knowledge, but not without effects, and indeed, otherwise there would be no reason to be interested in it. These effects are those of affects: *lalangue* affects *jouissance*.

This thesis is different from the question of the *jouissance* of *lalangue*. That one may enjoy *lalangue* is proven by the existence of the poet and the writer, and also by the schizophrenic who dispenses with the symbolic but not with *lalangue*. The later Joyce is proof of this.

What demonstrates that *lalangue* affects the living *jouissance* of the speaking being? How do we know it? This question needs to be posed since the thesis is far from being accepted by everyone. The twentieth century, said to be the century of language, is not the century of the effects of *langue*. In fact, it is the opposite, paradoxically, since it is widely believed that language is itself a product of the brain. Look at Chomsky and so many other upholders of neuronal man. I therefore appeal to Lacan's texts to tell us what proof there is that *lalangue*, in its difference from language, affects the living being. I'll set out the arguments.

That experience, with its lived *jouissances*, goes towards *lalangue* is certain, since a *langue* evolves according to living communities. It is interesting to note here the current problem of English and the major difficulties of translation between the English of England, the United

States of America, and Australia. We shouldn't forget the fourth English, disastrous perhaps but for us significant, the international English reduced to its usage as communication, for which it is built, but at the cost of a quite obvious impoverishment in relation to the versions of English I mentioned above. This impoverishment even shows that the function of communication is neither primary nor fundamental, and that a *langue* evolves by collecting words that arise from existence [*l'existentiel*]. Affect, in the sense of the feeling of the unsayable, produces words, a thesis that was already present in "On a question prior to any possible treatment of psychosis". We would also have to study the failure of Esperanto. That was an attempt to distance diplomatic *langue* from national powers and create one that was politically neutral. Its failure must be seen in the light of the rise of this international English, which as impoverished as it is, is not politically neutral.

Proof by affect

Another argument from *Encore*, closer to analytic experience, could be called "proof by affect".

We know that the effects of *langue* exceed anything that can be known of them, as we see from the fact that the speaking being, Lacan says, has all sorts of affects that remain enigmatic. This should be a warning to those who imagine that at the end of an analysis the subject would no longer experience discordant affects but only affects syntonic with their current situation. That was never Lacan's thesis: at the end of analysis, the subject remains "subject to unpredictable affects" (Lacan, 1970a, p. 26).

One of these affects is another satisfaction, linked to verbal chatter, to blah blah blah. This is satisfying—albeit in a strange way—in that something is both said and not said, and without us knowing why. This has nothing to do with the satisfaction of communication, of pseudo-dialogue. We have evidence of this, for example, in the fact, patent in analysis but also in everyone's experience, that a dream can change one's mood for the whole day, in one or another direction. A lapsus may delight or appal you quite independently of its consequences, etc. Satisfaction is obviously not *jouissance*. It is a phenomenon of the subject affected by speech, not a phenomenon of the body. It "responds" however (this is Lacan's term) to *jouissance*, more precisely to the enjoyed knowledge of *lalangue* that inhabits speech. The enigmatic unpredictability of the affect—I would say, its discordance—is a sign, according to Lacan, of what its cause is in the enjoyed knowledge of *lalangue*, a knowledge which exceeds anything one can know of it.

Here there is a major addition to the classic psychoanalytic theory of affects. The affect is neither an instrument for deciphering nor a compass for interpretation, as I often say. The thesis is Freudian, linked to his conception of repression: the affect is not reliable because it is displaced. And "not reliable" means that it does not reveal unconscious knowledge. A paradox, since for the affected subject nothing is more significant than what he experiences and which he often confuses with his truth. Lacan argued that metonymy is the norm for affects, but here we see something different: precisely as enigmatic, the affect becomes an epistemic index. Certainly it does not reveal a knowledge, but it does make a sign, a sign that an unknown knowledge which causes it is there. We are in the register of proof by affect.

At this point Lacan extends to the affects of blah blah—what he calls "other satisfaction"—his thesis about the affect of anxiety in the seminar he devoted to this theme. He recognised a special affect in anxiety, as I have shown, the only one which rightly has epistemic value, signalling the presence of the object *a* of desire as an a-phenomenological object. Incidentally, on the basis of this he paid homage to Kierkegaard, contra the complete trust of Hegel in absolute knowledge. The experience of anxiety arises in circumstances when, confronted by the enigma of the Other, the subject finds himself about to be reduced to this object, threatened by the imminence of what I have called a "wild subjective destitution". Some years later Lacan, taking account of the Real outside the Symbolic, broadened its function once more and redefined it as "the typical affect of every advent of the Real" (Lacan, 1975a).

Proof by treatment of the symptom

The main argument establishing the effects of *lalangue*—and for me, the most elaborated—is found in Lacan's 1975 "Geneva lecture on the symptom". Here it is a proof by treatment of the symptom.

That we can shift the *jouissance* of the symptom through speech, the first step of analytic experience, implies that it is in "the encounter of words with [the] body that something takes shape". Indeed, we must suppose a coherence between the method that operates on the symptom and the moment that the symptom itself is constituted. We have to link the fact that, on the one hand, it is during an early period of childhood that symptoms crystallise, and on the other, that we do not analyse without the associations of the subject (see Lacan, 1989, p. 12).

The method in question is the one that Freud invented and elaborated in the series of texts, *The Interpretation of Dreams, The Psychopathology of Everyday Life*, and *Jokes and their Relation to the Unconscious*. The method does not proceed via symbols or archetypes of discourse, as Jung believed, but through the subject's own, always unique associations. Interpretation relies on the material specific to each subject.

Now, if one evokes the work of Freud and reads the paragraphs devoted to the meaning of symptoms in the *Introductory Lectures on Psycho-Analysis*, this meaning is only interpreted accurately— "accurately" means with some effects of reduction of the symptom—in terms of the first encounters with sexual reality. That speech and sex are the two key elements of an effective interpretation allows us to conclude that there is a "coalescence" between these two fundamental givens.

They represent two distinct heterities [*hétérités*]. That's why Lacan adds the trauma of *lalangue* to what Freud took to be the trauma of sex (Soler, 2008c).

Firstly, sexual reality. Freud called it autoerotic, but Lacan disagreed with this thesis. This reality concerns the encounter with the erection, the little prick. "Encounter" means that it is not autoerotic but hetero, foreign. This is a first proof of an anomalous *jouissance* in relation to the body which, Lacan says, bursts the screen (a reference to Mishima who was so stunned by it). It bursts the screen because it does not come from the functional interior of the screen, which is silent. It is sometimes the object of a rejection when the subject is scared of it, as was Little Hans, for example, who made a phobia out of it.

Lacan makes a big deal of the fact that the child receives discourse before this very early period of life. But be careful, this is not an apprenticeship. It is an impregnation. "The unconscious is the way that the subject was impregnated by language, and bears its imprint". The term excludes mastery, active appropriation, and discrimination. It refers to this foreign thing, but we can note that without any doubt, before being able to compose sentences, the subject reacts correctly to complex expressions whose literal meaning he does not understand and does not know how to use. There is something here like a bizarre sensibility. From this receptivity to the otherness of *lalangue*, what Lacan calls the "water" of language, "some detritus" remains. The water of language connotes fluidity, the sonorous continuum of the a-structural heard. Detritus, debris (elsewhere he says deposit), all these terms that denote scattered discrete elements refer to something that is anterior to the use of quilting points. This debris is the Real, outside meaning, in the form of a sonorous One, received from what was heard. For do not forget that language is acquired through the ear. And it is, I quote, "some debris to which will be added later on the problems that are going to frighten him" (Lacan, 1989, p. 16).

Lallation, melody, the noise of sounds deprived of meaning but not of presence, operates before the quilting of language. This obviously raises the question of what those subjects who do not have access to sound—the deaf—find as a substitute. And they need to find something since they have access to language.

There is a coalescence between the impregnation by discourse and the moment of encountering the sexual, here the phallic. "It is in the way in which *lalangue* has been spoken and also heard by this or that individual in his particularity, that something will then emerge again in dreams, in all sorts of stumblings, in all sorts of ways of saying" (Lacan, 1989, p. 14). Such is the *"motérialité* of the unconscious" which accounts for the symptom.

The holophrastic unconscious

I would like to emphasise the step taken in this move from the causal incidence of language to *lalangue*.

The unconscious structured like a language was an unconscious made up of signifiers, but signifiers were not necessarily words. Lacan has for a long time insisted on the idea, based on the model of linguistic structure, that every discrete and combinable element functioned as a signifier. He gave the example of the slap that has become a signifier, and that runs through discourse from one generation to the next. *Lalangue* may certainly gather images from discourse, but its knowledge is nothing more than the ones of its *motérialité*, and the unconscious is conceived as the direct effect of these elements—one by one, word by word—that predate the child's own sentences. This is the first point.

The second point is that this passage does not exclude the function of the Other, which Lacan spoke of up till then and which is more well-known. Lacan takes it up again in this same lecture and elsewhere. I quote: "Parents mould the subject in this function that I call *symbolic*.

[…] The way in which a mode of speaking has been instilled in him (he is instilled with what impregnates him) can only bear the mark of the mode in which his parents have accepted him" (Lacan, 1989, p. 13). That strongly resembles the classic thesis that desire (including that of the parents) circulates in speech. But with *motérialité*, we are prior to the distinction signifier/signified, for the sounds that are distinguished from each other precede the meaning in what is heard: la, la, la, like one precedes any two in the chain. For this reason, the enigmatic ones in the song of what is heard have a direct effect when they are linked to the enigma of sex. Lacan hammered home often enough that there is no preverbal for the one who speaks, but there is pre-language in the sense of syntax. The song—or better still, the "melody"—of the parents is not the message of the Other and exceeds it, just as the unconscious as *lalangue* exceeds the unconscious as language. It is indeed why we must add, as Lacan did, the way in which the child hears to the way in which the Other speaks. What determines it? The analysand often asks "But why?" of this thing he cannot get rid of. No other reason than the irreducibility of contingency. There is also an encounter [*tuché*] in the way one hears, which greatly limits the responsibility of parents towards their children.

We could introduce here some considerations on transmission, which psychoanalysis has contributed so much to exalting. The objection to any mastery of transmission—a mastery that is the ideal for the educator while being the drama and the powerlessness of parents—an objection that Lacan first tackled through unconscious desire, is to be related more fundamentally to the primary antecedence of *lalangue*.

I will pause on Lacan's formulas: "a way of speaking" where previously he used to say "discourse of the Other": there is nothing vague in this notion. The signifier is heard [*s'entend*]; it's not between the lines. What is said between the lines, in the signifying interval, is interpreted and is called desire and phantasy. On the other hand, "a way of speaking" is a vague expression; it's both more general and broader, and we would be hard pressed to reduce it to terms of structure. It is no doubt necessary to take account of the fact that it is in a lecture addressed to an unspecified public. But I do not believe that this is the fundamental reason. A way of speaking includes the structure of language but adds something to it. In the structure of language, singularity is indexed through particular signifiers and the specific phantasy, both of which are relatively graspable. "Manner of speaking" adds to this something like the style of speaking—including phrasing, rhythm, breathing—that occurs at the level of the heard which itself involves the body, and sometimes partially raises speech to the dimension of theatre. In the relation with counterparts and in the judgements of sympathy or antipathy, this *di[t]-mension* is both very present and very difficult to define. This is why I used the word "song" of the Other to designate what is lallated—if I may make up this term from the Latin *lallare*— what is lallated in the emission of speech articulated by the Other.

Yet we must remember what I mentioned previously: in *lalangue* the One is indistinct. It comes from sound but nevertheless it is not reducible to the phoneme: it can go as far as the unity of a sentence functioning as a One. In other words, be careful: the holophrase precedes the sentence. The holophrase is defined as a soldering which suppresses the interval between the S_1s and S_2s of the sentence, and as a result makes the sentence function as a One. This is the holophrase which Lacan said in *Seminar XI* that it was specific to a whole series of cases extending from retardation to psychosis. Well, we can deduce that it takes on a broader and more basic function from these developments on *lalangue* in the mid 1970s. There is no more reason to reserve it for psychosis. The first spoken words can function as an enjoyed holophrase distinct from any message. To receive the message and to receive *lalangue* are two linked but different things, as are their respective effects.

What trauma?

Where is the traumatism in all this? Are the marks left by the coalescence of the debris of language with the trauma of the phallic sufficient for us to call *lalangue* traumatic, even when those who may have the feeling of being traumatised by it are scarce? On the contrary, many suffering subjects can say that they have found their salvation through words. We don't need to evoke Joyce here: Elfriede Jelinek, winner of the Nobel Prize in literature, testified to it in a recent interview published in *Le Monde des livres*. This is not a unique case. There are subjects who find something like a salvation at the level of *lalangue*.

The analysand complains about the discourse of the parental Other: on this point there is no exception. He complains about what the Other has and has not articulated, about what he has received from the Other and about what he has not received, or at least what he believes he has or has not received. Hence the emphasis on the transmission of the symbolic effects of speech from figures of the Other across generations. Conversely, he only rarely complains of *langue*.

In putting the emphasis on *lalangue*, Lacan does not reject the impact of the Other—particularly in the form of the parents as I have said—but he displaces the point of impact. From the weight of the discourse of the Other (articulated in language) Lacan moves to the weight of the *lalangue* of the Other, the *langue* heard from the Other. Well, it's a passage from the Symbolic to the Real. *Lalangue* is not Symbolic but Real. Real, because it is made of ones outside the chain and thus outside meaning (the signifier becomes real when it is outside the chain), and of ones which are enigmatically fused with *jouissance*. On the one hand, *lalangue* operates on the Real which the body enjoys and "civilises" it as symptom, Lacan would say. On the other, storing the signs left by experiences of *jouissance*, it itself becomes an object of *jouissance*. This is one of the main theses of the seminar *Encore*: to speak is in itself a *jouissance*. It's a subversion of the *cogito*: "I think thus it enjoys itself". The singular *lalangue* which comes to the subject through the Other is not without carrying the trace of the *jouissances* of this Other. Hence the obscenity of *lalangue*, about which one could say that it marks the subject with enjoy-signs [*jouis-signes*] both enigmatic and unprogrammable. From the very beginning, language entails for everyone who speaks a bond with the Other: not an intersubjective bond—one would even hesitate to qualify it as strictly speaking social—but a bond which has its roots in a singular bath of obscenity and which can later emerge as symptom, dream, and lapsus, etc. This is no doubt what allowed Lacan to evoke a sexual relation between generations, which is quite a different thing to the incestuous act.

The analphabetic symptom

Where Lacan relates the passage of the *lalangue* heard in childhood to the symptom through its fusion with *jouissance*, let us take the opposite path so as to see what the thesis implies concerning access to the unconscious in analysis.

I'll start once again with the symptom. At the beginning of analysis, it presents itself as a hole in meaning. Analytic work is driven by nonsense, a term used by Lacan in reference to Jaspers: it is generally the non-sense of a formation of the unconscious that challenges both understanding and will. But there is not only the symptom: there is the lapsus, the bungled action and the dream, so many phenomena that constitute units outside meaning. The analytic work of association consists in connecting this unit outside meaning with other associated signifiers that give it meaning. We thus pass from the erratic One that has surprisingly appeared to the chain of language. An analysis, Lacan said in 1973, delivers to the analysand the meaning of his symptoms, an always particular meaning, antithetical to shared common sense. The snag is that meaning does not resolve the symptom but can even make it worse. The symptom's resistance to the elaboration of meaning, and specifically to Oedipal meaning, was noted very early on in the analytic movement which seemed to be traumatised by the depreciation of its results. Freud was ironic on this point: something resisted, the unconscious closed up. Registering this, the analytic movement turned then to the analysis of resistances, which did not help. Only Lacan came to the conclusion, and again later on, that the analytic path was not that of meaning. When I say the path, I refer to that which leads to the fixation of the symptom as well as to that which leads to its reduction, the idea being that it's in fact the same thing. If the kernel of the symptom comes from the Real outside meaning of obscene *lalangue*, it can only be resolved through this same Real.

The symptom indeed comes from the Real, and doubly so: from the real of the substance of *jouissance* and from the real of *lalangue*. We grasp now how Lacan was able to arrive at a redefinition of the unconscious as real, as outside meaning. It concerns the unconscious as the "spoken knowledge" [*savoir parlé*] of *lalangue*, a knowledge that is at the level of *jouissance*. As I pointed out, there is the lucubrated unconscious, that is, deciphered, which allows the subject to appropriate some ones of the letters of his symptom—in other words, "to know a bit about it", but only a bit. And then there is the unconscious as *lalangue*, which is not of the Symbolic, but Real, ungraspable. In *Encore*, Lacan evokes "the mystery of the speaking body" (Lacan, 1998, p. 131), in the sense of the mystery of the body affected in its *jouissance* by the knowledge of *lalangue*, affected in an always singular, and I would add, incalculable way. In this sense, if the subject as speaking is inscribed in the genealogy of discourse, the symptom that divides him as an "event of the body" has no genealogy, even if it carries the imprint of maternal *lalangue*. With the event of the body, we are neither at the level of logic or of language, nor even of the phantasy, but at the level of an accidental encounter between the word and *jouissance*, produced according to the contingencies of the first years of life and which, having stopped through the encounter not writing itself, will henceforth no longer stop writing itself, and which the subject will assume or not. If we consider Freud's example where, through linguistic equivocation, the glance at the nose and the shine on the nose become equated one, this shine became fixed as the condition of erotic choice.

I can reply here to a question that I raised some years ago and left in suspense, a question concerning the analysis of those analphabetic subjects that quite young children are, still in pre-language.

I would ask today if there is anyone who isn't analphabetic among analysands? What must be said is that the symptom, being written in letters of the unconscious as *lalangue*, is always itself analphabetic. It knows nothing of orthographic writing. It is writing without spelling or syntax, it is the letter that comes before this dematernalisation of *langue* that is the learning of spelling. Thus the symptom is always misspelled, by definition.

This is why dysorthography is on the whole a quite special symptom. Today, it would be worth reflecting on its increasing frequency in our culture. And rather than incriminating the new inefficiency of schools, we would perhaps then see that its powers at the time of the *Belle Époque* of the Third Republic came to it from somewhere else. Dysorthography—or if you prefer, sinn-graphic [*sinngraphique*], with the two *n*s of *sinn* that evokes "sin" in English from which Lacan picked up the term *sinthome*. As we know, there are no other sins than *jouissance*, nor ortho-sin either. I would conclude that to analyse is to seek the analphabetic. This is not the same as saying to seek the infantile, for the thesis does not imply that the child is infantile: on the contrary, just closer to the real. It is the adult who dreams wide-awake. We aim to lead the subject right to his point of analphabetism. And write *analphabêtisme* with the circumflex accent so as not to forget that the signifier is stupid [*bête*], which means contingent and outside meaning.

We can apply the schema that Lacan used for the lapsus to the symptom. In 2006 I commented on the remarks that open the "Preface to the English-language edition" of *Seminar XI*. In terms of the definition of the unconscious, these remarks are at odds with the first chapter of the seminar on the unconscious. Applied to the symptom they say, if I may put it briefly: when the signifier—the One of a symptom—no longer carries any meaning, it is only then that we are sure that we are in the unconscious, the real unconscious, the enjoyed unconscious.

We see to what this reference to the real unconscious responds in its distinction from unconscious meaning: conceptually, the real unconscious contrasts with the unconscious supposed by the transference, and practically, in the diachrony of analysis it is in position as the end of the transference.

I said that Lacan did not stop looking for a way to conceptualise what could stop the flow of analytic blah blah under transference, as well as the endlessness of deciphering which, in its recurrence, can always tolerate one more cipher. He sought an end that did not reproduce the Freudian bedrock.

This is what led him to formulate, beyond the schema of the pass via the object, presented in the "Proposition of 9 October 1967 on the psychoanalyst of the school" (Lacan, 1995), what I have called "the pass to the Real", which he gave, I believe, a reduced model in 1976 in the first sentence of this text. We still need to consider the impasse to which it responds: that of the transference.

Note

1. There are many references: *Encore, Television*, "La troisieme" (end of October 1974), The Geneva lecture on the symptom (October 1975), and then some further comments in "*L'insu que sait d'l'une bevue s'aile a mourre*" and "*Le moment de conclure*".

CHAPTER FOUR

From the transference towards the other unconscious

"The unconscious is a fact inasmuch as it is supported by the discourse which establishes it"

The transference, a name of the unconscious

To say "impasse", to bring up the necessary "fall" of the transference if not its "liquidation", should not lead analysts to chant the well-known refrain about the detrimental effects of the transference, especially as this critical note is dominant in contemporary discourse where it is only spoken about as a power likely to obscure reason and paralyse the will; a sort of public danger that is often confused with that of sects. This should already alert us and above all put us on our guard.

Indeed, we must not forget that analysis owes everything to the transference: there is no psychoanalysis without the postulate of the subject supposed to know. Everyone agrees on this. What is apparently less well understood is that without this postulate there is no unconscious either, for the unconscious, as I have said, is not just one thing among others. It is the transference that makes it supposed. Lacan produced a matheme for it, written in accordance with the algorithm signifier/signified (Lacan, 1995). The subject supposed to knowledge, a knowledge itself supposed from the signifiers of the unconscious, is written at the place of the signified of the analytic address. In this sense, the transference is a name of the unconscious, but the unconscious as supposed; hence the fact that it is essentially tied to belief. We could even say that it is in essence itself belief. This is indeed, outside analysis, what it is reproached for: its credulity. The term "supposition" was a way of giving epistemic dignity to the transference by raising it to the status of a scientific hypothesis. The term, introduced in the seminar *The Four Fundamental Concepts of Psychoanalysis* (Lacan, 1981b), should be paired with another expression from the same period, the "position of the unconscious", which already shows that it is not enough to suppose the unconscious in order to position it. The supposition belongs to the analysand, the position to the analyst. The analytic act—whatever its manifestations—is this: to position an unconscious, which in itself is not positioned, and from this fact the analysand will be able to suppose, for supposition is a retroaction of positioning. Hence the idea—which is not paradoxical if we know the link of the unconscious to speech—that psychoanalysts are responsible for the unconscious.

But, you might object, the dream, the lapsus, the bungled action, not to mention the symptom, are they not obvious expressions of the unconscious? No doubt, but only in the retroaction of Freud's act, he who first posited them as such in claiming that a truth was at work there. The specificity of Freud is that with him the supposition and the act of positioning were linked. Between the manifestations I just mentioned—called "mistakes" ["*méprise*"] by Lacan—and the assertion of the unconscious, there is the saying of Freud. And that is why psychoanalysis remains appended to this saying. The result is that when confronted with those who hold these expressions of the unconscious in contempt, those who thus scorn the mistake [*qui méprisent donc la méprise*], there is no convincing argument, nor can so-called clinical demonstration convince them or make them agree.

The series of mistakes—lapsus, bungled action, symptom—should be completed with free association. Association, according to Freud, is a way of speaking uncoupled from intentional mastery, and which aims to make the intrusion of unexpected signifiers possible: a way of speaking in which the subject accepts not knowing what he is saying. We know that a subject who does not accept this register of "I am speaking, but I do not know what I am saying" renders any interpretation ineffective. This is why I so often say that the call for confessions, testimony or opinion, so prized today, and about which statistics are created, is in itself a denial of the unconscious, since testimony is a form of speaking reduced to saying what one knows, or believes one knows.

Lacan insisted, following Freud, that free association is the knowledge supposed to the analysand subject and not to the analyst. At the start, the analyst knows nothing about the unconscious of his patient. All he knows is to make it appear through speech and it is only at the end of an analysis that he will know a little bit about it.

The analysand presents himself beneath a signifier that Lacan calls the signifier of the transference. What is it if not simply what the subject presents to the analyst? It is what is unthinkable or unmasterable for him, and which thus makes a hole in what he thinks he knows about himself, as well as in what he thinks he can "manage", as people say nowadays, regarding his suffering and helplessness, for the symptom resists management. The transference, beginning with a signifier outside meaning, establishes the supposition of knowledge. This is why it appears in the analysand who is affected by the non-sense of the symptom, in a temporality of expectation: expectation of the knowledge that will provide a solution to the hole produced by the subject's mistakes, and specifically a solution to his symptom. It is this expected knowledge that is in a way transferred onto the side of the analyst and somehow expected from his interpretation. The transferential signification thus oscillates from one partner to the other: the analysand expects from the analyst via interpretation the very knowledge supposed to free association by the analytic procedure. From the phenomenology of the procedure, we see what is constant—the supposition of knowledge—and what varies—the subject to whom it is imputed.

The effect of free association on the supposition of knowledge is rather ambiguous.

I said expectation of knowledge, but in what form is this expectation presented? Each, let us say naïve, analysand does not refer directly to knowledge. What he expects over and above therapy is to make sense of nonsense: in other words, to find the truth that it contains. The expectation of knowledge actually takes the form of the expectation of meaning. We should recognise the importance of this fact in order to connect Lacan's formulas to the analytic experience itself. The expected meaning is latent in the series of associated signifiers that emerge in the analysand's speech, and can be taken as the response of the unconscious itself.

In fact, as Lacan said in the "Introduction to the German edition of the first volume of the *Écrits*", analysis delivers to the analysand the meaning of his symptoms. Indeed, but the meaning is singular, specific to each person. It does not constitute a transmittable knowledge. There is no shared meaning of any symptom, only particular truths. Truth and meaning are nonetheless linked. They have in common, firstly, that both are phenomena of the subject (there is meaning or truth only for a subject), and secondly, that neither can add up to knowledge: truth because it can only be half-said, meaning because it flees, irreducibly.

Analytic discourse, as Lacan formulates it, puts knowledge in the place of truth. This means, firstly, that in the speech of the analysand there is no solution to the half-said. It certainly happens that a subject gets fixated on some production of truth and gives it a consistency to the point of making it his last word, but essentially the more that the saying of truth occurs, the more it accumulates, the more the analyst receives them as so many fictions of truth, not a signified truth that would be equal to knowledge. There is thus an impotence of truth. Secondly, however, the half-said of truth would not exist without the signifiers of the unconscious, not without its *motérialité*. Hence the strange and disconcerting formula in the "Preface to the English-language edition" of *Seminar XI* that the unconscious function—and he is speaking here of the real unconscious—"fiddles with the truth" (Lacan, 1981a, p. viii). The term "fiddle" is sexually suggestive, implying that it [the truth] does not go as far as the consummation of the wedding night.

Free association is a tantalising structure. On the one hand, it supports the transferential supposition through the recurrence of the emergence of truth; on the other hand, it contests this supposition through its equally recurrent powerlessness to find the other half of half-said truth. A mirage of truth, Lacan says, to emphasise that it never arrives at the oasis of completeness, at the whole truth, but rather gets lost in what he rightly called the "desert of analysis".

What is shown in the analysand's speech is that there is no marriage between the subject's articulated truth and knowledge, and that knowledge itself has no boundary. Cantor, help us! But the analysand is not Cantor, and the series of associations is not the series of transfinite numbers. The more that truth is articulated, making the meaning of the symptom emerge—and that's the product of the elaboration of the transference—the more that unconscious knowledge is proven to be real, ungraspable. Lacan suggests this well before 1976. In 1970, in "Radiophonie", he already said that the more that discourse is interpreted, the more it is confirmed as unconscious. And later, that to elaborate the unconscious is to make it even more unconscious.

We can already conclude from this that the transference, which supposes a subject to expected knowledge, is also a kind of denial of the unconscious, as the unconscious is precisely "knowledge without a subject". That there is a divergence of supposition between the transference and the unconscious was pointed out in 1967 in "The mistake of the subject supposed to know". I said that science has prepared us for this idea of knowledge in the real, but the difference is that it is precisely in psychoanalysis that knowledge without a subject fiddles with the truth, that is to say, with the subject. It even "dreams" of the truth, Lacan would say. The whole problem is to move to the real unconscious through the work of the transference.

Reduced model of the pass to the RUCS

Lacan took the trouble to provide a schema of what I call the pass to the Real in the "Preface to the English-language edition" of *Seminar XI* to which I have just referred.

I'll pause at the first sentence: "When the *l'esp* of a *laps*, that is, since I only write in French: when the space of a lapsus, no longer carries any meaning (or interpretation), only then is one sure that one is in the unconscious. *One knows*" (Lacan, 1981a, p. vii). I have already commented on this sentence several times since 2006. Lacan is giving, I believe, a reduced model of what we call the fall of the subject supposed to know, namely a pass to the real unconscious that I will from now on write as RUCS, to get rid of the usual signifieds of the term "unconscious".

I leave aside the implicit and ironical allusion to Kant's transcendental aesthetic of time and space, as well as the play on writing with its resonances in what is heard. A lapsus, a blunder, is the moment of intrusion in the subject's guarded discourse of a signifier that all of a sudden—*laps* [lapse]—usurps the place, *esp.* [space] of the word the subject intended to say. It is quite simple. But its status, between a simple error and lapsus, is ambiguous, for one could think it were nothing if not for the transference.

What is the space of the lapsus? Nothing other than what is joined to it: the chain of associations through which the subject tries to give meaning to this incongruous signifier. Lacan's topology had always linked space, understood as extended, to the deployment of the signifying chain, and hence his first approach to the subject in terms of a surface, albeit moebian. To associate in order to give meaning is to try to reappropriate the "intrusive" signifier, to try to make it a signifier of one's truth by connecting it to other signifiers. In other words, it is to attempt to reduce the mistake. Free association moreover has in general this double function: to allow signifiers to make a surprise appearance and then to appropriate them by giving them meaning through the addition of other signifiers.

The space of the lapsus is in fact the space of the transferential work that supposes a subject of the lapsus and that attempts to reach its truth. This is the space of the "hystorisation" of the subject. It is in this space of giving meaning that the unconscious fiddles with truth, which is always the subject's truth. This could be written synchronically with the matheme of the transference:

$$\frac{\text{Laps [lapse]}}{s(S_1, S_2, \ldots S_n)}$$

Except that in the text I am commenting on, Lacan formulates it in terms of a temporal sequence, corresponding to what happens in the analytic elaboration and adding a moment of time that is not written in the matheme of the transference.

Three times, then:

1. *laps*. 2. space of *laps*. 3. the real unconscious.

The third time is there to say that when this space of hystorisation no longer carries any meaning, we exit this transference and enter the unconscious, the real unconscious. I said, *this* transference, for it is the transference grafted onto the lapsus. What then remains of the *laps*? Only its word, an element of knowledge which has not only emerged in spite of the subject, without his consent, but which finally remains in its facticity, as an isolated signifier disconnected from the articulated truth of the subject. Outside the chain and hence real, it testifies to the unconscious working all alone, outside meaning but not outside *jouissance, quasi* neological. The real unconscious is neological if neologism consists in giving to words the weight of an ineffable and personal *jouissance*. Made of signifiers outside the chain and implanted in the field of *jouissance*—that the lapsus shows without deciphering—it is the psychotic kernel of every speaking being. I will come back to this.

We could say that the real unconscious is not constructed in the way that the unconscious as phantasy is, and we encounter it at the moments when it makes surprising appearances.

In the matheme of the transference, the unconscious only figures as supposed. The word of the lapsus can ultimately be said to be real, first as a signifier that no longer calls any S_2, and hence quite isolated and disconnected. This is the first definition Lacan gave of the signifier in the Real, in relation to psychosis. But there is more: it is also real in that the signifier is situated at the level of *jouissance*. This is the thesis of the seminar *Encore*. And doubly so, because it affects *jouissance* by negativising it on the one hand, transporting it metonymically—the Other of the signifier also has its place in the living body where it has its effects—and on the other, the signifier is itself enjoyed. This is what Lacan argued from 1973 on: "The unconscious is the fact that the being, by speaking, enjoys" (Lacan, 1998, p. 105). This word of the *laps* outside meaning, real and in the Real, does not fiddle [*tripote*] with the truth. I would say rather that it knocks about [fricote] with *jouissance*. And here we could evoke the expression that Lacan uses, "impact of meaning" [*portée de sens*], which is not identical to "effect of meaning" and which—beyond the production of meaning—connotes the satisfaction attached to meaning and to truth.

Where in this sequence are we to situate what in 1964 Lacan called the Freudian unconscious, this Euridycean unconscious of pre-ontological status that makes a surprise appearance in subjectivity? I think it should be situated it in what he calls the space of the lapsus. Let us say that this is the unconscious as truth, which of course does not go without the structure of language. But the unconscious of 1976 is not simply the unconscious as truth. Like it, no doubt it speaks, but elevating speech to the status of the operator that governs *jouissance* it makes the "*parlêtre*", who speaks "with [his] body". How could we not recognise the radicality and novelty of this thesis compared to the earlier formulas that had become canonical? It is true that Lacan invoked the real from the start of his teaching, but not in the same sense. What he situated as real at this moment was the real of the cut, an unconscious as truth that came into being in the gap of the subject, in the repetition of the cut.

Let's go back to the 1976 text. In time 3, one is therefore *in* the unconscious, namely, there where there is no subject. The "one" is thus well justified. It would not be possible to say, "*I* am in the unconscious", since the real unconscious is knowledge without a subject.

I rewrite this sequence that goes from the transference to the real unconscious:

$$1.\ \frac{Laps}{s}\ ;\quad 2.\ \frac{\text{(Space of associated Signifiers)}}{\text{(meaning, hystorisation, UCS as truth)}}\ ;\quad 3.\ \frac{\text{Signifier of the }Laps}{\text{RUCS (outside meaning)}}$$

So, at first, the *laps* with its supposed subject; then the space of the transferential hystorisation with its effects of meaning; lastly, the reduction of the *laps* to a signifier, outside meaning, detached from any supposition of a subject. This is why I say that it is a reduced model of the fall of the subject supposed to know, a fall that makes the signifier of the *laps* emerge as real.

But caution, this is not a place where one can get settled. I quote: "But one has only to be aware of the fact to find oneself outside it". Indeed, awareness—at least that's how I understand it—is a phenomenon of the subject, an expression of his opening to the world, which in itself poses questions. Bringing back the question of the hole in meaning, it reopens the space of transferential associations, which means starting this process again, "like the sea, always starting again". So to be in the unconscious does not promise the subject any knowledge of the unconscious: the place is not a tourist attraction. There is no friendship that will last.

When one is there, "one knows", says Lacan. The verb is "to know" [*savoir*], but that does not constitute a knowledge [*un savoir*] (here, the substantive) that can be elevated to the level of the universal. It is the major and radical objection in these years around 1976 to the ideal of complete transmission, linked to science, on which Lacan had for such a long time wished to model psychoanalysis. The unconscious as *lalangue* implies rather a complete non-transmission: "The analytic thing will not be mathematical" (Lacan, 1998, p. 117), says the seminar *Encore*. In other words, the real unconscious is not teachable, and is only verified for each person in the singular experience of the elaboration that is their analysis. There are two conditions here: that the unconscious is at first presupposed (transference), and that the analytic act supplies "the partner who has a chance of responding" (Lacan, 1975c, p. 16).

Before an analysis one may be in transference, in the unconscious as supposed, but not in the real unconscious. This unconscious is only experienced in an analysis, and nowhere else, but one cannot capture it, one cannot recognise oneself in it, one cannot communicate it, and it won't result in any "friendship". This is another way of saying that there is no desire for knowledge. We are at the limit here of what analysts can exchange with those who do not have this experience. The discourse on the unconscious is not only a discourse condemned in advance, but also a discourse that excludes the unconscious. This is the whole problem of educational courses on psychoanalysis and it would be better not to forget it when we wish to speak to other discourses, and especially to those of the neurosciences!

The flaw of the subject supposed to know

In analytic experience, unconscious knowledge without a subject begins where the supposition of the subject stops. Flaw, Lacan says. The fallacy of the supposition of a subject to knowledge is revealed here. Note the different terms he used over the years to speak of this fallacy: transference is only a signification, thus imaginary; an unreal; a postulate; lastly, a lure. But neither the subject nor knowledge is imaginary; what is imaginary is the supposition of their union.

Flaw here is not a vague metaphor: it is very precisely the flaw between the subject and the unconscious. On the one hand, a subject who runs after truth but misses it because truth is never whole, the awareness of which reveals the lie. On the other hand, this knowledge manifests itself as affecting being through its intrusion, but it does not belong to the subject. The flaw points to an impossible conjunction of the impasses that mark the two edges: on the one hand, speaking the truth, I miss it; on the other hand, the real unconscious can be neither subjectivised nor exhausted.

However, this flaw does not herald the end of the transference. It is only a necessary condition. Besides, is there ever only One end to the transference (whatever the phenomena outside the transference may be)?

We see this first at the level of the sequence, since attention to the unconscious inevitably brings back the transference. Only just denounced, the lure of the subject supposed to know is reconstituted. And how can attention not be focused on this "without a subject", since it belongs to the subject and does not leave him indifferent, shearing through his thought, his will and his body? This sequential balancing between elaboration of truth and real unconscious is thus reproduced in analysis. Approaching the unconscious destitutes the supposed subject yet summons it as well.

This occurs not only in the experience of an analysis, since any real knowledge raises the question of the place it occupied, this "nothing but knowledge". We are back to Descartes, summoning God as guarantor of his arithmetic, but also to Cantor. It is the thesis of "The mistake of the subject supposed to know": the subject supposed to know is latent in every theory. Since to theorise is to seek a knowledge that gives an account of a real, a knowledge which is not yet available but which one supposes is there to capture. Such is the transference. This allows us to understand how the transference can be spoken of in the case of the analysed analyst, provided that we distinguish between the analyst who operates—by his act—and the analyst who thinks or tries to think the analytic experience. The certainty of the act is no doubt outside the transference. Within transference, when it comes to the act there are only passages to the act. But the analyst who tries to think psychoanalysis, to theorise the experience, is necessarily under transference: in other words, an analysand.

CHAPTER FIVE

The royal road to the RUCS

In following Lacan's trajectory, I realised that his references to the formations of the unconscious changed over time.

We could say that he commented on them all methodically. We have the main developments on the dream, the *Witz*, the lapsus, the bungled action, the forgotten word, etc. Then there comes a time when he has more or less finished with his return to Freud and where he evokes the triad: dream, lapsus, and joke. There are many examples in the texts of the 1970s: "L'étourdit" (1973), "Introduction à l'édition allemande des Écrits" (1975c), and later in others.

Then we have the famous text I have just referred to and at which I paused, the "Introduction to the English-language edition" of *Seminar XI* where the lapsus appears on its own. We are in May 1976, just before the start of the seminar *"L'insu que sait d'l'une bévue s'aile à mourre"* which emphasises the unconscious as lapsus. Lacan notes that a blunder [*bévue*] is difficult to define, but the definition he gives of it is after all still "one word for another".

I asked myself why the lapsus would be privileged as the gateway to the unconscious since the formations of the unconscious are not the unconscious but only the roads that lead to it. It seemed useful to tackle this question in order to gauge what it is that changes with the RUCS.

Motérialité *of the unconscious*

"When *l'esp* of a *laps*, namely the space of a lapsus, etc." This handling of "*motérialité*" to which Lacan devoted himself in the last years, this fragmentation, trituration, this play between sonority and written form—as in the title "*L'insu que sait d'l'une bévue ...*"—is generally attributed to Joyce. But Joyce himself follows the mode of unconscious processes, those that Lacan seeks to illuminate in these last years in particular. He never uses them, as far as I can see, without a precise intention, and here he distinguishes himself from Joyce, for whom word games are directly connected to *jouissance* without passing through meaning, which obviously gives them an enigmatic status.

I see two very different intentions here.

The first one, inconspicuous and introduced quietly thanks to the *esp* of the *laps*, is epistemo-political. Lacan extracts a single syllable by fragmenting the two words "space" and "lapsus". I would not say a single phoneme, since in French "lapse" [*laps*] is itself a word that has a meaning. The *laps* refers to time, even a measure of time, next to space.

The beginning of this sentence thus evokes, in the latency of its significations, the two categories of space and time of Immanuel Kant's transcendental aesthetic, through which Kant tries to give an account of the universality of Newtonian physics in his *Critique of Pure Reason*.

In the background are the multiple developments of Lacan's continued contestation of Kant's transcendental aesthetic. We can ask: in the name of what and of whom? Einstein and quantum physics, no doubt, but above all Freud. With regard to the first, the argument is developed in response to the second question in "Radiophonie". With regard to the second, how many times will Lacan need to repeat that the topology of the unconscious made it necessary to revise Kant's transcendental aesthetic. He is severe with it, going as far in "L'étourdit" as describing it as inept and idiotic.

Now, for Lacan, epistemic debates always have a political dimension. With regard to Kant, this is made explicit in the "Introduction à l'édition allemande des Écrits" where, speaking of common sense which dominates politics, he says: "I do not have to remind you of it speaking as I am to the German public which has traditionally added to it the meaning of critique"—Kant here again—"Without it being useless to here recall where it led to in 1933" (Lacan, 2001b, p. 555). I do not believe that it was to rekindle an old quarrel, but rather so we do not forget that to think proceeds via an ethical path and always involves politics, whether outside or inside psychoanalysis. Thus whether to think or not to think the unconscious has consequences.

The second aim is more analytic.

In his act of breaking up the words "space" ["*espace*"] and "lapsus", Lacan reminds us of what he had already proposed years previously, even before *Encore*: that the phoneme is the minimal sonorous unity of *lalangue* and thus of the unconscious. When we read that in a text from 1976 we should not be amazed for he did not discover it there.

It dates from the time of the seminar "The formations of the unconscious". He picks up the point again in 1968 in "From an Other to the other" (Lacan, March 2006, pp. 51ff) in the session of 27th November, where he takes up his graph of desire (Lacan, [1960b] 2006, p. 692). He insists on what he had proposed in 1958, citing his text, that his graph with its two horizontal lines of the signifiers of the Other and the signifiers of the unconscious, and the retrograde curved line which intersects them, is made up of three signifying chains (contrary to what is often said) when we make the retrograde curved line the line of the

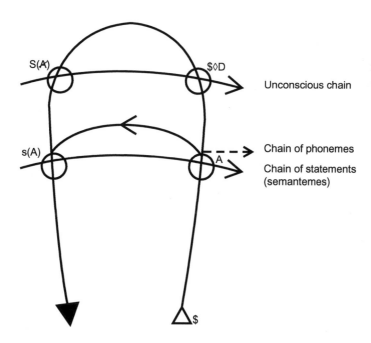

Graph of the *Witz*

signified crossing that of the signifier, as is the case in the structure of speech. Lacan corrects this reading as if in anticipation: it concerns three signifying chains but with two states of the signifier.

On the lower horizontal chain is the signifier as semanteme, that is to say, defined by a rule-bound even if never univocal use: thus, words which have a meaning. Let us say that this is the line of the dictionary, of the *langue* we exchange. On the curved line, he says, the signifier is at the level of phonemes, in themselves devoid of meaning and recombinable without consideration for the rule-bound uses of the dictionary.

It took me quite a long time to grasp the grounds for this assertion. In fact, the thesis is there for a precise reason, Lacan tells us, but without further explanation. It is necessary in order to explain how jokes are possible: these specific blunders that seem to be calculated. Thanks to phonemes, a second chain may be latent in the chain of semantemes, that is to say, in statements. Here then is what opens up the question of a differential assessment of blunders, for all the failures through which the unconscious comes to us do not all perhaps have the same value.

Failures that do not have equal value

The dream and the lapsus are only ever of value to the extent that they elude a particular person's consciousness. They pertain to one's irreducible singularity, and their interpretation only has value for one individual, although that may not please Jung. Among the formations of the unconscious, the joke, on the contrary, has the particularity if not to collectivise at least to function beyond the particular, at least for all those who share a language and a culture. It thus offers the general model of the possible latency, to use the Freudian term, of the unconscious. Functioning at the level of common speech, on the lower chain of the graph, the joke testifies to the possible presence of another discourse within speech, the latency of another saying within vigilant speech. The laugh, as it surprises us, indicates that the combinatory of the ones of *lalangue*—let us say, the ciphering of the humourist—has opened the door of the unconscious.

However, to quote a remark from 1967, it's the door "beyond which there is nothing more to find", and the laugh authorises the "way that has been spared" [*chemin épargné*]. I had always wondered about this sentence and I understand it better with the 1976 text that I commented on above. The way is that of transferential space.

It is not a particularity of the lapsus to open the transferential space. It is the case for every "symptomatic formation of the unconscious" to "demonstrate [the] relation to the subject supposed to know" (Lacan, 1990b, p. 43). Indeed, every blunder may be treated like the One, the one lacking meaning since it emerged without being summoned by consciousness, and from that time on it opens the space of the call for meaning.

The particularity of the *Witz* is that rather than opening transferential space it contracts it in a punctual effect of meaning, closing as soon as it is opened. And we know that any gloss kills it. Beyond laughter there is no meaning to find. In other words, we are immediately at the end of the reach of meaning.

The lapsus, in contrast to the *Witz* does not spare us the way of the transferential elaboration of the search for meaning, at least when the analyst is there to support the transferential quest. As for the speaker's intention, a blunder opens the door of the space to pass through, the space, let us say, of its reading. This reading stops on the threshold of the door beyond which there is nothing further to find, when there is no longer any scope for meaning. This is the door to which the *Witz* led directly and which opens onto the real unconscious.

What then remains? Nothing other than an emergence of this knowledge without a subject that inhabits *lalangue*, the knowledge that works on its own without a subject but not without effects. Impossible to master, it is "without a master". The defeat of Descartes: the subject of psychoanalysis is perhaps the Cartesian subject of science, but the knowledge of the unconscious is not the knowledge of science.

So in what way would the lapsus be superior to the dream as a manifestation of the unconscious?

The lapsus—which is like the dream but unlike the *Witz* in that it is specific to a given subject—is a purely linguistic phenomenon, situated entirely at the level of "*matérialité*". This is not the case with the dream. The dream is not purely linguistic. Without a doubt Lacan, following Freud, made every effort to show that in spite of its imaginary scenarios the dream was a ciphering, and that provided it was deciphered it could be read differently. In this sense, Freud totally renewed the traditional approach to the dream.

But note first that this did not stop Jung from searching for the key to dreams, which, moreover, had been sought long before psychoanalysis. Analysts may very well turn their noses up at this, but if it exists and withstands time it is because it is possible, and if it is possible it is because the dream lends itself to it. On the other hand, no one could imagine that there would be a key to the lapsus, with its own vocabulary and interpretations.

A second remark: deciphering, from which we deduce the linguistic nature of the dream, is always risky. To decipher is firstly to determine the vocabulary before later extracting the message. The operation is always "problematic", liable only to lead to lucubration, as I said.

The lapsus, in contrast, is not lucubrated: it is epiphanic because it is in itself a ciphering. It makes an unexpected sign emerge in speech, not programmed by vigilant speech. A blunder is always possible: a chosen word stops writing itself to the benefit of another that imposes itself. It is not deciphered but actually given meaning, by recombination through association with other ciphers that have come from consciousness, up to the point of the exhaustion of meaning.

Does this mean that the space of the dream has no end? That could well be the case. We would not exit from the interpretation of a dream for it can always be deciphered differently, and sometimes over a whole lifetime.

I was intrigued by a remark of Lacan's at the beginning of "L'insu que sait d'l'une bévue s'aile à mourre" which marks the dream's difference from the lapsus. He notes that the dream is a blunder, except—my emphasis—that we can recognise ourselves in it. Idem for the Witz. Here then is another sorting principle between the aforementioned failures.

If as a manifestation of the unconscious the advantage remains with the lapsus, it is precisely because we do not recognise ourselves in the lapsus, which has no more scope for meaning. It places us in the heterity of the real unconscious, outside meaning, and without the subject that constitutes the speaking being.

I will conclude. The dream is the royal road to the Freudian unconscious. I would add that this road goes no further than the truth signified by the signifiers extracted from it. More than the dream, the lapsus is the major manifestation of the Lacanian unconscious, the real unconscious. If Freud distinguished the dream from all the other blunders as the royal road, it is because it occurs when consciousness sleeps, testifying to another psychical activity. But with the lapsus of langue, if I may say, the spoken knowledge of lalangue is revealed in a blunder that testifies to the real unconscious in pure form.

CHAPTER SIX

The Borromean *aleph*

After the period in which the unconscious is formulated in terms of language, the signified of which is sought, it was a major step to uncover the real unconscious made of "incarnated" ones, outside the chain and outside meaning, challenging the idea of the unconscious as symbolic. The RUCS is a-structural: far from being constructed or interpreted, it is encountered in emergences that are always punctual and which defy both awareness and communication.

Let's remind ourselves of the steps that led to this thesis: they go from the structure of signifying representation stemming from the linguistic conceptualisation of the Freudian practice of deciphering, to the unconscious "knowledge without a subject" implied by this same structure, a knowledge which if not determinant of the subject determines his *jouissance*. This was first thought of in terms of object *a*, as the lacking object or as the object of surplus *jouissance*, then in terms of *lalangue* as the place of this "spoken knowledge" [*savoir parlé*] which civilises *jouissance* by giving it its linguistic form.

Such an advance could not fail to affect the entire Lacanian corpus, in a series of cascading re-workings of all the notions previously used: the opposition between the real and meaning, a devaluation of the lying truth, the promotion of the notion of the *parlêtre* as another name for the real unconscious, a new light thrown on interpretation, the aims, means and end of analysis, a re-evaluation of clinical categories, the function of affect, the nature of love, transmission, etc.

To weigh up these repercussions, we need to take into consideration the new analytic questions introduced by the reference to *lalangue* and its effects. The crucial point for me is that *lalangue* is what I would call an uncertainty principle. As I have stressed, the One of *jouissance* that would not be merely one among others is uncertain, hypothetical, for the "spoken knowledge" of the unconscious challenges any capture in knowledge. To put it another way, the part of knowledge that emerges from analytic work appears in deficit in relation to knowledge of the real *lalangue* and, besides, is liable to be only imaginary.

At one time, Lacan would encourage questioning the unconscious until it gave an answer that was not ineffable, in the form of the phantasy or the signifiers spelled out from the symptom. A nice programme, but tricky for the unconscious as *lalangue*, which is never wholly decipherable and whose deciphered part remains hypothetical.

How can this unconscious respond? If the effects of *lalangue* go beyond us, and we can agree with Lacan that they do, then is not psychoanalysis brought back to the double pitfall of the ineffable and uncertainty? This is the failure of the matheme, as Lacan notes in *Encore*. He who had made such a big deal of the "mathematics of the signifier" states, as I have said, that "The analytic thing will not be mathematical". Poetic perhaps? Except that the poem is already composed, every analysand being a poem more than a poet, but a poem that is impossible to read in its entirety. With *lalangue*, it is not a question of either mathematics or logic but of the signifier in the real that is not possible to exhaust.

After the fragmentary responses that are deciphered from it—let us say, its letters, since the letter is defined as a fusion of *jouissance* with a linguistic element outside meaning—how are we to approach this real unconscious?

Lacan's focus on the real, as I have said, comes well before the concept of the RUCS. Since the flow of speech and the endlessness of deciphering do not have any full stop, Lacan at first referred to the barriers that "function as real" in the analysand's speech in order to formulate the finiteness of the analytic process. As I said, we can follow the successive formulas by which he defined the real. The first two bring up the logical category of the impossible: the impossible to say, then the impossible to write.

The real unconscious is something else. It can't be proved, it is not reached through logic; it emerges. That's why I have used the Joycean term "epiphany". The real unconscious has its home in *lalangue* and does not stem from the structural approach that precedes it in Lacan's teaching. The effect of *lalangue* is doubly real: its Ones are outside the chain and thus outside meaning. They have passed into the field of the Real outside the Symbolic, that of the living substance. The snag is that this unconscious spoken knowledge makes knowledge fail—an uncertainty principle, as I have said.

The recourse to the new framework of the Borromean knot— introduced at the same time as the emphasis on the function of *lalangue*—responds in part to this difficulty and finds there, I believe, one of its strongest justifications.

The linguistic matheme, S/s, whereby the unconscious as phantasy could be formulated, did not allow for the Real of the living being to be situated, the Real which is outside the Symbolic and outside the Imaginary, which is not a signified and which owes nothing to the subject. "The Symbolic only makes things phantasmatically", Lacan will say. Now, symptoms are not phantasmatic but well and truly inscribed in the Real "which the body enjoys" (Lacan, 1975a). As we see through analysis, their enjoyed *motérialité* points to both the real of *lalangue* and that of the living being. In representing this Real, which is truly unthinkable despite the efforts of the life sciences, Lacan performs a kind of Cantorian operation—his own *aleph zero*—with one of the three rings of string of which the knot consists. For with the knot, this absolute referent, without being known, becomes theoretically manipulable. The Borromean knot is an instrument with which to formulate the Real that is neither imagined nor thought, in order to reveal its place and possible function.

To the interlocking of the two dimensions of the Imaginary and the Symbolic, first approached by Lacan within a linguistic framework, the knot adds their three-fold interlocking with the Real. As I said, he presupposes the autonomy and equivalence of these three dimensions, and a renewal of the definitions of these three *dit-mensions* is thereby opened up. Between Imaginary and Symbolic, there is meaning, the unconscious as phantasy, what Lacan is going to call "mentality". Mentality is thus a combination. It is no longer that of the hierarchical signifier and signified of the period of "The agency of the letter". Instead, it implies a knotting of these two dimensions. This mixture that chattering involves—whether in psychoanalysis or not—made up of representations and signifiers, is described by Lacan as feeble-minded—"man thinks feeble-mindedly" [*l'homme pense débile*], he said to indicate that we have no purchase on the Real outside the Symbolic.

It also opens up a new combinatory, that of possible knottings and their effects. In fact, Lacan spent years studying possible ways of knotting in the hope of discovering their translation into the clinic.

The real *jouissance* disconnected from the subject must be knotted to the word, between Symbolic and Real, in order to be decipherable in analysis. Marked by *lalangue*, which fragments, partialises, and absorbs it, it is spliced [*se schize*] purely in schizophrenia, leaving the subject in the isolated autism of his *jouissance*.

If this real unconscious is knotted to the Imaginary it becomes fixed, while in turn it "limits" the Imaginary, mooring it sufficiently for the subject not to be completely in the delusion of mentality. It is not a coincidence that from 1975 onwards Lacan developed the notion of mentality from which he produces a new diagnosis—"the illness of mentality"—to designate an Imaginary without the ballast of the Real and which rambles along ruled by circumstance.

The necessity of a new framework that allows the unthinkable Real to be situated is not in doubt. However, handling it is not without difficulty when it is a question of thinking about the analytic experience.

This difficulty is due to the fact that a knot presents a synchronic structure whereas analysis takes place within time. In its diachrony, which proceeds only through words, the real of the unconscious, as I have said, is approached as an end and limit point of the sayings of truth. This is what allows us to assert that the joke spares the way, or that Joyce, with his treatment of *lalangue*, went directly to the best of what we can expect from the end of an analysis. With the knot, Lacan tried to retranslate what happens in the time of an analysis, no longer in terms of metaphor and metonymy with their anchoring or vanishing points, but in terms of a knot being made, being transformed, being undone, etc. Hence the expressions such as the knot "is already made", "lapsus of the knot", suture, splicing, knot of paranoia, etc., which refer to the knottings that are altered through speech, in its diversity.

This change of paradigm becomes a bit clearer if we think that a metaphor is a stitching together of signifier and meaning, this meaning that Lacan places exactly in the knot between Imaginary and Symbolic, a stitching that occurs through speech but not without the contribution of *jouissance*. However, there is nevertheless a "but"; no one has as yet produced, for example, the knot of the entry into the transference, the knot of the exit, the knot of what Freud called working-through, or of the time it takes, etc. That could be a project.

On the other hand, the clinical fecundity of this new framework is judged by the new contributions it inspires. It has produced a lot, and allows us to rethink the classic notions of inhibition, symptom and anxiety; to distinguish the symptom from the *sinthome*, as well as the real symptom from meaning; to theorise differently the classic clinical structures—neurosis, psychosis, and perversion; to introduce a new category of psychosis—the illness of mentality; to rethink the suppletions [*suppléances*] of psychosis; to resituate the Father function as *sinthome*; and also to replace the various types of interpretations. In this re-evaluation, I will begin with the introduction of the new term "*parlêtre*".

CHAPTER SEVEN

The *parlêtre*

This term echoes the emphasis on the function of *lalangue*, its link with the real of *jouissance*, that is constitutive of the real unconscious. It is preceded by the introduction of the new Borromean framework, basically starting from *Encore*. It does not get rid of the notion of the subject as want-to-be, but adds to it by indicating that the subject only has being from what comes through the incarnated effects of *lalangue*.

The term *parlêtre* is introduced in the second lecture on Joyce published in 1979 in the volume *Joyce avec Lacan* (Lacan, [1979] 1987). The date of the writing of this lecture has not been established, but I am sure that it is contemporary with the seminar on Joyce and is probably even a bit later. I note, indeed, that the introduction of *lalangue* and the Borromean knot in Lacan's teaching immediately follows a new emphasis from 1970 on writing and the letter.[1]

With the periodisation of Lacan's teaching, a prejudiced reading occurs which suggests several, successive Lacans: first, the one of speech and language, then, that of the object *a*, finally, that of *jouissance* and of the Real. Not the Real as the limit of formalisation—"which does not stop not writing itself"—but the Real that is well and truly there, as it is inscribed in the Borromean knot. A facticity outside the Symbolic, thus also outside meaning, and even outside enjoyed meaning, outside "I think, therefore it enjoys itself", this is the Real that is not all, not universal, resistant to representation. But with this term "*parlêtre*" we immediately see that the function of speech that was present at the beginning is still there at the end.

Inventoried speech

Is it a question here of a return to speech? I do not think so because it had never been forgotten. But perhaps it is not the same function of speech. Periodisation, leading us to expect what will come at the end, sometimes has a pedagogic value, but it does not respect what to me seems to characterise Lacan's epistemology. This certainly brings together startling speed and progress, but in an elaboration that proceeds by continually revising the previous set of notions, without negating them. Sometimes it even keeps the formulas, but can also render them unrecognisable by changing their framework in the style of a generalised theory, showing a coherence that shifts and renews itself in a spiralling progression.

The speech referred to in "Function and field of speech and language" is a speech of solution. Constituting the unconscious as repressed speech which returns, the "full speech" restored in analysis gave the quilting point that at the end of analysis assured one's identity with one's being. Thus analytic experience was situated entirely in the triangle of stifled speech, the "it speaks elsewhere", and full, restorative speech.

This speech of solution quickly fizzled out in Lacan's teaching. The major text here is "The direction of the treatment", which concludes on the impotence of speech. You chatter and chatter … The text re-elaborates the Freudian thesis of unconscious desire as the signified of all that is expressed through the speech of the subject and his formations of the unconscious, but it asserts "desire's incompatibility with speech" (Lacan, [1958] 2006, p. 535). As signified, desire haunts speech. It gives it its meaning, the meaning of the inexpressible object, but full speech is useless. Desire, the effect of speech and that which constitutes the being of the subject, is in itself inarticulable. The indestructible unconscious, as Freud said.

With the notion of the *parlêtre* new powers of speech are revealed. The text of the last lecture on Joyce establishes this. I quote: "Whence my expression of the *parlêtre* which will be substituted for the UCS of Freud (unconscious, we read it): move over, it's my turn now. To say that the unconscious in Freud when he discovers it—it is discovered all at once, still after the invention the inventory has to be done—is a knowledge that, as spoken, is constitutive of *LOM* (MAN)" (Lacan, [1979] 1987, p. 33). This spoken knowledge is certainly that of *lalangue*, for elaborated knowledge is ensured through writing and can do without speech.

Calculated dysorthography

The first paragraphs of Lacan's lecture gives the theoretical context for this thesis. He is engaged in an exercise of pastiching Joyce. To do this, he needs to play on the letter, specifically by undermining orthography, disconnecting what is heard from its agreed written form: *L O M* [*l'homme*-man], *eaubscène* [*obscène*-obscene], *Hissecroibeau* [*Il se croit beau*-he thinks himself beautiful]. That's not all, but I will pause at *l'escabeau* [stepladder]. The stepladder forms an image, a talking image, if I may say, for all that allows one to emerge as an individual—*the* individual that Joyce quite particularly incarnated. Here there is an echo of what Lacan, at the beginning of his teaching on the mirror stage, situated as the function of stature, and even of the statue on its pedestal, raising the erect and rigid form of the body to the One of the Imaginary. The stepladder of the last years is much more than this: it concerns this real subject that I am speaking about, affirming himself through his desire and his being of *jouissance*.

Stepladder: Lacan writes *hessecabeau* with the *h* of "*homme*" [man] and the *esse* of "*être*" [being], in order to say that the *escabeau* [stepladder] makes the man. Why this play of calculated dysorthography? There are others that are possible as well, as I noted long ago in my previous studies on Joyce. We could just as well write: *est-ce cas beau?* [is this case beautiful?], or *es-ce cabot?* [is it a mutt?], to show the imaginary and narcissistic dimension, or even, as Lacan does, *S. K. ... beau* by using the letters that get rid of meaning, etc.

The interest of this trituration of *motérialité* through writing only takes on its sense and its significance when we link it to the real unconscious, the unconscious as "spoken knowledge" [*savoir parlé*].

It uses the difference between speaking and writing to illustrate a specific use of writing as distinct from speaking. *Lalangue* only exists as spoken and thus also as heard. The signifier is indeed heard in *lalangue*, but *lalangue* is like chewing gum, a multiplicity in which, I remind you, the unit elements are problematic (from the phoneme to the proverb). Dictionaries exhaust themselves making inventories of already established usage. The signifier that is heard in speech is only isolated by the letter, the "localised structure of the signifier", the "precipitation of the signifier" in its link with *jouissance*. Here then is the undoing, or redefinition, of the classic quilting point of the signifying chain as the direct knotting of the word with *jouissance*. I said "renewed function of speech", but it is speech that somehow calls for the renewed reference to writing as an instrument with which to isolate its problematic *ones*.

But of what value are these painstakingly deciphered letters of the unconscious if they are only a "lucubration of knowledge"? As I said, Lacan's thesis applies even to linguistics for signifier/signified, S/s, suppose writing, and *a fortiori* the unconscious "structured like a language" which results from the effort to isolate and differentiate the elements as units.

The question is thus to know what *"parlêtre"*, as the name of the unconscious, adds or changes to the Freudian unconscious defined as the meaning of desire. Lacan did not reject this definition, still referring in *Television* to "The unconscious, namely the insistence through which desire manifests itself [...]" (Lacan, 1990b, p. 8).

"Parlêtre will be substituted for the Freudian UCS (unconscious, we read it)". He thus contradicts his own *Television* in which, questioned about the term "unconscious", he said that Freud had not found a better one, and added: "it's not to be revised". The new term brings back the question of knowing what the unconscious is, for it is not only the times that have changed in the last decades of the century but also the orientation that Lacan gave to psychoanalysis.

Does that mean that the Lacanian unconscious is different? This is a big question. Lacan could sometimes say: "The unconscious is Lacanian", but the text I chose states otherwise: what is discovered is discovered in one go. The invention is Freudian; then comes the inventory of its conditions, its manifestations and what it is. No one could say that Lacan is showing off in crediting himself with a more thorough inventory.

For all that however, he does not minimise his contribution: move over from there, it's my turn now! The formula evokes neither the idealisation of sublimation nor the narcissism of the stepladder. Rather it signals a reduction to emulation and competition, in line indeed with our time. But if the "there" of the "move over from there" marks the place of the unconscious as thing, we can see how after taking stock of its effects the name of the thing may change.

The UCS is "a knowledge in as much as it is spoken constituting *LOM* (MAN)". It is knowledge, most certainly, since it can be deciphered, but knowledge harboured in spoken *lalangue*. In this it is very different from the knowledge of science that only comes about through writing. Now speech, unlike *langue*, is not dead speech, it is, on the contrary, obscene, as I said. As spoken, knowledge is at the level of *jouissance*. It is *jouissance* that the term *"parlêtre"* in fact suggests, the *parlêtre* who is not the subject but rather the *jouissance* being of this subject as want-to-be.

Should we then suppose that in Lacan's teaching, the effect of *jouissance* of the 1970s is substituted for the effect of desire of the 1960s, to give a chronology that negates at each step the one that has preceded it? I do not think so: the reference to knotting does not result from the work of negativity. Besides, isn't object *a* inscribed at the heart of the Borromean knot? This latter would not be of any analytic use if, besides the three dimensions, it did not knot the various successive elaborations by Lacan, if it did not condense the stages of the inventory which was not created all at once. It is neither science that only knows its present, nor is it the negativity on the move of Hegelian history. It is therefore not about choosing between the want to enjoy [*le manque à jouir*], first designated as the effect of the symbolic, desire, and object cause.

The mystery of the speaking body

We grasp the reason why Lacan evokes LOM, Borromean man, if I may call him, constituted as One from the knotting of the three consistencies and which the writing in three letters almost visualises. The definition of the *parlêtre* is thus itself Borromean: speech, until now defined as a vehicle of meaning, is, via the ones of knowledge that it articulates, connected not only to enjoyed meaning [*sens joui*], but also to the field of the Real, to real *jouissance*.

Lacan had stated: "The unconscious is what the being in speaking enjoys". Yes, but how, since I the speaker know nothing of this enjoyed spoken knowledge? Lacan's reply is: "I speak with my body". Man has a body, he speaks with his body; "he is a *parlêtre* by nature" [*il par-l'être de nature*]. I recall this sentence from *Encore* that on first reading is so surprising: "The Real is the mystery of the speaking body, the mystery of the unconscious" (Lacan, 1998, p. 131). But it is only surprising if the body is reduced to its imaginary form and if we forget that the Symbolic, without which there would be no unconscious, has effects on the Real. The first step of this thesis dates from *The Ethics of Psychoanalysis*, from the Thing defined as "what of the real suffers from the signifier". Lacan insisted: "I speak without knowing it. I speak with my body and I do so unbeknownst to myself. Thus I always say more than I know" (Lacan, 1998, p. 119). "La troisième" took this up literally: "The unconscious [is] a knowledge which is articulated from *langue*, the body which speaks there only being knotted to it by the Real which it enjoys" (Lacan, 1975a). In other words, the *jouissances* of the body are speaking ones. Obviously, we are in a totally different function of speech here. And that's not all, for the speech that we say is *of* the subject is "enjoying speech". There is a satisfaction in the blah blah blah, in what is or is not stated in the ordinary sense of the term. It responds, on the side of the subject, to the *jouissances* that *lalangue* civilises on the side of the substantial body.

I speak with my body. The thesis would require a return to the function of the symptom as message, but even more so, to the drives as the effect of the speech of demand on needs (Lacan, [1958] 2006, [1960a] 2006), and thus, as Lacan later formulates it, "the echo in the body of the fact that there is a saying".

Indeed, what responds to the question of the subject in analysis, what enables us to deduce what *I* want in what I say, if not the drive, either in metonymy or in act, and the symptom as "event of the body"? "To speak with one's body" goes together with the Lacanian hypothesis I have often emphasised. The subject is not a being because his being is always elsewhere—there is no *Dasein* here—but there is the being of the *parlêtre* who has a body to enjoy. That does not make an ontology, however unpleasant this might seem to Heidegger.

It remains to be seen whether this may make a "jouilogy" [*jouilogie*], or an economy of *jouissance*, as the notion of "the Lacanian field" from the seminar *The Other Side of Psychoanalysis* might have led us to hope. Lacan himself gave the answer: there is no energetics of *jouissance*. Neither the figure nor the letter is equivalent to the numerical constant that defines energy in the field of science. There is no more a science of *jouissance* than there is a science of object *a*. From that I conclude that interpretation still has a future!

Note

1. With "Lituraterre", first, and then *Encore*, where he described writing as "an Other mode of the speaker in language", and *RSI* with its redefinition of the symptom as a function of the letter, and also the postscript to the *Four Fundamental Concepts*.

PART II

ANALYSIS ORIENTED TOWARDS
THE REAL

CHAPTER EIGHT

The end pass

I come now to the consequences of the RUCS regarding analysis and its end. If there is no end to the possibility of the transference and no end either to the real unconscious, how therefore is an end to analysis possible? There is no end to the transference, but in its space there may be several passes to the real, of which the lapsus offers us the reduced model. What would the end pass then be? This question runs through all of Lacan's teaching. It was at stake in his construction of object *a*, it remains at stake in the RUCS, which could not leave the pass of 1967 unaffected.

I will take things from the side of the symptom, for if there were only the lapsus things would have been easier for Freud. Actually, the word of the lapsus is homologous in the diachrony of speech to the letter of the symptom in its synchrony. But more than the lapsus, the symptom is what best shows us that the real unconscious, outside meaning, has a use value—that of *jouissance*—but no exchange value. With the real unconscious, the "no dialogue" ["*pas de dialogue*"] does not even have its limit in interpretation.

And yet, we can apply to it the reduced model constructed for the lapsus. Every time a parasitic element surfaces in intentionality, it will summon the associative work that produces meaning by revealing the phantasy. But here we are in the real unconscious. At the entry into analysis we speak of the analytic symptom. It is not just any old one: it is a symptom under transference, that is, elevated to the status of an enigma to be solved. It is a symptom, as we say, that poses a question. We question it because we wonder where it comes from, what it wants, and what it means. It is thereby elevated to the status of the signifier of the transference. It is thus the symptom which we believe in: we suppose that it can say something. It's what is more commonly called subjectivisation of the symptom.

The space of the symptom can be defined exactly like that of the lapsus. It is the range of its association with other signifiers that gives it meaning. This is the space of hystorisation where it fiddles with truth. When this space no longer carries any meaning, the symptom is disconnected from all subjective truth: it is real, unhooked from the transferential postulate. So what remains of it? The intrusive element (the letter, Lacan said in 1975) lodged at the level of *jouissance*. It's why I could pastiche and say: when the *esp.* of a *sympt.* no longer carries any meaning, we are in the unconscious, the real unconscious, outside meaning. The symptom has been reduced to its neological kernel. Clinically, let us say, it is the end of questioning and a shutting down of the transference. We should no doubt raise here the question of interpretation according to whether it is adjusted to the scansions of truth—as Freudian interpretation essentially was—or whether, in making instead a hole in meaning, it aims at the real unconscious. I will leave this point on hold.

But if one is no longer in transferential expectation, if one no longer believes that the symptom can say something, is this because it has said everything?

Is it that it could not say still more or something else? Ad infinitum. Yet to suppose that it has fallen silent, won't it begin to speak again? This is the perspective of analysis without an end or of analysis resumed. This question is justified. It is structurally based, which is why it re-emerges repetitively. It is based on the fact that the unconscious as *lalangue* is inexhaustible, and that even what is isolated as the letter of the symptom is only ever hypothetical. And there's no possibility that the unconscious can tell us how far to go in its own exploration. It's not it that will mark as the last signifier any of the signifiers surfacing in a blunder or insisting in the repetition of the symptom. The unconscious no doubt speaks but it does not conclude. Between the lie and the mistake, at the level of language there is no inherent end on the side of the subject to hystorisation, and no exhaustion of the unconscious as *lalangue* thinkable on the side of the real.

So what decides the end? Neither the RUCS nor truth but the third partner that is added, one that is not of the linguistic order. In this 1976 text, it is called "satisfaction". We see the paradox in relation to any structural definition. This reversal of everything that comes before in Lacan's teaching is very late. We can consider that he introduced the real unconscious in *Encore*, but we have to wait until this "Introduction to the English-language edition" of *Seminar XI* for the idea of an end by a specific satisfaction. The term does not figure in the "Proposition of 9 October 1967 on the psychoanalyst of the school" on the end by the pass. And not even in "L'étourdit" where admittedly he evokes a mourning that ends in a "substantial" therapeutic effect (Lacan, 1973, p. 44), after passing through a rather manic-depressive phase, but without invoking this term "satisfaction". Now, indeed, as I noted previously (Soler, [November 1989] 2000, p. 429) the so-called *passants* who agree to make a testimony in the procedure of the pass, do not speak about this depressive moment but rather about a satisfaction at the end. I had hypothesised that this could be an artefact of the procedure, but Lacan's text gives it a foundation.

The flaw seen in the subject supposed to know ensures the real unconscious but is not sufficient to ensure the end of analysis. The additional condition for a conclusion to be possible is on the side of the affect generated in the sequence that ensures the pass to the real unconscious. Indeed, the analysis is at its point of closure when there is no longer, let us say, any "analysand libido", since "analysand libido", caused by the object which is lacking, is that which runs after truth. Out of gas, we could say. If I am not mistaken, I already emphasised this point long ago. It is why I was interested in Ferenczi's remark that "the analysis must die of exhaustion" and not through a decision. This could very well be another one of Ferenczi's brilliant anticipatory intuitions. For in fact, "exhaustion" like "satisfaction" is not in the register of elaboration.

Why this term "satisfaction"? Up to that point we had the end by the object. It referred to *jouissance* since *a* is the object lacking to *jouissance*; then the end by the symptom which also refers to it. The term "satisfaction" can be found in *Encore* in the form of what Lacan calls "another satisfaction", that of speech. Satisfaction (just as well as dissatisfaction) is the affect that on the side of the subject responds to *jouissance*. Once the coalescence of the signifier and *jouissance* was postulated—without which moreover no literature would be thinkable—Lacan can propose that there is a satisfaction obtained from speech and that this satisfaction of the blah blah blah is what responds to phallic *jouissance* (Lacan, 1998, p. 64). Satisfaction and dissatisfaction define the reverberation in the subject of what is happening on the side of *jouissance*, the side that is not that of the subject. Likewise, in the expression "identification with the symptom", the term "identification" designates the response of being. The modality of *jouissance* reverberates in subject effects. And this thesis applies to transferential speech.

What then is the satisfaction at the end? It can only be situated in relation to the satisfaction of the journey. It is different from "the other satisfaction" which Lacan speaks about in *Encore*. The transference sustains the satisfaction obtained from truth and even in the race for truth, which, between lack and expectation, mimes desire and makes what Lacan calls "the mirage of truth" glitter. That satisfaction has no more a principle of limitation than the truth that speaks, except the satisfaction at the end—"to be provided urgently"—that is expected to put an end to the mirage of truth and the satisfaction of the race. In other words, it ends the "love affairs with truth" that the "Note to the Italians" attributes to Freud. This is coherent. But it should not be imagined that the end of the love affairs with truth is the start of the love affair with the unconscious. There is no friendship there!

The expression "identification with the symptom" also designates a point of arrest of the analysand's libido, of the love addressed to knowledge. For the benefit of an acquired knowledge, if you wish, but only because of the unconscious, because there is the unconscious. It does not go further than that. It is not a knowledge about the unconscious since the snatches that we get hold of would not exhaust it: in a word *lalangue* objects.

I stress how much, in invoking this fall of satisfaction in the race for truth, Lacan introduces a factor that challenges any idea of a fixed ending. In 1967, Lacan stated that the algorithm of entry into analysis corresponded to the algorithm at the end. In 1973 he provided a model of the pass to the Real through the repeated fall of meaning. But the new thesis here is that this is never enough to ensure the end of analysis. What must be added is a change in the subject's satisfaction. Now on what does the factor of satisfaction or dissatisfaction depend? It defines being, but it is incalculable and thus unprogrammable. It is in vain that some go to a great deal of trouble in analysis to seek out some origin in the past, and that, outside analysis, the whole politics of prediction is an attempt to foreclose the unconscious. This incalculable side of the subject, that we can call ethical, justifies Lacan in saying that the request for satisfaction at the end is urgent, but that "one is not sure of satisfying it". And he adds: "except to have it weighed". This term "to weigh" is very interesting. Whatever the case, to weigh is not to calculate.

This weighing aims to anticipate what is expected beyond the "point where every strategy vacillates", this point structurally guaranteed because of the gaping hole of truth and the real of the impregnable unconscious. Beyond this point, there is no supposed knowledge, just the *quantum* of satisfaction. It is the point of challenge for the cartel of the pass: the subject is incalculable and remains so. The type of satisfaction for a given subject, namely, the type of affect that answers to this structure, does not pertain to any calculation, with the consequence that we can neither predict the satisfaction at the end nor the analytic act. I would also conclude that it is the incalculable of the ethical subject that makes the procedure of the pass, with its paradox, necessary. We expect from a *passant* that he testify to the lying truth: in other words, that he hystorise his analysis. And it won't be enough that he lists the productions of truth that have punctuated this analysis, for that would only be the novel of an analysis. It would be necessary for him to show how the lie glimpsed in truth has cured him of the mirage and made him sick of the race for truth, and that even when in order to say it he has no other medium than speech with its lying truth.

So what can it be to weigh the request? I think that Lacan is referring here to the preliminary interviews which he saw as so important, and which are handled badly when they are prolonged and not distinguished from the associative work that ought to be reserved for what follows. I do not think that to weigh the request means to evaluate it, since the incalculable would block this as well. Hence, indeed, the imposture or illusion of the diagnostics of analysability on entry. To weigh it would rather be to make sure of the actual weight on entry of an expectation of something other than truth.

A last essential point: if the satisfaction at the end is incalculable and un-programmable, what is the weight of the analytic act and of the mode of interpretation on the production of this fall of love affairs with truth, without which there is no end, and which an insight into the structural fault is not enough to produce? Can the analyst wash his hands of it in the name of the incalculable?

Speaking of transference love, Lacan defines it as "love addressed to knowledge". The expression condenses the two aspects of the transference, epistemic and sentimental, which are closely intertwined and inseparable. Phenomenologically, the mixture differs greatly from one subject to another. It oscillates between two extremes: some are astonished at not experiencing transference love, and others love but are astonished at not seeing the relation to knowledge.

Lacan asserts that this love is a subversive love. But not because it would go towards knowledge, quite the opposite, it goes very well with hatred of any interpretation that disturbs the love affairs with truth. Only in analysis is this form of love subversive. I have stressed the distinction between two loves, the commonplace and the transferential—the love of the One, well spotted by Freud, and the love of the S_2 of knowledge—but in reality the difference is less essential than discursive. If it is subversive in analysis, it is because "it gives itself a partner who has the chance to respond, which is not the case in other forms" (Lacan, 1975c, p. 16). In fact in the other forms, between parents and children, or between lovers, how could the partner respond with the effect of the pass to the unconscious?

This thesis of the "partner who has the chance to respond", applied to analysis oriented towards the Real, refers all the responsibility of this reduction of the mirages of truth to the analyst, even though he is not the master of it and even though he cannot anticipate what in the subject is going to respond. Thus the question arises of the specific means that an analytic technique oriented towards the Real can employ. Interpretation and the handling of time are at stake here.

CHAPTER NINE

The time that isn't logical

The essential part of Lacan's elaboration concerning the time of analysis was in the framework of his return to Freud, and focused on the analysis that Freud had introduced, that is, an analysis oriented towards articulated truth, a truth that speaks in the structure of language through the analysand's words but also through the symptoms of his body. It is the dialectical time of *rambling speech* which the variable length session corresponds to. It is the time of the chain which produces the surprise return of the repressed, the time of the future anterior of the subject, stretched between anticipation and retroaction, and governed by the quilting points of his discourse, which will allow him to retroactively refind the marks of the first contingencies of his life.

However, the real unconscious is not dialectical and calls for other modes of intervention. I would ask if the Lacanian short session and the length of time needed for analysis do not share the same causality, even if in practice the generally long duration of analysis seems separate from that of the sessions which vary greatly depending on current practices.

It is in so far as psychoanalysis as a practice of speaking mobilises the Imaginary and the Symbolic—namely the field of semblants—that the

Real becomes a question. We can wonder whether, as Lacan stated at the end, it is not a "shared delusion" ["*délire à deux*"]. I noted the different steps which aimed at the Real and which led Lacan to question the metaphors of his early teaching one by one, passing from the signifier to the sign and to the letter, from language to *lalangue*, and to question at the same time the scientific model of psychoanalysis as the condition of transmission.

Lacan put forward three elaborations of this real that could emerge in speech and that could put an end to the infinite drifting of both truth and deciphering. These elaborations involved three definitions of the final pass and not just one. In the three cases we have a principle of conclusion by a real: that of the impossible to say for the pass to the object, that of the impossible to write for the pass to the Real of the non-relation, "specific" to the unconscious, and that of the outside meaning for the pass to the RUCS. So should we say that in these three cases the time needed—which we find so long—is the time of access to the epistemic conclusion by the Real? Certainly not.

The non-epistemic variable

From 1949, with the notion of the "time for understanding", unanticipatable as it can never be reduced to a thought process, Lacan had marked out the place of what I call today the non-logical variable. It is absolutely clear with the real unconscious: without even evoking the symptom, how many lapsus linked to the real will there have to be in an analysis to go beyond the mirage of truth and to recognise the real unconscious?

This is because another non-epistemic variable is at play in every case. It's why, indeed, the ways to a conclusion via the act are never simply those of the necessities of logical deduction. Thanks are due to Gödel on this point, and to Lacan who made this clear at the end of his school, when he said that everyone would conclude "according to his desire". And there we have one of the names of the variable which decompletes logic, so that the concluding that resolves the complaint of impotence will involve a leap. In other words, concluding at the end from the perspective of the epistemic conclusion is only ever a possibility.

It is not the absence of a principle of concluding that makes analysis so long: it's that in every case the principle of concluding is unbearable, protected by "the horror of knowing". From an insight into the frame of the phantasy, whether in a lightning flash or not, to the conclusion of the impossibility of the relation, to the real unconscious of *lalangue* as unknown knowledge, the knowledge acquired is the knowledge of an end to the aspiration to knowledge: the synonym for castration. From now on it comes up against a refusal, an "I don't want to know anything about it" which resists the conclusion. "It needs time to get used to being" [*"se faire à être"*] as Lacan said in "Radiophonie". In this context it would mean: to be the object that is in internal exclusion to the subject. The "to get used to" evokes "to make do with" [*s'y faire*] and suggests the patience to bear, to accept the Real which elaboration of the supposed unconscious brought to light.

An index of this non-logical variable, and of an end that is only possible, is found also in subjects who, as I've noted, having come to the end of the relation to knowledge that is the transference, are alleviated of their own "horror of knowing" by converting it into hatred (Soler, 2008b): hatred of analysis as well as of its henchmen, Freud and Lacan, and certainly also of one or more of those who have accompanied them on the journey. There are many other indices of the non-logical variable whose place Lacan always marked and which he in fact inscribed with the word "ethics".

This suggests that with this non-logical variable one cannot anticipate the time an analysis will require. "One" is not only the analyst: it is the subject as well. And how many times will we not be surprised that the resolute analysand at the beginning is the most recalcitrant at the end? The opposite is also true and one may see the sceptic at the beginning become the most resolute at the exit.

The epistemic principle of the end by the Real is required in order to close an analysis, but that it is required does not make it sufficient. An additional and necessary condition is a response of being that does not belong to logic. We could rightly call it ethical if the term were not so debased today. A clear sign of this condition is indeed to be found in the time of mourning that marks the end of analysis, as Lacan explicitly noted in the "Proposition of 9 October 1967 on the psychoanalyst of the school", as well as in "L'étourdit": it follows the moment of the glimpse of the Real, pushing beyond the end of an analysis.

This response of being, which determines the fundamental options of a subject in relation to the Real and which may or may not override his horror of knowing, is the only thing to introduce the margin of freedom without which everyone would only be the puppet of their unconscious. It is not only unpredictable, as I have said, but also unable to be expressed as a statement and only allows itself to be approached through signs. Lacan would ultimately place these signs on the side of the affects generated by the pass at the glimpse of the Real, and for that he himself needed time.

Didactic affects

From that point on, it is not enough for an analysis to have gone to its epistemic end to make an analyst. The desire of the analyst is not deduced from acquired knowledge. This is the thesis of the "Italian Note" of 1973 and the "Introduction to the English-language edition" of *Seminar XI* in 1976.

According to the "Note", there is an analyst when the analysed subject, the one who has situated his very own horror of knowing, has moved to enthusiasm. Others, on the contrary, can move from horror to hatred. Experience shows this. But there are other alternatives as well, the most frequent being the move from horror to forgetting. The lightning flash of revelation, when it occurs, is generally short-lived and the descent into therapeutic ends is an ever available and handy accomplice.

In 1976, slightly shifting his terms, Lacan proposes that the pass evaluate not enthusiasm but "the satisfaction that marks the end of analysis". The definite article indicates that it is not contingent, that without it there is no end and that it is constitutive of the end. It emerges when there is no longer any satisfaction taken in lying truth. Could this be a change of taste, a satisfaction taken in the outside meaning of the real unconscious that would come to limit the satisfaction taken in truth?

This is also to say that with this principle of evaluation that bears not on the didactic effect but on a response of being to the didactic effect of analysis, we are very far from the idea that every analysis taken to its end point produces an analyst: in the sense of an analyst who enjoys the Real. There is no automatic enthusiasm or satisfaction at the end. Beyond what is prudently called the clinician, it is only the non-logical variable that makes the analyst possible.

We must consider the change of perspective that Lacan introduced and the double devaluation it implies: of truth in relation to the Real, and of logical structure in relation to the position of being. This cannot be without practical consequences. The hard-working analysand is an analysand who enjoys inconclusive truth, with his hystorisation with a "y", and this is a euphemism: for to be hystorised and to enjoy one's phantasy are one and the same thing. This is why Lacan says that the analyand consumes phallic *jouissance* and that the analyst makes himself consumed. From then on, the love of truth appears for what it is, symptomatic and defensive—the profusion of chatter, the saying of endless stupidities sustained by a satisfaction that defers the moment to conclude.

A session adjusted to the real unconscious

Hence the question of the means to be adopted by an analysis oriented towards the Real and the responsibility of the analyst. If he favours the movement towards this destitution of truth, what can he do?

Here I return to the problem of the Lacanian session and also to that of the specifically Lacanian interpretation. Regarding the Lacanian short session—I have already spoken about this in the text "A practice without chatter" (Soler, 2007b)—I will just say that it targets the Real at which Lacanian analysis aims.

The question is not to object to Lacan that the unconscious demands time to articulate itself, as he was indeed the first to have explored this in all its forms. It is rather a question of knowing if the pulsating opening/closing movement of the unconscious that is produced in the transference is isomorphic to the alternation—within a session/outside a session: in other words, to the presence of the analyst. The whole of analytic experience shows that this is not the case.

Take the commonplace example of the analysand who arrives quite animated to his session and who says that he has been speaking all day and night to his analyst, but once he's actually there all his lucubration collapses, or he is silent or he hears himself saying something completely unexpected. Conversely, once outside the door, an empty session often generates some new and important material. The time of the unconscious and the time of the session, whatever its duration, cannot be superimposed.

The short session—and this is the crucial point—in no way prevents as some say, the articulation of the elements of the unconscious, scrap by scrap. Scrap by scrap is the effect of the scansions. These effects are in some respects incalculable, but the elements which are produced and which scansion allows to be extracted, are limited and can be objectified. The difference—and there is one obviously—is not the capacity of either the one or the other to elaborate the unconscious. They both do. Beyond this, we are no longer in psychoanalysis but in the large field of "psy" with which it should not be confused.

The difference is that the Lacanian short session makes the cut function as an interpretation of that which inhabits the truth articulated by the subject. But why not then put this interpretation into words? It is not forbidden, except that the other satisfaction, precisely, always risks reducing the effects of the interpretation to the satisfactions of the blah blah blah. The cutting of the session that cuts into words is the "finger pointed" towards the *jouissance* that ballasts the hystorisation of the subject in analysis. The analysand who told me that the short session is like *coitus interruptus* did not realise how well she put it. In "The direction of the treatment" Lacan had put forward the idea of a silent interpretation, the finger pointed towards the signifier of the lack in the Other (Lacan, [1958] 2006, p. 536). At the end, it is the finger pointed towards the Real that comes into this place.

But actually, I think that what counts in a session, be it variable or short in length, is its end, as it is moreover for the analysis as a whole. There are conclusive ends of the session that bring out a quilting point that generally satisfies; ends that question by emphasising a term that revives the transferential question; and then there are ends that I have called suspensive [*fins suspensives*], that neither conclude nor question but which cut the chain of speech and shear through meaning. The quasi-punctual, short session practised by Lacan adds to this by realising the razor of the cut between the space of what's said, semblants, and real presence.

The first two—conclusive or questioning—push towards the hystorisation of truth. The second two, in contrast, push towards the real. These have affinities with the Lacanian apophantic interpretation which, like the oracle, "neither reveals nor hides, but makes a sign", a sign of what ex-sists to the hystorisation of the subject. Hystorisation is brought about through the times of the so-called opening of the unconscious in which truth unfolds. This theme is well-known and has made the times of its closing seem negative. But the Real, whatever its definition, manifests itself in the times of the closing of the unconscious, even in that of the rejection of the chattering unconscious, *Sicut palea* [as dung]. The real unconscious is a closed unconscious, closed on its ones of *jouissance*, autistic and neological, as I have said.

However, we do not have to choose between the unconscious as truth and the real unconscious. There is no analysis without the hystorisation of the subject. In diachrony, the Real is at the end of the process, that of the session as well as that of the analysis, where it functions as the limit and thus as the end point of the lying truth, the fall of meaning. In synchrony, the Real and truth are, let us say, knotted, which rules out the possibility that one can escape from truth completely, however much it is devalued. "Analytic discourse puts truth in its place, but does not shake it up. It is reduced, but indispensable" (Lacan, 1998, p. 108). Moreover, the real unconscious "fiddles" with the truth, Lacan says. This is so true that at the very moment that he asserts the real unconscious, he reiterates the idea that the pass consists of testifying to the lying truth.

The satisfaction at the end

Here is what allows the satisfaction at the end to be clarified. It does not simply substitute a satisfaction that would be taken from the Real outside meaning for one taken from truth in the process of free association.

What then of the affect at the end, the famous satisfaction of this pass to the Real? Satisfaction or dissatisfaction, it is what responds in the subject to a state of *jouissance* that is not of the subject but of the body.

Lacan spoke positively of *gay sçavoir* but we must not be deceived. If the Real is in the right place, the satisfaction at the end refuses *gay sçavoir* as much as it does sadness. Moreover, we could already deduce this from *Television* if we read it carefully. Why? Because the *jouissance* of deciphering that defines *gay sçavoir* returns us to sin in every case, says Lacan: in other words, the relapse into guilt and sadness that it generates and that prevents us from locating ourselves in the unconscious. Indeed, in deciphering we do not locate ourselves: we drift endlessly in phallic *jouissance*. This assertion is consistent with the idea that the love of knowledge that is the transference—the love that sustains the deciphering aimed at meaning—does not sustain the desire to know. An end of analysis is also the end of the joys of deciphering.

The satisfaction at the end is acquired with use, the use of a particular, Lacan says. There is thus no point in trying to give it a definition that holds for everyone. We can only say what conditions it, and its function.

This is linked to the logic of language. It is this logic that determines that, as a user of analytic work, I will repeatedly experience two limits after the satisfactions taken in the mirage of truth and in the moments of waking up to the Real. Firstly, the lie of truth that Freud described with his *proton pseudos*, that is, its powerlessness to touch the Real— the real of *jouissance*—and to conclude. With truth I never get there: castration is guaranteed. On the other hand, the unconscious without a subject imposes itself and exceeds me, working on its own, outside meaning, in each of its *fixions* of *jouissance*.

We can describe the affects generated by the race after truth and by the emergences of the RUCS. On the one hand, the expectation and hope that evolve in a time that moves from enchantment to disappointment: truth speaks, but does not go beyond a half-saying which makes a mirage of the half that isn't said. On the other hand, the affects of the emergence of the real, from the lapsus to the symptom, oscillate between astonishment, in the strongest sense, to anxiety. Anxiety is the typical affect of any advent of the real.

How could a double despair not emerge from these two ordeals— reiterated over the course of so-called free association—as the subjected [*asujetti*] subject does his work: or if you prefer, a despair with two sources. We can see this in the final phases of analysis—or at least where the pass lays down the requirement for an end of analysis. Indeed, a thwarting of the transferential expectation occurs as these two ordeals are revealed by analysis, and we know from experience the protests that this stirs up. However, these pitfalls are not necessarily dead ends.

The exit that is possible depends on the way in which the entangled pitfalls of truth and the real oscillate, says Lacan. I understand this to mean that it is through passes to the outside meaning of the Real, moments of awakening on the model of the lapsus that I have described, passes which put a stop to the fictions of truth; and conversely, through the rebounding of truth in successive fictions, which each time produce the expectation of a subjectivisation of the unconscious, the truth and the Real alternately object to or rather counterbalance the satisfaction that each engenders—awakening or hope—each compensating in alternation the dissatisfaction produced by the other. From there, with use, a third satisfaction emerges, one which is not due to the beauty of their symmetry. It alone is the sign that the subject has acknowledged the real unconscious that resists any capture by knowledge. In acknowledging the Real, we lighten its burden, while at the same time ending the false hopes generated by the mirage of truth. So this pass truly belongs to the Lacanian field and is different from the pass of 1967. Let us say that it supplements the latter with the Real that was lacking there. It is remarkable, indeed, that it changes its temporality. Where the first evoked the instant of perception, the lightning flash of the breakthrough, the second involves a long period of reworking *jouissance* that is quite different from the discontinuities of the cut.

Yet perhaps we should qualify this. All the constructions of 1967 on the pass and the act that it conditions already situated the end of analysis in reference to *jouissance*. But this was only conceptualised through object *a*, which Lacan called real. Why didn't Lacan stick with that? What made the steps that followed necessary for the Lacanian field to be established? Chronology is not enough: we must find its mainsprings.

Lacan was not able to stick with the elaborations of 1967 for a fundamental reason, which he himself perceived and formulated in various ways (I will not list them here): that object *a*, the *a* which is in the position of cause in the subjective economy and the analytic bond, is powerless to put an end to the half-saying of lying truth, in other words, to the flight of meaning, of enjoyed meaning. Rather, it is this object that is always fleeing through the hole of discourse, and its installation in the place of the semblant in analytic discourse does not make the latter a discourse of the real. There is no discourse that is not of the semblant. There is certainly a topology of object *a*, but what topology locates as most real are holes. This is at least how I understand Lacan's strange sentence which says that analysts who authorise themselves only from their dislocation [*égarement*]—thus the opposite of the analyst oriented by the real—will find their happiness in topology (Lacan, 2001a, p. 314). I think that this verdict of inadequacy was indeed present in the "Proposition" when Lacan says: "The vain knowledge of a being who slips away [*se dérobe*]." It cannot be said of the RUCS—however unknown and without a subject it is—that it slips away, since it appears not in the flight of meaning but in the very tangible modalities of *jouissance*.

Now I believe that the conceptualisation of this Real is necessary in order to see what triumphs in capitalist discourse, and even to counter it. Lacan was in tune with his times, doubtless knowing that the Symbolic never wins against any Real, and that the alternative is played out between the real unconscious and the real of capitalism.

However the question that remains is that of the subject produced by analysis beyond any possible final pass.

CHAPTER TEN

Terminable analysis

Separation identity

The question arises of what analysis leaves the analys and beyond its therapeutic effects. The problem of identity is posed not only at the exit but also at moment of entry into analysis. However, the question goes far beyond the analytic framework and is useful to determine its general framework.

The names of identity

I have chosen to begin with its relations to the name and to nomination. I am not starting from nothing since there is already a thesis according to which the symptom is the name of the subject's identity, his true and proper name which usurps the patronymic name.

I am not going to run through this thesis but will just make two remarks. We can find a simple indication of it in the fact that some subjects manage to rename themselves through their work. But what else is a work than the product of the knotting between a desire and a mode of *jouissance*? It is the same for both the subjects' deeds and misdeeds. Thus we say: a Fragonard, Gödel's Theorem, Zorro the Avenger, but also Jack the Ripper and, of course, Joyce the Symptom. From there it is only a small step to the idea that an analysis aims at finding one's true proper name. But this is also to suggest that each subject has at least two proper names: his patronymic name, which obviously has major subjective resonances, and his private name, that of his being of *jouissance*.

The patronymic name is received from genealogy: it is a transmitted name. Let us say that it comes automatically from the Other. *Patronymikos*, indeed, comes from *pater* and *onoma*, as if language recorded paternal genealogy. We know however that this attachment to the father is not universal; there are matronymic rules of nomination. Moreover, the practice of generalised nomination for all subjects is relatively recent in history, because for a very long time, since Ancient Greece, the patronymic name was reserved for great families. There are also atypical cases where it is the social body which names: for example, foundlings, or those born with an X. It is as if today the obligation to register birth, to inscribe each child with a name in the State register of births, marriages, and deaths, had, beyond an obvious function of social control, that of welcoming each new living being, a function in some way homologous at the secular level with Christian baptism.

Unlike the common name whose referent is generally a class of things, one expects from the patronymic name that it index an existence and one only, independently of any quality other than descent and sex. Within this limit, the patronymic name is not a signifier for it tends to designate independently of any attribution. Certainly a patronymic name can have a meaning: Mr or Mrs Baker, Miller, Beauregard [the name indicating a class position], and why not Soler, which in its original language refers to the ground whereas to the French ear it is to the sun! But in every case, in its function as proper name, meaning is elided.

The first name, which is added to the patronymic name, is quite a different thing: it is not transmitted automatically but inscribes a choice. It is always the mark of the desire of the Other towards the new arrival, a signified of the Other (s(A)) which carries the trace of his/her dreams and expectations—look how many Venuses, Ophelias, and Marilyns there are!—or the trace of mournings when it is the first name of the dead child or of the lost grandparent, or when it is a unisex first name that deletes the actual sex. Subjects know this so well that some, rejecting the mark, decide to change their first name in spite of the requirements of civil status.

The practice of first names, and even of plural first names, also obviously aims to increase the identifying power of the patronymic name. However, its discriminatory power is conspicuous in its poverty. Witness the majority of homonyms to be found in directories and the practice of changing one's patronymic name when it is felt to be ridiculous or offensive, or even dangerous. Unless it is simply, in some places at least, that in being a woman one becomes a wife. In short, the proper name in the ordinary sense is insufficiently identifying and does not succeed in fulfilling the program of the true proper name: to allow one and only one individual to be identified.

This impotence of patronymic names indeed reflects the difficulties inherent in defining a proper name in relation to its referent, what I am going to call the "named". We assume that we name something that "there is". Remember the Genesis story: God, after having created each thing gives them each a name. But if one names what there is—thus a referent—several questions immediately arise. This "there is", how does one distinguish it from every other thing—in other words, how does one identify it in its unicity? Is it even in existence, since it is possible to speak of that which, such as Pegasus, does not exist or only exists in imagination? Hence the wish of Willard Quine for an "ontological immunity" which does not speculate about existence but which sticks solely to the question of identity: this "there is", what is it? These questions, which I am simplifying, have led to considerable elaborations in logic. John Stuart Mill had already stressed in *A System of Logic* that with the name, denotation and connotation are separated. Later elaborations roughly divide up in two groups. The first, that of the so-called descriptivist theories that begin with Russell—and are extended with Frege, Searle, and Strawson—comes from Russell's theory of descriptions. It consists of linking the function of the proper name to a description, fixing an essential property of the referent, or a bundle of properties. The example given by Russell himself is of Sir Walter Scott, the author of *Waverley*. Or again, Kripke's example of Nixon, president of the United States of America in 1970; or Hitler, the man who killed the greatest number of Jews. There we see that it is a matter of supplementing the patronymic name with an identifying trait of singularity, which allows the One of identity to be reached without any possible confusion.

Now, let us not forget that these questions which might seem to be quite abstract in fact have a very concrete import, as is always the case. Think, for example, of the police investigation where we cannot do without the distinctive traits that allow an unequivocal identification. The identity card, for example, which adds a series of traits to the patronymic name, is related, without knowing it, to descriptivist practices: date and place of birth, and also the individual signs, as we say, to designate bodily marks such as fingerprints, which are not of the subject but of the body, today supplanted by DNA thanks to science. There are other more ambiguous marks between body and subject, sought at first in phrenology and then in writing, where the written form makes a singular and unfalsifiable trace, especially in the signature, and similarly with science, the frequencies of vocal emission beyond the audible accent. Why not add here the inimitable and unknown style detected by the feminine eye that Lacan evoked in his seminar with "the professor's shoes" (Lacan, 1992, p. 296).

The second group aims, on the contrary, at eliminating every connotation. Kripke is its most eminent and innovative representative, and he tries especially in *Naming and Necessity* to split the proper name from any identifying property, from any singularising trait. What he calls a pure "rigid designator" separates reference from any meaning, and identifies a referent without saying what it is. It is difficult, however, to arrive at an identity name without any property. The singular statement of pure existence creates a problem and it is very difficult to hold to this view in psychoanalysis.

I will pause at the first of Lacan's developments on the proper name in "Subversion of the subject and the dialectic of desire". There the proper name designates what of a being is not identified and is not identifiable by the signifier. If the subject is represented by the signifiers that he assumes, these signifiers are however only representatives that do not say what he is in himself, outside of representation, which thus remains an x. The proper name is precisely not a signifier that represents the subject but the index of what he is as "unthinkable", what of him does not pass to the signifier. The two names of this unthinkable in Freud are "libido" and "drives"; in Lacan, at first, "desire" and "symptom", then the specific Borromean knotting which defines a *parlêtre* that he calls *sinthome*. In this way, the proper name is more the name of the thing than the subject. And when Lacan says of the neurotic that he has a horror of his proper name, that he wants to know nothing about what he is as thing, he is reformulating what Freud called neurotic defence as fundamentally the distance taken thanks to the signifier from the place of the Real.

The name "symptom" is a true name of identity insofar as it names from the point of one and only one singularity. It is the case in the examples I mentioned at the start. And this takes me back to the renowned (*renommee*). This is the word for celebrity. The fact of being famous (*fama*) evokes a second operation of nomination, "to make a name for oneself" when one has one already. The "renowned" name brings off what fails with the first name: that is, to jointly index an existence and its traits of unicity, in knotting the patronymic name to a distinct singularity. It is difficult to consider it as a simple "rigid designator" denoting an existence without connoting anything of its specificity; it is, rather, the only name that can fix an identity as singular. What could one call this singularity that appears in works or in notable deeds, good or bad, if not symptomatic singularity? Provided of course that we remember Lacan's last elaboration which names the symptom not as an anomaly but as the knot specific to each person that allows the body, *jouissance*, and the unconscious to hold together. To rename oneself thus always has a Borromean function, and it is through it that a subject signs with his unfalsifiable signature. Proof by Joyce.

For him, however, there is a specificity to his symptom name, besides his genius. Lacan did not say Joyce *les langues*, or "*l'élangue*" as he put it in the seminar of 18th November 1975. That would have been to name him by his symptomatic relation to language, the rather maniacal style that peaked in the writing of *Finnegans Wake*. With "Joyce the symptom" he names not the symptom that he *has* but the symptom that he *is*: that is to say, the fact of "accomplishing himself as symptom" (Lacan, [1979] 1987, p. 35). The infinitive "to accomplish" implies time and effort maintained asymptotically towards his symptom being. This symptom being consists in renaming himself and thus deploying the Borromean function to make up for the deficiency of his father. By doing this, he adds a name—"the necessary son"—to the series of Names of the Father (Lacan, [1979] 1987, p. 34), which does not stop writing itself as "the uncreated spirit of his race".

I would like to explore the basis of Lacan's shift, in the years around 1975, from the Name-of-the-Father to the Father of the name, for I do not think that it is only a taste for punning that inspired him. The "to make a name for oneself", which seems to leave all the responsibility for the name to the subject himself, must not conceal from us the fact that there is no auto-nomination. This means that a proper name, even that of the symptom, is always linked with a social bond. In every case, there has to be what I am going to call the offer of nomination, the positioning of the subject [la mise du sujet]. But look at Freud's case of the Rat Man: we can say that "rat" comes from his unconscious as the name of a jouissance situated in his phantasmatic relation to the lady and to the father, but it required Freud to designate him as the Rat Man, and thus to give him his name of entry into analysis. Likewise, it is Lacan who names Joyce the symptom. It is also the case for the name that he first gave himself: the artist, who to exist, had to be confirmed by the public: let us say, the century. Without this bond, he would only have been the megalomaniac Yeats had seen in him when he met him in his youth. This means that the name is at the mercy of the uncalculable encounter. It thus involves, in part, a contingency—just like love.

Who has access to the power—it is a power—of nomination? Since contingency is at play, the power to nominate becomes relatively dispersed.

Think of the hateful insult. It is an attempt at a forcing towards the name of "jouissance" but which does not really make a name, for it is immediately refused. There are also unworthy names imposed by the Other without consent, such as M. the Accursed [the French title of Fritz Lang's film M]. And then, above all, there is the love that names. This theme runs through Lacan's teaching. He begins with the notion of full speech inhabiting intersubjectivity: "If I call the person to whom I am speaking by whatever name I like [...]" (Lacan, [1953] 2006, p. 247) he will answer me until "there is love only of a name" (Lacan, 2004, p. 390).

The poets saw this long ago. I have already quoted Claudel in Partage de midi [The Break of Noon]: "If you call me by a name that you know and that I am ignorant of [...] I would not be able to resist" (Claudel, 1967, p. 1005). The love that names raises the anonymity of the object cause of desire to the elective unicity of the bond. We see here to what extent the name is bequeathed, but it in no way fixes a specificity of the one named. Let us think of Marguerite Duras with "your name of Venice in deserted Calcutta", etc. There are certainly other types of nominations: those made from "properties" of the named that are skills, in the same way that we name a responsibility or reward outstanding behaviour (an order of merit, as we say). These are socialised and socialising nominations that inscribe the being identified in the social bond. When it is love that names, on the contrary, the properties of the named are not evoked: the received name is not the name of the symptom of the loved one, but on the contrary of the lover, the name of the symptomatic object that I am for the other. The "you are my wife", says it plainly. These names say more about the one who names than the one who is named.

The question is obviously raised here as to what specifies the Father who names. I will come back to this. It is clear that his saying is not limited to the saying of heterosexual love. Like this latter, he names a woman as the symptomatic object, but his half-saying adds another object to it that is the issue of this woman-mother, thus knotting together the ties of sex with those of generation, those ties about which current scientific advances suggest are not so inscribed in nature that they cannot be undone.

The Names of the Father, announced in the plural, went well with this function of saying, for saying is an existential function, thus contingent and pluralisable. This function of the signifier in the singular, that of the Name-of-the-Father that Lacan never rescinded, can be inscribed, but it is not a signifying function. The plural Names of the Father are in fact the names of various different sayings bearing the function. Lacan gave a few examples. Woman, Wedekind's masked man, and I add here, thanks to Joyce, the necessary son. We know the interest Lacan had in Wedekind, attributing to him an even greater perspicacity regarding sex than Freud's. Lacan's *Introduction to Spring Awakening* takes up this question of the plural in a way that is worth our while considering. The Father, he says, has so many names that none suit him. He has no proper name except the name of the name of the name, or the name as existence. In this assertion, the Father designates the function, because in terms of what a father is, the one who carries the function through his *père*-version, he has a proper name like every subject.

So, what about the name of the name of the Name-of-the-Father function? To this triad we can apply the logical game that Deleuze applies to the name of Lewis Caroll's song in his *Logic of Sense*. "Father" is a name which has an ordinary meaning; "Name-of-the-Father" is a name of the name which designates the function; and all the particular names of this name of the name, "woman", "the masked man", etc., constitute the series of Names of the Father in the plural, the series of manifestations of the function. This means that if existential saying is able to lay down the law, and even an ironclad law when it is the superego, there is no law of saying. The paternal saying which names is hence rather epiphanic, as I have already argued. It reinforces the injustices of nature by the contingencies of its emergence, but its contingency also separates it from the avatars of the conjugal family. And in all cases of saying, the nominating saying has a Borromean function. It knots the three consistencies in hooking the Real into an imaginary-symbolic social bond. It is thus both knotting [*nouant*] and *nou(s)ant* [knotting us], if I may write it that way.

End identity

Lacan's successive formulas concerning the subject at the end of analysis are numerous: the end by assumption of "being towards death", by subjectivisation of castration, by subjective destitution of the pass, and finally by identification with the symptom. This variety, that follows the elaborations of structure, is precious because it forces us to choose and can thus have anti-dogmatic qualities. But it leaves us with a question: that of the "saying", of the unique saying to be inferred from the many different things that are said.

If we turn to Freud on terminable analysis, it seems that the actual end is purely pragmatic. This is not the case with Lacan who never gave up defining the conclusive point of analysis, at first in terms of acquired knowledge and then finally in terms of the affect produced by the epistemic effect.

The constant that runs through the variety of Lacan's theses is thus particularly important to me. One claim is never altered: that there is a definable conclusion, that this is inseparable from the production of the analyst, and that it has an essential political impact.

What is sought in his various formulas is what I have called a separation identity (Soler, 2004). The expression is not Lacan's, but since 1964 with *Seminar XI* where he produces the notion of alienation to the signifying chain, he opposes to it what he calls separation by the object. Separation identity is to be understood in its difference from the identifications of alienation. These latter are run through in an analysis and are, as we say, summoned in order to fall. They come from the Other and borrow from it its signifiers: they go from the ideals, I(A), big I of big A, up to the phallic signifier. They certainly attempt to "crystallise" in an identity—the term is Lacan's—but they are just the screen, if I may say, of a subject who is only supposed and who is not identifiable in the Other where he only functions as lack (−1). Analysis, however, reaches its end in a separation identity. It cannot come from the Other, and it is expected from the analytic metamorphosis. This is the invariant saying of Lacan on this point, conveyed by the various formulae that go from the "you are that" of the 1949 text on the mirror stage up to this famous identification with the symptom of the years around 1975.

"You are that."

In 1949, in his text "The mirror stage as formative of the *I* function", Lacan concludes by saying that analysis accompanies the patient up to "the ecstatic limit of the *'You are that'*" (Lacan, [1949] 1966, p. 100). If this is not a formula of identity, what is it? A separation identity, as the term "ecstatic" indicates.

In the following decade, it is the famous "assumption of being towards death", the pathematic resonances of which eclipse the true structure. As analysis is being defined as the restitution of the chain of words constitutive of the subject, we might infer that the notion of intersubjectivity developed in the two great texts "Function and field of speech and language" and "Variations on the standard treatment", would only produce an alienated identity. But it is precisely in relation to this that Lacan describes death as an "external centre of language"—in other words, real—and more precisely as a paradoxical real, quilting point. Lacan evokes here the subject who "says no": no to the productions of the Eros of the symbol and no to the chain, in favour of a "desire for death" whose three major forms are not to be confused with the death drive. He describes these forms that indicate—Lacan says it explicitly—that being towards death is the "assertion of life", the only true one according to him that inscribes one's own unique being. Subjectivisation of being towards death is here understood as the establishment of unique difference. It passes to the act in the suicide of Empedocles, whom Lacan will later make the paradigm of separation identity and who provides the model of the act through which the subject finally becomes identical to himself. We are not far from Valéry's famous line: "As into himself at last, eternity changes him [*Tel qu'en lui-même enfin l'éternité le change*]".

"The solution to interminable analysis" (Lacan, [1958] 2006, p. 537).

What would we make, then, of the end by assumption or, as Lacan sometimes says, subjectivisation of castration, that he will elaborate a few years later, starting from "The direction of the treatment"? The end is conceived as the fall of the ultimate identification with the phallic signifier, the end of the famous "being the phallus" in the desire of the Other! An effect then of de-identification. Is this not very close to an effect of separation since the phallus is the mediating signifier of the relation to the Other, the relation to its desire? It is true that this effect does not identify, since it leaves the $ (the barred subject) to be discovered, so to speak, and we could think of this as an end by the indetermination of a without-identity [*un sans-identité*]. This idea had a currency and is still sometimes repeated today, but it is because what came later was not correctly read, and in particular the lines that followed. They are certainly very coded but not indecipherable if we work at them, especially when we have access to the later work.

What do these say? Firstly, that the effect of separation, which is that of phallic disidentification, is the condition for putting imaginary castration into play in the erotic relation to the Other: to give and to receive the phallus. Let us not forget here that the Freudian bedrock, in chapter VII of "Analysis terminable and interminable", is the rejection of this putting into play, and stasis for the man in the despair of protest or for the woman in her demand. "To make castration subject" ["*Faire de la castration sujet*"]—according to the expression Lacan used in his summary of "The analytic act"—is already a solution to the Freudian bedrock.

Certainly this does not yet make an identity, but it is not all. In the last paragraph the text concludes on what Lacan calls the "solution to infinite analysis", a solution to the Freudian bedrock. This is a solution provided by Freud himself, according to Lacan, the Freud who in 1937 begins to write for the first time about what he calls *Spaltung* [Splitting]. To put it simply, according to the two formulae that I have suggested, that there is no penis, but there is the fetish. In this fetish which for Freud was the displaced penis, Lacan recognised the first Freudian introduction of the consideration of an object that he himself had not yet written as object *a*, but which he had already seen as the solution.

To conclude on this text, we don't exactly have an end by separation identity, but an end that is not without an effect of separation, and already an indication of the element that will respond to the indetermination of the subject: namely, the object itself. In this sense, the text is like an unfinished play, which close to the last sentence leaves us on the threshold of the additional elaboration that is to come.

Destitution

There remains the famous "destitution of the subject" of the period of the pass, the true nature of which it is difficult to misconstrue. Lacan clarified it himself, notably in "Le discours à l'EFP" in December 1967. Contrary to what the term "destitution" connotes, it is not a negativisation but a positivisation. It is only conceivable in relation to the institution of the subject supposed to know that marks every entry into analysis. But destitution only institutes the subject as want-to-be, as x of desire, the enigma of indetermination, and therefore as irreducible by the signifying chain as Freud's primal repression. It is to this non-identifiable x that destitution gives identity, through the equivalence of the $ with the object, the latter being the only thing to respond to the "what am I" of the entry into analysis. It is the non-identity of the subject supposed to the chain that is destituted.

However this objectal identity is paradoxical. Indeed, since the object, despite its imaginary and real bodily consistency, is not an object of reality that can be grasped within the coordinates of the Kantian aesthetic, identity by the cause of desire becomes unrepresentable. It has no representative. Destitution produces being where there was a want-to-be. It determines that which was indeterminate, giving being through the object-cause that determines the subject's desire: that is what a resolute desire means and what I think Freud also meant with his "indestructible" desire. But this object-cause remains unrepresentable. And at the end of his whole elaboration, Lacan gives his verdict that, it must be said, has given rise to error: "Vain knowledge of a being that slips away" ["*Savoir vain d'un être qui se dérobe*"] (Lacan, 1995, p. 10).

Separation identity, then, but one that slips away. We are not far from the ecstatic limit of 1949. You are this object that is not signifiable in the Other—separation—you are that which does not cease to chatter about all your statements and acts—constantly—but which no statement represents, no act can staunch, and which thus only manifests itself as an act. It is not surprising that just after this is the seminar on the Act!

Identification with the symptom

With this notion that surprised Lacan's students so much at the time, we can see that the inversion of perspective—introduced by taking *lalangue* and the real unconscious into account—does not negate the constant of the saying about the end of analysis by separation identity. It reinforces it. The formula is new but the saying is not, and it never varied.

The symptom in the singular, a formation of the real unconscious, is not on the side of the Other: it comes from the Real, from *jouissance* and from *lalangue*. Lacan defined this identification in a way that could not be simpler. It consists, he says, in "recognising oneself in it" (*s'y reconnaître*). What does this mean? The expression should be balanced with another from the same period, which says that you can never recognise yourself in your unconscious.

Obviously, to recognise oneself in one's symptom one needs to have at least localised it, recognised it as a specific modality of *jouissance* beyond any therapeutic changes. It is the condition for managing it—"to know how to use it" [*savoir y faire*]—says Lacan. For the neurotic, who by definition does not recognise himself in the symptom, who defends against it and thus complains about it, even if he pretends to be cynical, it is progress.

To recognise oneself in the symptom is to assume what must be called an identity of *jouissance*. This has nothing to do with identification to the Other. It is thus the symptom reduced to "what does not stop writing itself", the response to the "what am I?" of the entry into analysis. The precursor to this thesis is found at the end of the seminar *The Four Fundamental Concepts of Psychoanalysis*, where Lacan, evoking a special type of identification to object *a, was* already formulating a separation identity by *jouissance*. Indeed, what the symptom determines is not the simple subject supposed to the signifier, but on the contrary, as I have pointed out, what Lacan designated in 1975 as the "real subject", the subject well and truly there, the "pathematic" subject: that is, the individual *parlêtre* who has a body, both substantial and real.

Lacan's trajectory thus goes from ineffable identity, asserted from 1949, up to the identification of 1975, the one that the letter of the *jouissance* of the symptom tears out of the ineffable, the letter being the one thing in language that is identical to itself. I will come back to this point for it is more complex than it seems.

Ethics, never individualistic

Identity is the opposite of dispersal; separation, the opposite of alienation. It is astonishing to see to what extent Lacan produced misconceptions and was misunderstood by his first pupils. The latter valorised certain concepts into an ideal: lack, castration, disbeing [*désêtre*], destitution, not forgetting, of course, non-knowledge. Hence their stupefaction when they saw identification with the symptom appear, which nevertheless only gave the final quilting point to a thesis that had been present since the beginning. Lacan himself diagnosed this misunderstanding when he evoked those analysts "who only authorise themselves from their dispersal".

Now, without this fundamental thesis of separation identity, how can we explain a massive clinical fact—which, indeed, the enemies of psychoanalysis often bring up—the fact that those said to be analysed, for whom analysis has changed everything, remain nevertheless at a certain level the same, if not even more hardened.

The time for understanding that is too long has drawbacks. Clinically, of course, but also in as far as the conception of the end of analysis has a decisive political impact.

From the beginning, speaking of psychoanalysis, Lacan proposed that "ethics is not individualistic" (Lacan, [1955] 2006, p. 346) and that it involves *a contrario* effects of current civilisation. Rereading the totality of these texts, I was struck by the number of virulent remarks about the times that could be applied perfectly to the beginning of this twenty-first century. Put briefly: times of social hardship, the barbarity of the Darwinian century, producing touching victims: this is "Aggressiveness in psychoanalysis" (Lacan, [1948] 2006, p. 99); objectification of discourse which banishes the meaning of the subject: this is "Function and field of speech and language"; then the ethics of the superego and terror: this is "The remarks on Daniel Lagache's presentation". "The Proposition of 9 October 1967 on the psychoanalyst of the school", furthermore, forecasts a future of segregation into camps, and that's not all, right up to "La troisième" in which we are all identified as proletarians in no longer having anything with which to make the social bond.

Parallel with each of these diagnoses, the mission of psychoanalysis is redefined: "we clear anew the path to his meaning in a discrete fraternity [...] with this touching victim" (Lacan, [1948] 2006, p. 101); that "the subject's satisfaction is achievable in the satisfaction of all" (Lacan, [1953] 2006, p. 264); freed from the ethics of the superego through the silence of desire (Lacan, [1960] 2006, p. 573); and then, to make use of his castration in "Subversion of the subject and the dialectic of desire"; to escape from the "herd", to leave the capitalist discourse in *Television*; and finally to take the real into account—as I understand it, the real of the proletarian social symptom in "La troisième".

We see that in each case, and we must follow this progression in more detail, the prescribed purpose goes in the direction of restoring a social bond beyond the resolution of the alienation to the Other that analysis strives to bring about.

On this point, what is it in identification with the symptom that concentrates the most intimate aspect of autistic *jouissance*? Does it not intensify compulsory individualism and the dereliction of the modern proletarian? Some have asked, after the year 2000 when today's subjects are in the grip of capitalistic values, how we could still want "to meet at its horizon the subjectivity of one's time", as Lacan advocated for the analyst at the end of "Function and field of speech and language" (Lacan, [1953] 2006, p. 264). It is that these same people who no doubt supposed that identification with the symptom was homogeneous with the regime of what I have called the generalised "narcynisism [*narcynism*]" of our time. There, I think, is the error. The social symptom of "all proletarians" which globalises the relation of all with the products of the market is disruptive of the social bond, establishing only a single link, hardly social, between each person and some prescribed surplus enjoyment. This is not the case with the fundamental symptom or, better still, with the *sinthome* that in no way excludes the social bond if it is, as I will show, a Borromean symptom. This symptom knots desire and *jouissances*, the Imaginary, the Symbolic, and the Real for each person in a singular and never global way.

CHAPTER ELEVEN

Identification with the symptom or ... worse

The symptom is what via the unconscious makes up for the foreclosure of the sexual relation. It is thus structurally out of the question that the fundamental symptom be absent at the end of analysis, whether we know it or not. That does not rule out the therapeutic effect, which consists of modifying one part of the symptom, that to which meaning can be given via deciphering. Look at the paradigmatic case of the Rat Man: at the end of the deciphering process, his obsession disappears, but the fundamental symptom of his relation to the sexual partner is neither resolved nor elucidated.

This symptom is not just any old one. At the beginning, and during the course of an analysis, we are faced with plural symptoms which are multiple and varied, and that establish themselves in opposition to the conventionalities governing established discourses. In contrast, the symptom in the singular is the one that establishes the social bond where precisely there was none. And where is this if not in the "enclosed field" of the relation to sex or to different objects that can be substituted for it: in other words, in the "love affairs" about which Lacan could say in *Television* that they are severed "from every established social bond" (Lacan, 1990b, p. 38). This means that just as the schizophrenic is confronted with his organs, and even more so to his life, without the aid of an established discourse, so too very *parlêtre* is confronted sexually to the Other of sex without the aid of an established discourse. The symptom is a suppletion. At this level everyone is incomparable. I have called this symptom fundamental in analogy with the fundamental phantasy. I could also say the last symptom, since it is this symptom that in the field of *jouissance* makes up for the last word lacking in the field of language.

Analysis necessarily proceeds from the symptom at the start to the establishment of the symptom at the exit, and thus it is imperative to know in each case what the position of the subject is in regard to his fundamental symptom at the end, what he knows about it and how he bears it. When Lacan says that it would be better to identify with it, he obviously means that there are other possibilities … worse ones.

I will explore the alternatives. First of all, the excluded alternatives. With the Borromean symptom we cannot say "either the symptom or desire", nor "either the symptom or the social bond", as we sometimes hear. It is a symptom that links beings to each other by establishing a knot between *jouissance* and desire, between the Real and semblants. It is inaccurate to imagine, as we sometimes hear, that Lacan's last elaborations negate his theses on the subject of lack and of desire.

A symptom that creates a specific social bond between bodies includes desire and the phantasy underlying it. This thesis is clear when, in his development on what *a* father is that supports the Father function, Lacan situates his female partner simultaneously as the cause of his desire and as the symptom of his *jouissance*. We can no longer oppose the Eros of the desire that would be socialising—by sustaining object relations—to the symptom that, withdrawn into its own *jouissance*, would be asocial. There are no doubt autistic symptoms, but equally there are also quite asocial strangled desires which empty the relation to the other of its substance, and which illustrate well enough, without having to look very far, the internment of the obsessional and the annihilating quest of the hysteric.

From this I will draw a first conclusion: the question is simply of knowing, in each case, what type of *jouissance* is linked to what cause of desire. Lacan replied clearly to this question in the case of the Father as symptom [*symptôme-Père*], the father version [*version père*] of perversion [*perversion*]. There are other versions, of course: those bachelor symptoms uncoupled from the other sex; those of the spectrum of non-father type heterosexual symptoms that culminate in Don Juanesque positions that tolerate the woman but not the mother.

A second conclusion: the opposition of "crossing the phantasy" to identification with the symptom needs to be rethought. It is true that in the chronology of his teaching, Lacan at first emphasised the crossing of the phantasy as that which would show the subject his being as object, and that his conception of the moment of the pass is built from there. But identification with the symptom, which goes together with the real unconscious, does not exclude this but includes and completes it. Let us not oppose them under the pretext of doing something new at all costs.

Alternatives: to identify with one's symptom is the alternative to another identification, the identification with the Other, the big Other in its various manifestations, albeit the famous final identification with the analyst promoted by the IPA. To an analysis demanded by the subject because he is flailing beneath inconvenient identifications—subjective perception of the symptom being relative to the identifications—with this final identification, he is given the objective of rectifying these identifications in favour of others supposed to be more compatible and acceptable, the analyst putting himself forward as the measure of the norm. This treatment of the identifications of alienation through other identifications is more than a paradox. Remodelling the analytic discourse on that of the discourse of the master reinforces alienation by restoring in a different way the dominion of the Other.

We can give a weak definition of the final identification with the symptom and say that it consists simply of accepting what we have not been able to transform. This dilution of the notion into simple resignation is scarcely of interest. It only has import if taken in the strongest sense and it is defined, I think, by two features: it is not a matter of merely consenting, or even of ceasing to complain, which would already be progress; much more essentially, and this is the first feature, it is a matter of no longer suffering from the symptom. But this result, when it is obtained, is the sign of another change, involving the crossing of identifications. Let us not forget that the suffering engendered by the symptom has been produced in large part by the division of the subject between the ideal and the drive, to use Freud's terms again, the drive which prevents compliance with the prescriptions of discourse. To produce a symptom, which I would dare to call a "happy" one against the background of the curse of sex is not impossible, since the fundamental symptom is the solution given by the unconscious to castration. The latter is a universal misfortune, however masked it may be by the pretreatment imposed on it by discourse. A happy symptom, then, without forgetting the tone appropriate to say this.

But this is still not its principal feature. The second feature is epistemic, not pathematic. To identify oneself with the symptom is, if you like, to recognise oneself in it. With the Freudian unconscious, it is as out of the question to recognise oneself in it as it is to know it, because of what, according to Freud, is primordially repressed: *Urverdrängt*, as indestructible as it is impossible to subsume in saying. The perception of the incommensurable effects of *lalangue* intensifies this impossibility, which only the fundamental symptom makes up for. In it alone can the subject find his principle of consistency, and constitute it as the answer to the question at his entry into analysis: what am I? I am that *jouissance*, or more precisely, that modality of knotting between a desire about which it is impossible to say all and a *jouissance* that fixes a letter of the unconscious, albeit unknown. In this way, the fundamental symptom is alone in being able to create identity, a truly proper name, which all the identifications fail to do.

Without this, we could well be with what Freud called the negative therapeutic reaction. In his definition, we see two traits that I have just ascribed to identification with the symptom, but inverted. Freud notes that in this reaction, whatever his progress the subject continues to suffer. Freud even specifies that the more that progress is confirmed, the more there is renewed suffering. This is not all. The negative therapeutic reaction is not just content with not ceding misery, it clings to ignorance. Freud continues: the subject says "I am ill", which signifies that he claims his troubles do not involve his unconscious. This formula "I am ill" rejects any recognition of the symptom as the subject's doing: it carries a refusal. I could say, a rejection of "subjective attribution", to take up again a term used for psychosis. And it signifies that what I suffer from is so strange to me that I am unable to recognise in it anything of "the obscure decision" of my being. The negative therapeutic reaction as described by Freud, and without confusing it with the final end point of analysis—besides, he devotes two different chapters to these—is the direct opposite of identification with the symptom. There where identification with the symptom fuses a satisfaction and an insight, the negative therapeutic reaction involves a renewal of misfortune and a refusal of knowledge.

We should add that the therapeutic reaction has various degrees that distance it from its extreme form, in which sadness and the "I want to know nothing about it" can be combined in different ways. When the subject does not give up on what he would like to be, or on what he imagines others are—when he will not give up on these dreams—when he continues beyond the first therapeutic effects to reject not only the real of the impossible to avoid castration but also the necessary solution his unconscious has already given and which does not stop writing itself, then we have all the gradations of ends that I would readily describe as ends by disenchantment. This is the repeated choice of neurosis. I note that these ends are rarely heard about in the procedure of the pass, doubtless because this procedure selects, as it were automatically, subjects who think they can testify positively, something I already noted some years ago (Soler, 1994, p. 181).

Another alternative is that of the transference symptom. The expression is justified insofar as in the analytic discourse the partner cause of desire, the analyst, is also the condition of the *jouissance* of the unconscious.

There are several ways of enjoying the unconscious. The fundamental symptom is one that involves the RUCS. Free association is another way of playing with the plural declension of what I could call the rosary of signifiers. What is enjoyed there is not the fixed letter but the series of ones that drift in speech. This enjoying of the unconscious via free association pertains to a temporality in which the series dominates, and belongs to the modality of infinitude, of the infinite recitation of the unconscious with the effects of meaning it engenders. It goes together with belief in the symptom, a point that I have previously developed. On the contrary, the fundamental symptom is not a fluctuating being of the chain; its constancy is a fixed point that stops the drifting of the chain of language. It belongs to the modality of finitude, of the limit, and identification with this symptom ends the belief that was attached to it and to the expectation that it will still say something via the race after truth.

To identify with the symptom at the end of analysis is thus to change the symptom: to swap the transference symptom for the fundamental symptom, and to pass from indetermination to consistency, from evasiveness to assertion, and also from the want-to-be to the being of *jouissance*.

But why privilege the second terms in this series? Why should consistency, assertion, and atheism of the symptom be better? They are not better but their opposites—the culture of uncertainty, evasiveness, want-to-be, and belief—are correlated with a specific alienation: alienation to the real presence of the analyst as condition of enjoying the unconscious. This alienation to the real presence is a different alienation from alienation to the signifier of the ideal, which also exists in analysis but which precedes and masks it in the sequence of the treatment. I think that this real presence is already evoked in different terms by Lacan in "The direction of the treatment", when he spoke of satisfactions that are so difficult to unknot in the final phase of analysis. The question is not new. Had not Freud already said, with his priceless humour, that after having gone to enormous trouble to keep patients in analysis he now had to go to enormous trouble to make them stop? Indeed I note that the question first raised about the length of time of analyses is posed in a more general way, for it is not only in the treatment that the presence of the analyst as symptom can be used. In the institution, outside analysis, it can also be used as a prosthetic symptom (Soler, 1999).

I therefore conclude that the true benefit of identification with the symptom is to produce the effect of final separation. This resolves the transferential relationship without going back to identification with the big Other. Lacan first evoked this separative effect in *Seminar XI*, then in *"L'étourdit"*, in terms of mourning for object *a*, but it can be reformulated in terms of the symptom, as I am doing here. It has the advantage of including in the formulations the true mainspring that stands in the way of the separation effect: namely, another symptom, condensing another *jouissance*, that of the transference.

The two alternatives that I have just examined—the negative therapeutic reaction or the perpetuation of the transference symptom—already allow me to say: either identification with the symptom, or worse, the failure of the finished analysis.

Many questions could be developed here, questions that, it seems to me, open up a vast program of the differential clinic, for it is likely that some symptoms lend themselves to identifications more than others.

The masculine clinic, which is much less discussed than the feminine clinic, could be refined by these questions about final identification. Is it not observed, for example, that for a man to identify with his symptom—when it is a father as symptom—is what allows him the greatest probability of getting rid of that obsession with the father that so often possesses the neurotic man. And even of getting rid of the identification with the traits of his dad? In other words, don't we observe that identification with the dad is in indirect proportion to identification with the father as function? In this case, we must say: to do without the father on condition of making use of the father as symptom.

Obviously, questions about the differential clinic are also raised in relation to the sexes. How would it be otherwise since on the woman's side a female version of the exception does not exist? In other words, there is no exception of one who provides a model of the solution to castration. I use the word "model" in the sense that Lacan used for the father, but here as model of the function. The model of the function for a woman is necessarily on the other side, stretching from the man to God, with the question, in each case, of knowing whether this fundamental partner is more in the register of the Father version [*version Père*], the one of limited love, with or without the hysteric's strike of her body (Soler, 2007a), or, whether it moves away from it and flirts with the side of the limitless and opaque Other of the mystic. Strangely, the famous ravage is produced mostly in the first group of cases, that is to say, in the woman coupled with a father as symptom. I note that the mystics, in as far as we have their testimony, do not belong to the ravaged nor, I think, to the masochists. Perhaps it is precisely because in being made the symptom of a divine Other, or in being annihilated, these mystics do not encounter the objection of the phallic limit.

Let's take up finally the question of becoming an analyst, since the analyst is also reduced to lending his presence and thus also his body as a symptom. For the analyst, as for the woman, a model of the function is lacking. It is true that everything indicates that the analyst is tempted, for lack of any typical version of the analyst as symptom, to cling to the father version, especially when he is a man. To Freud's credit he had already perceived and articulated this problem. However, there is no more a typical version of the analyst as symptom than there is of a woman as symptom. And like this latter, the analyst lends himself to the other, to the analysand, becoming the symptom, but provisionally, we hope.

This thesis is set out in the seminar on Joyce and raises the question once more of what may impel someone to it. For the woman, the question does not occur, as the benefits of *jouissance* in being the symptom appear obvious enough. But for the analyst, who like the saint is not supposed to enjoy his function, the question should preoccupy him. I think it preoccupied Lacan. Plenty of ethical and clinical problems arise here.

We can wonder whether there are not fundamental symptoms that favour the choice to become an analyst as symptom. Would this not be for the psychotic the prosthetic social bond where the autism of the real could dwell? As for the neurotic, what would be the benefit here? Is it that the analysed neurotic is so struck by what he has discovered that he would desire to have it discovered by others? Or, on the contrary, is it because he has not given up on his transference symptom so that, identified not to his real symptom but to the not-all truth, he is satisfied to refer the effect of castration to the other, to the analysand? Whether it is one or the other way, or one more than the other, will obviously greatly affect the style of analytic practice.

CHAPTER TWELVE

The identity at the end, its aporias

I said that the question of identity was at the entry into every psychoanalysis. But we should recognise it under different terms. When Lacan formulates the step of entry into the transference in terms of a "*Ché vuoi?*", when he adds a "What am I there?" where the signifiers of the Other are lacking, these are questions of identity.

The references to the *cogito* of Descartes imply that identity poses a question, since the "I think, therefore I am" does not say what I am. It poses—I should say: sub-poses—an existence, not an identity. Hence the following step by Descartes—"What therefore am I?"—which is a question about identity, not about a particular subject but about the universal subject. Translated into psychoanalysis as a practice of speech, this *cogito* would become "I speak, therefore I am", except that I do not only speak through my mouth but through my symptoms. Identity in the social sphere is first of all a policing problem, to know who is who etc. It is also for each subject a problem of social integration. We know this only too well. The question is intrinsic to psychoanalysis and constitutes the entry into psychoanalysis precisely because of symptoms.

The subject who addresses the analyst knows the indices of his social identity—profession, sex, income, religion, etc.—but what he presents are the uncontrollable repetitions, inhibitions, anxieties, both painful and incomprehensible, which are imposed on him and run counter to his intentions. All that he does not manage to do—impotence and everything that he does not manage to prevent—constraint: these are the manifestations that we can subsume under the term "symptoms", which social identity does not accord a place to and which can become obstructions. Indeed, the person who is in harmony with himself and his world does not come to analysis.

The *cogito* of the analysand on entry into analysis could articulate itself in this way: "I have symptoms, therefore I am ... but what am I?" Not as a social being, but as affected and thus represented by these symptoms.

We invite this subject to speak in the specific modality of free association, to say all the thoughts emerging in the transferential relationship. We thus enjoin him to represent himself only through his speech.

First aporia

The first paradox emerges here. It is that with his statements, which of course suppose language, the subject cannot accede to his identity.

The signifier, without which we could not speak, is not suited to fixing identity. Its differential structure, established by linguistics and notably Jakobson's phonology, contests this. Because each signifier is only defined in relation to another signifier, it is never identical to itself. It certainly represents the subject who utters it, and we can certainly reply to this subject: you said it, you cannot unsay it, but the signifier still represents him in relation to another signifier. In the chain of his statements, the chain of language, the subject is thus never One but always "some two", according to Lacan's expression.

The symptomatic subject, the one we suppose to the decipherable chain of his symptoms, lacks identity, in as much as he speaks. He is "a without identity" [*un sans identité*], a being whose being is always elsewhere, vanishing, as Lacan says repeatedly, even in the seminar *Encore*. He does not know what he is, he does not know what he wants, and he hopes that analysis will tell him. Is this the case, and if yes, how so? This is the whole question.

Note first of all that what is of a subject at the beginning of a psychoanalysis is also there at the beginning of his life, or rather, at his entry into language, since he first receives the discourse of the Other which, in saying what he is, in wrapping him in a series of attributes, raises in a latent way the question of what he is in himself, separated from all the judgements of the Other. He thus searches for himself, but at first through identification, in other words, by borrowing the traits that might define him. He borrows them at first from the other, the counterpart as supplier of images, or from the Other who speaks and transmits its signifiers to him. Whether the identifications are imaginary or symbolic—the first being governed by the second—they provide what can be called an identity that I'm calling here an aliena- tion identity, an identity established on loan and which the subject experiences as such. Especially given that the social other judges, this alienation identity[1] is what actually constitutes the ego, the kernel of which is identification with the image of one's own body and which then gets dressed in successive skins via the ideals of the Other, and whose alienating function in relation to the subject Lacan emphasised from the start.

Yet we must not forget that identification does not necessarily pro- duce conformity, and that the division of identity is indeed reflected just as well in non-conformity. Many subjects choose a counter-model and believe that this allows them to separate from the Other although they are just as captive to its dominion as are the most conformist sub- jects. We thus sometimes see siblings who are diametrically opposed to each other, though derived from the same core injunction.

Analysis counts and challenges these pro or contra identifications. Lacan even says that it "denounces" them in order, I think, to empha- sise their function as prosthetic identities. It is what we evoke when we speak of the fall of ideals in analysis, those ideals which are always linked to the desire of the Other, for "identifications are determined by desire" (Lacan, [1964b] 2006, p. 724). After the crossing of these identifi- cations, analysis then brings the subject back to the question of what he is as desire, "*ché vuoï?*" and thus to the paradox which I evoked earlier, namely that language is not suited to respond to this question. Desire "is incompatible with speech" (Lacan, [1958] 2006, p. 535), despite the fact that it haunts it, and we could say, taking a more logical path, that since the subject is supposed to a signifier which represents him but does not identify him, he always has the value of minus-one in the chain of language.

If this were the last word, psychoanalysis would not respond to the question of the entry into analysis due to the incompatibility of the linguistic instrument it uses. It would only bring the analysand back to his essential destitution. Only this is not the last word, just the first.

If language is unsuited for identity, where are we to find a principle of identity? Nowhere else than in that which, in experience, is not language. Indeed, the subject is not the whole of the individual. He is the effect of speech, but the individual has a body, a body to enjoy that is to be distinguished from the subject. It is thus on the side of the symptom that we can look for the solution.

Solution by the symptom

Lacan's hypothesis at the end of the seminar *Encore*, but presented well before this, is that the enjoying substance of the body is affected by language. This latter may be unsuited for identity, but it is still an operator that has effects in the Real. It subtracts from *jouissance*—object *a* is a name for this subtraction—but at the same time it governs the configurations of this remainder and becomes itself an apparatus of *jouissance*. Furthermore, without this hypothesis how are we to conceptualise the hysterical conversions discovered by Freud? Certainly, Freud only evoked the effect of thoughts and representations, *Vorstellungen*, to explain them, but what are they other than language?

The symptom is the main manifestation of the organism affected by discourse, and Freud, once again, situated it first of all as a way of enjoying. Lacan at first stressed that it was a way of speaking since it was decipherable as a message. But that does not stop it from also being a way of enjoying. If we condense the two di(t)mensions we get the "I think, it enjoys itself" that I have already mentioned. And this is more than *a* way of enjoying: it is the *only* way, as I have said, there is no other. The symptom, as a modality of *jouissance*, makes up for the relation that is foreclosed for everyone. There is no sexual relation but there is the symptom, the linguistic modality of *jouissance* specific to each of us: a fixed *jouissance*, determined by one or more elements of the unconscious as language, the elements that we try to decipher in analysis. Again we must not forget the effect of the two unconsciouses that I have distinguished, and differentiate the symptoms of the unconscious as truth from those of the RUCS. The Borromean knot knots these, and each involves *jouissance*: for the first, the *jouissance* of meaning, of the phantasy; for the second, the *jouissance* of the incarnated ones planted in the field of the Real.

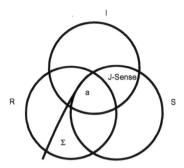

Knotting of the two unconsciouses

Lacan sought how what I have called separation identity, or even a will to separation, could be established. How could one not be reduced to the clothes of the Other that one wears? Lacan recognised the paradigm of this will in the act of Empedocles, who is supposed to have committed suicide by throwing himself into the volcano at the edge of which he had left his sandals. An extreme act. Obviously we expect from analysis a non-fatal separation of the subject that would give him his identity, and notably his sexual identity.

In the Other and in social discourse, there are only semblants, signifiers, images, norms, and prohibitions about sex, but nothing which says how each one of us enjoys. At the hour of truth, when the subject makes semblants pass to the act, there are many surprises. At the end of his elaboration, Lacan concludes that it is the real symptom that gives the subject his own identity, the true proper name that distinguishes him from everyone else, the only one that does not have a homonym.

We could thus say that analysis answers the opening question: I am my symptom. This is why Lacan speaks of "identification with the symptom".

Second aporia

Is this to move beyond the impasse linked to the linguistic instrument? I'm not so sure, as I have only recently understood, but it is I think of major importance.

I'll propose a formula of this second stopping point: that one identifies with one's symptom does not imply that one has identified one's symptom, contrary to what I at first supposed. If it is true that the effects of *lalangue* exceed all that the subject is able to grasp, it is the real unconscious, the unconscious as *lalangue* which blocks us from identifying the symptom other than in a hypothetical way. For the incarnated One, the one that would be the letter of the symptom, remains undefined, from the phoneme to the word to the sentence, even to the whole of thought. In other words, the unconscious that we decipher does not know everything, but only a bit.

We may have taken the measure of our own inertias of *jouissance*— for "fixation" means "inertia"—without being able to articulate the one that fixes them, or only to do this hypothetically. Analysis leads to the assumption of an identity at the end, but to assume is not to know. I even think that this is what justifies the expression "identification with the symptom".

The identity at the end is clarified by the non-identification at the start. The Rat Man suffers from his obsession but does not recognise himself in it; he dissociates himself, he does not want to be the bad *jouissance* that appears there. Hence his demand to Freud. This non-identification is what Freud called defence. It refers, as does the identification at the end, to the position of the subject at the place of the *jouissance* that is at stake for him, according to whether he recognises or not what he has that is most real.

The real symptom, disconnected from meaning, is not disconnected from language: it is a mixture of *motérialité* and *jouissance*, of the word enjoyed or of *jouissance* transferred to the word. Lacan wrote its structure in the seminar *RSI* as a function of the letter one. Now the letter, in its difference from the signifier, is characterised by identity to itself. The final identification with the letter of the symptom seems to resolve then, as I have evoked, the ineffable quality of the "you are that".

A possible program for analysands stems from this: find the letter of your symptom. We saw and heard that repeatedly on certain panels, the sympathetic Eureka of analysts fresh from the pass before the split of 1998, announcing "I have found the letter of my symptom". We can only salute the efforts of good will, ultimately pathetic, for being led by peer pressure. But how can we not see in every case the derisorily "lucubrated" dimension, to take up Lacan's term, of this trophy, of this fetish even, and the lie organised around the irreducible point of opacity?

These Eurekas forget to coordinate the thesis of the RUCS with that of identification to the symptom. If we put a little bit of thought into it, we will no longer be astonished that Lacan refers not to a knowledge of *lalangue*, but to a "know how [*savoir y faire*]" with *lalangue*. It is precisely the correlate of the non-knowledge of the One incarnated in the unconscious as *lalangue*. It is not that there is no certainty concerning the Real, but that it bears on the presence of the *jouissance* element, on the "I am my modality of *jouissance*", and not on the *one* which fixes this and which remains being "indistinct" [*indécis*] for whoever is its support. I am the letter of my symptom, certainly, but I can only approach it hypothetically. Let us say more positively that I can invent it by successive intersections that approach the effects of *lalangue*. What the subject has that is most real is his symptoms, says Lacan. This is not only because these symptoms are *jouissance*, but also because *lalangue*, which "civilises" this *jouissance*, is itself, as I said, real, a-structural, and the Real is not made to be known.

Don't we recognise how much closer this perspective is to the actual experience of analysands who are reaching the end of their analyses? Is there a single person who can believe that he has completely reduced the opacity of his being? For that he would need to have settled his score with the unconscious.

Note

1. What Lacan calls alienation in *Seminar XI* is something else, which is linked not to the presence of the discourse of the Other but to the structure of language, which imposes a forced choice which implies, in every case, a loss.

PART III

A RENEWED CLINIC

CHAPTER THIRTEEN

The status of *jouissances*

The real unconscious that makes the parlêtre is the most shared thing in the world, although, as I said, only in an analysis can it be proven whether or not it can be knotted to the unconscious as phantasy.

We must consider the consequences here at theoretical, clinical, and practical levels. They are multiple, and they require that we simultaneously complete the theory of the symptom, reorder our diagnostic categories in relation to the function of the father, and question anew the impact of the exchange of speech, of love and the very aim and function of psychoanalysis at the beginning of this century.

However, we cannot situate Lacan's advances in relation to the symptom and the status of *jouissances* without returning to the beginning, the Freudian beginning.

Freud's saying

We know the first thesis: in deciphering symptoms, Freud discovers what he calls sexual meaning, but this is coded in terms of the repressed partial drives: oral, anal, etc. The symptom is thus a sexual substitute: due to repression, it is a paradoxically unpleasant way of enjoying.

Freud hears, in the adult who speaks to him through his symptoms, the voice of the little "polymorphous pervert", enjoying his own body autoerotically without any partner. This is the first model of what I have called the autistic symptom, in order to designate a bodily enjoyment that does not pass through another partner, one that relies only on the excitation of the erogenous zones.

If the drives do refer to *jouissance*, they ignore the difference between the sexes. According to Freud, this is introduced into the unconscious only via what is called the phallic phase and this is not so much tied to the discovery of anatomical difference as to the masturbatory *jouissance* of the organ. This implies correlatively the maternal lack, and more precisely that the mother is deprived of the organ that "concentrates in itself the most intimate autoeroticism".

I thus return to the notion of generalised perversion that I have already developed, not in order to say that it is a phenomenon of our times, nor to generalise the clinical structure of perversion, but in order to question the mode of *jouissance* of the speaking being. Generalised perversion, as the name indicates, concerns each *parlêtre* and it is consistent with Lacan's famous assertion: "There is no sexual relation". Yet we need to measure its exact scope, its implications for the couple, as well as for psychoanalysis and its practice. The formula does not mean that things go wrong between men and women, as is so often said.

The sexual non-relation, if one believes Lacan, is "Freud's saying", never formulated by him in an obvious way, but one that can be inferred from everything said by the unconscious that he knew how to gather. The formula is assertive and homophonic: the *"il n'y a"* [there is no] can be confused with *"nia"*, the past tense of the verb *"nier"* [to deny, repudiate]; however, this *"n'y a pas"* is not a negation, it repudiates nothing. It affirms in the negative mode: *"y a pas"* [there is not].

For Freud, what can account for this saying if not what I have just evoked in relation to sex: the unconscious only has two components, the partial drives and phallic *jouissance*. The symptom is a mode of enjoyment that localises that part of the original polymorphous perversion of the little speaker that is never renounced. In other words, the *jouissance* of the symptoms in phobia, hysteria, and obsession, but also in perversion as a clinical structure, is nothing other than the *jouissance* "deemed perverse", the one that Freud discovered in the phantasies that he deciphered in each symptom. This says nothing about genital matters. How can a sexual couple be established without the genital drive? Now, that is precisely what is in question in the expression "sexual non-relation". This aims at neither desire nor love, but at the body to body of the act and the *jouissance* that is specific to it in the orgasm—the sole emergence of *jouissance*, apart from the symptom, to come into the space of the subject, if we are to believe Lacan.

Freud saw clearly that there was nothing given about the sexual couple and that with the discovery of the drives, its possibility became a theoretical problem to solve. The footnotes added over the years to his *Three Essays on the Theory of Sexuality* prove this clearly. His solution is the appeal to the Oedipus complex, to the figures of the parental couple inducing behaviours through identification and to the separating effects of the threat of castration.

Lacan, apparently, did not disagree. The 1964 text, "The position of the unconscious" bears witness to this (Lacan, 2006 [1964a], p. 720). The text proposes that sexuality in its relation to the unconscious is split in two, the side of the living being and the side of the Other. The latter is that of the Freudian Oedipus, with its ideal signifiers and the identifications which it governs. This is the space of "order and the norm"; in other words, of the *semblants* of man and woman, of the phallic signifier and of the father. The side of the living being is that of the body-to-body of the act and of the *jouissance* that it involves.

The real question, however, is of knowing where to place the castration that Freud made so much of, and how to formulate it. Here, Lacan separates from Freud, for whom the castration complex is on the side of the Oedipus: castration caused by the father. For Lacan, beginning at least with the seminar *L'angoisse* of 1962–1963 (Lacan, 2004), whatever the predominance of the imaginary father-castrator might be, castration is without the father, the function of the father being something else. Real castration begins on the side of the living being marked by *lalangue* and is the castration of *jouissance*. In the "Position of the unconscious", the myth of the lamella articulates this; it is as much a substitute for the biblical myth as it is for the Oedipal myth. It is a myth that is not only without the father but, I would say, without the Other of language. It claims to mythify the enigmas of life in as much as life is reproduced by means of sex, at the price of a loss of life, as is illustrated by individual mortality, and which establishes the vector of the libido, the libido in which Lacan includes even the sexed animal kingdom. Hence his reference to ethology that he parallels with hysteria. He has moved on here from the simple dialectic of phallic lack through which, in 1958, he gave an account of the couple. It is now a question of the libido in so far as it seeks a complement for *jouissance* via the partial drives. And here is his conclusion as far as the sexual act itself is concerned: "there is no access to the Other of the opposite sex except via the so-called partial drives wherein the subject seeks an object to take the place of the loss of life he has sustained due to the fact that he is sexed" (Lacan, 2006 [1964a], p. 720). It implies the homology of the *jouissance* of the symptom with the sexual orgasm. Here, we are already beyond Freud.

Concerning so-called genitality, Freud was interested in its symptomatic failures: frigidity, impotence, the disjunction between love and *jouissance* in debasement, masculine insensitivity, etc. But of its "successes", there is almost nothing in all his work: no theory of the embodied couple, only some scattered indications that we should of course take into account in order to nuance what I am arguing. First, we can take the evocation of the *jouissance* of the sexual act as the *summum* of *jouissances*. This shows how much Freud distinguished this *jouissance* from "the brevity of autoerotic *jouissance*", even though both pass through the same organ. And then, there is all his questioning about how the partial drives can or cannot be integrated into the preliminary pleasures of the act. Finally, there are his remarks on the obstacle that the respect for women constitutes. There is nothing systematic, however, or even consistent, on what conditions the orgasm or on its function.

The relation as symptom

Lacan's thesis applies to the sexual act and goes well beyond it. It does not identify the lack of the sexual relation with the symptomatic failures of the act itself, but, on the contrary, it holds that it is the success of the sexual act that produces the failure of the relation. As he says in *Television*, "this failure of which the successful sexual act consists" (Lacan, 1990b, p. 38 [trans. mod.]). The thesis is already explicitly present in the seminar of 1962–1963, *L'angoisse* (Lacan, 2004) where there are numerous passages devoted to the orgasm and the identity of its success with the failure of the relation. Our thesis is the following: it is because Lacan went beyond Freud in questioning the couple of the sexual act, not only in its failures but also in its successes, that he can affirm "there is no" ("*n'y a pas*") with all that this implies of a generalised perversion, and that in attributing it to Freud he overpays his debt, rendering to Caesar more than is his due.

The *jouissance* of the *parlêtre* is denaturalised by the blade of language that limits it, fragments it, and stops it prior to any prohibition. This "primary castration", as he calls it in *L'angoisse*, reduces our *jouissance* to being that which is considered perverse, what is certainly "permitted", which does not mean that it is authorised—by whom would it be?—but that it is not impossible, not impossible to write. Language inscribes only phallic *jouissance*, one *jouissance*, and a *jouissance* of the one, just as surplus *jouissance* of objects tied to the drives is integral to it, but as I have said, nothing of an other *jouissance*. This means, as I have already formulated it, that "the unconscious knows nothing about women". "Sex" as it was called in the classical era, is not inscribed there, if we mean by that what characterises it as *jouissance*. The signifier "woman" remains, of course, and the semblants that relate to it according to culture, but nothing of her being of *jouissance*, except for the index of the suspicion that it exists. Indeed, how could we ignore that the aforesaid woman is defamed? Lacan did not fail to emphasise this.

As for the sexual act, it is clinically obvious that its link with anxiety, this exceptional affect, is a sign that allows us to recognise the place where orgasmic *jouissance* and castration—not imaginary but real castration—meet in a single experience. Such is the thesis of *L'angoisse*: the orgasm is *jouissance* for both sexes, but it reiterates the effect of castration each time through the eclipse of the phallic organ. Some years later, in *Encore* (Lacan, 1998), Lacan sticks to his guns in speaking of the sexed couple in terms of the impossible encounter of the idiot and the madwoman: in other words, on one side, the castrated *jouissance* of the phallic one, and on the other, the other *jouissance*, unplaceable and enigmatic.

From here, I will set out a series of conclusions and remarks.

I'll remind you first of all that for Lacan the drive is different from what it was for Freud, even though he builds on the latter's formulations, and its function is double-sided. In its structure, according to Lacan, it comes from language: more precisely, from the discourse of demand and its effects on need. But, as an activity, the drive both compensates for and reinstates loss. Speaking of its circuit around drive objects, he specifies that "the activity in the subject called 'drive' (*Trieb*) consists in dealing with these objects in such a way as to recover from them, to restore to himself this earliest loss" (Lacan, [1964a] 2006, p. 720). The *jouissance* "deemed perverse" of the drives, is, let's say, castrated *jouissance*, of which the object *a*, defined as the object "which lacks", is the condition.

Thus the very action of the drive includes an effect of castration, the same one that I called "primary castration", and which is also at play in the orgasm. There is nothing of this in Freud. This does not mean, however, that for Lacan the adult heterosexual remains the little polymorphous pervert that he once was, characterised by the dispersal and juxtaposition of the partial drives. In some discreet but decisive remarks, Lacan adds a supplementary condition that, curiously, has been very little commented on: genitality, if it passes by way of the partial drives, presupposes the interdependence of their co-presence. The access to the partner is thus only assured if the partial drives are constituted in a set, in the logical sense, by the operation of the Other (Lacan, 1973, p. 49).

Whatever there might be of this supplementary condition, the fact remains that the *jouissance* of the act is still the *jouissance* "deemed" perverse, the same one that Freud detected in the symptom. In other words, the closed field of the sexual relation is not excluded from the field of the symptom. As a result, it is logical that the most normative heterosexual *jouissance*, that of the father for example, might be called a father version [*père-version*], to be written in two words to signify the father version of perverse *jouissance*. It is *a*, surplus *jouissance*, and which write this, the Other of Sex remaining unattainable. Our mode of *jouissance* "which, henceforth, is only situated from surplus *jouissance* is, in fact, no longer expressed in any other way" (Lacan, 1990b, pp. 32–33, [trans. mod.]).

To summarise, we can say what makes a couple. At the level of desire, there is indeed a couple: that of the phantasy, $\$<>a$, united with meaning; at the level of love, if one believes *Encore*, there is a couple, subject to subject, $\$<>\$$; but at the level of *jouissance*, there is nothing, no couple. *Jouissance* does not bind; isolated, it does not establish social bonds.

Why then qualify this *jouissance* as perverse if it is structural and thus applies to everyone? In saying *jouissance* "deemed" perverse, Lacan indicates a reservation. I see in this qualifier "perverse" what remains of the original term "perversion", from the beginning of the last century in the work of Krafft-Ebbing, where perversion is defined in relation to a norm that is assumed to be natural, and designates all the behaviours of the *jouissance* of the body that are not channelled through the heterosexual act. An anomaly with regard to the zone and the object of the drive, says Freud, who shared something of this perspective. Perhaps it is necessary to see in the term the index of the dissatisfaction that it generates and the latent dream of a fusional *jouissance*. As a consequence, if it is the success of the act that makes the non-relation, the failure of the act evident in the symptoms studied by Freud—or its concerted avoidance by those who abstain from it, those *sexless* subjects of whom I spoke in the 1990s—becomes clearer: it is precisely to short-circuit the inconvenience of the non-relation with its subjective effects. As Melville's Bartleby says" "I would prefer not to".

More important, and this will be my third remark: what is the *jouissance* at stake in the social bond, let's say in reality, if not the marriage of phallic *jouissance* and surplus *jouissance*? The *jouissance* of power in all its forms (political, epistemological, artistic etc.) is the definition of phallic *jouissance*, which goes hand in hand with having the fetishised objects of consumption. Generalised perversion includes the sexual act, but it extends over the whole field of discourse and it is today out in the open, no longer covered by the semblants of tradition. Without doubt it is this which produces the banalisation of the act, this loss of secrets and shame that makes some people believe that they are dealing with mutant subjects. There is thus no exception to generalised perversion, save perhaps—and I will return to this—the "other *jouissance*" of the woman, foreclosed from discourse, which does not pass through the object *a*.

Fourthly, let's return to the sexual relation. How can we explain, within the framework of this thesis, the well-attested fact that satisfaction linked to the orgasm in the sexual relation is in general quite distinct from the one that accompanies masturbation? I use the word "satisfaction" rather than "*jouissance*" precisely because the position of the subject relative to this specific *jouissance* is involved here, the more general question being that of knowing how diverse *jouissances* are reflected in distinct subjective effects.

With his notion of the psychoneurosis of defence, Freud thought he could correlate the difficulties of sex with social repression, that is to say, with the discourse that uses the signifier to limit *jouissance*. But there is also an order of inverse determination. If I have used the expression "the commandments of *jouissance*" (Soler, 1998), it was precisely in order to say that *jouissance* in its various guises has subjective effects. In allowing the emergence of the *jouissance* called perverse, the contemporary discourse we call "permissive" modifies the notion of the psychoneurosis of defence. To remain at the level of phenomena, we could almost believe that it renders Freud's notion obsolete. As Lacan said, everything that is not forbidden becomes obligatory, and I would add: by the effect of imaginary induction. As a result, emulation of the practices of *jouissance* will follow, particularly in adolescents and in various groups based on affinity. We should not be deceived by this, however; the defences immanent to the speaking subject are not so much reduced as modified in their form. The analytic experience of the unconscious continues to attest to them for they depend less on the historical contingencies of discourse than on the irreducible effect of language.

It is obvious that generalised perversion goes hand in hand with a whole series of subjective manifestations specific to our times. These contrast with the proclamations of those who, following Foucault, believe that the time has come for self-generation through each person's free choice of their *jouissances*: rising depression, suicides, and, *a minima*, solitude, morosity, lack of meaning, etc. Perverse *jouissance*, in order to be *jouissance*, is essentially no less than a *jouissance* that dissatisfies the subject. It is the *jouissance* "that you don't need", as Lacan says in *Encore*, for Eros to make the One of dreamed of fusion out of two, that evokes the division of the subject and the lack central to the non-relation.

In this context, where does the satisfaction specific to the sexual act come from? I note at first that this satisfaction is not as common as one might believe—let's not forget the increase in the number of the "sexless" and, more generally, the ethics of the bachelor. However, it seems to me that the orgasm has a subjective function. I think that it touches on the problem of sexual identity without resolving it, while at the same time reproducing in the relation with the partner, *mutatis mutandis*, the double import of the partial drives. There is no sexual act, wrote Lacan, "which has the power to affirm for the subject the certainty of what he is as a sexed being" (Lacan, 1984a, p. 16). On one side, the success of the act is the experience for each one of the two, of being for the other, albeit differently and only for an instant, in the place of the unattainable thing; while on the other side, the moment of satisfaction itself is the restoration of the separation which does not make one out of two. Depending on which side one positions oneself on, the question becomes whether to haunt once again the borders of the thing (the usual way), or to avoid it (the way that is increasingly being chosen today, it seems to me). Without doubt we must specify the differences due to sex here. We can note that the disparity between being a man and being a woman also has repercussions for the subjectivisation of the act. Not to mention the fact that the other *jouissance*, the only one not to be included in perverse *jouissance*, has its own repercussions, which I have already described (Soler, 2006). So could we expect spoken communication, especially words of love, to temper these impasses? That is another question.

What you could not choose

Classical theory saw very clearly that the phantasy was at stake in the creation of erotic links with the counterpart, the object of the phantasy underlying "object relations". However, it is well-known that this link of desire guarantees nothing about the response of *jouissance*. The symptom as emergence of the real unconscious, is "an event of the body". The term "event" suggests the manifestation of a non-programmed *jouissance* that is imposed on the subject who submits to it. The orgasm illustrates this at the level of the couple, and to say that the partner is symptom is to say that they are the cause of the event of *jouissance*: "A woman is a body that is the *jouissance* of another body" (Lacan, 1979, p. 35).

Up to what point does the symptom of the real unconscious determine the subject? Between the iron law of the effects of language on the living being and the contingency of the encounter that makes the body event, what margin is there for any liberty? Between what does not stop writing itself of the effect of castration and the chance of the event, does a place for choice remain? Or is the subject only there as the puppet of the unconscious?

This is not today's debate, but it is still more topical than ever. Freud, speaking about the psychoneurosis of defence, could evoke what he called a "choice of neurosis", for the very notion of defence implies a position of the subject in relation to what constrains him: according to Freud, his drives. In 1946, when Lacan was fighting against the organo-dynamism of Ey, he wrote "Presentation on psychical causality" (Lacan, 2006 [1946]) denouncing a conception of mental illness that excluded the dimension of freedom and which reduced the subject to being nothing more than the product of malfunctioning organs. I will pass over the diverse forms in which this perspective has appeared both in the past and today, with the increase in the ideas of cognitive behaviourism. The question remains of what psychoanalysis is able to oppose to it. We know that from the start Lacan evoked even in madness what he called "the obscure decision of being", and some decades later he did not recoil from saying that subjects "have a choice" regarding their sexual identity. More generally, putting forward the notion of an ethics of psychoanalysis and even of a sexed ethics when he spoke of the "ethics of the bachelor" excludes determinist thought. But on what grounds?

For Freud, man or woman depends strictly on anatomy. There is a place for subjective alternatives but they are at another level, essentially that of each person's response to the experience of the castration complex (we know that for women, Freud distinguished three possibilities) and also at the level of object choice, homo or hetero. But for him, in all these cases it is anatomy that functions as the real basis for all the particular configurations. This thesis seems closer to common sense.

Lacan's conception is completely different. The very term "sexuation" that we now use frequently, and which suggests a process, already implies that. We could remember some striking formulas from his late work: subjects have a choice between the side of man and the side of woman, he said; and later, even more strongly: sexed beings authorise themselves.

There is thus a major disconnection between sex and anatomy. Anatomy implies much more than the form of the image, for it is linked with the living organism as sexed. The anti-naturalism of these formulas is clear and could obviously give rise to the suspicion of anti-realism, even of anti-biologism, as if the denaturation through language in the speaking being were such that his position as sexed owed nothing to the living body. This is strange, if one remembers that in the 1960s, between the seminar *L'angoisse* (Lacan, 2004) and the text "Position of the Unconscious" (Lacan, [1964a] 2006), Lacan had made much of the real of the sexed reproduction of life, of its link to death, and of what castration owed to the characteristics of the functioning of the male organ.

Here, there is something to consider and evaluate in Lacan's conception.

It is new, as much in relation to common sense as in relation to Freud. In addition, the term "choice" must not lead us to think that the thesis is Foucauldian. We know that Foucault did his best to emphasise the idea of the free choice of pleasures as the principle of the auto-fabrication of sex. This was an attempt to disconnect the question of identity, a question so central to our civilisation, from that of sex. So it was a way of denying that there was something like a sexuated identity, and denying that there were any real constraints in the field of sexuality. This attempt should be distinguished from those theories of gender that make sex a social product.

With his formulas of sexuation, Lacan puts forward the idea that the identity man/woman neither follows anatomy nor even semblants— the images and ideas of woman and of man that are not lacking in any discourse to which the theories of *gender* refer. One is a man or a woman according to the mode of *jouissance,* that is, depending on whether for a given subject its *jouissance* is all or not all phallic. I developed this point in 1992 in London, in a talk called "Otherness today". We could say that man is any *parlêtre* who is all in phallic *jouissance,* whatever his anatomy might be; and woman is any *parlêtre* who is not all in phallic *jouissance,* regardless of anatomy.

This thesis is difficult to handle and it is very obvious that we handle it badly, for while repeating the formulas that I have just quoted, we continue to speak of women according to common sense. Far from calling women those who are "not all", we attribute, on the contrary, the "not all" with its other *jouissance,* to those who are women according to their anatomy or civil status, assuming that it is the same thing. This produces some comic effects that I have already had the opportunity to emphasise, since it allows those who are visibly the most wholly phallic to adorn themselves with a pseudo not all, as if it is their right.

The evaluation of the anti-naturalism that I evoked will thus depend on the conception of *jouissance.* We can already say that this anti-naturalism is not an anti-biologism; it does not neglect the Real, the Real outside the Symbolic, the one that Lacan inscribed in his Borromean knot, which includes precisely all that is called life, without being able to represent it. *Jouissance* is linked to this real of life and not to the ana-tomical form of the body, that is, the Imaginary. When it is all phallic, this Real bears the mark of the letters of the unconscious. When it is not all phallic, when it is Other, it remains unmarked, inhabiting the body-substance, for in order to enjoy, it is necessary to have a living body. In all cases, *jouissance* is anomalous, foreign to the homeostasis of the organism and to the organisation of semblants. It is disturbing, for it perturbs the pleasures that are called natural and the good order of things, which is that of discourse.

So I can be more precise: the thesis of the choice of sex is neither an anti-biologism nor an anti-realism. Its presupposition, the postulate that grounds it, is that the Real is heterogeneous, that it is naturally

untied from the intertwining, if I can use this term, of the Symbolic
and the Imaginary which discourse organises, and which regulates the
right dosage of pleasure and the balancing of satisfactions.

This still does not tell us in what way sexuated speaking beings
authorise themselves. The thesis seems very paradoxical. It is true that
with regard to their sexuated identity, many subjects do not trust their
anatomy. On the contrary, they develop all the doubts we know about
being a man or a woman, sometimes to the point that they challenge the
civil status that recognises only their anatomy. The feminine masquer-
ade and the masculine display seem to affirm sex in using the images
and symbols of man and woman, but these are, rather, fine covers for
the question that often torments them: Am I a true woman? Am I really
a man? Most subjects are far from having a sense of choice. Indeed, the
whole of clinical practice immediately confirms the fact that they suffer
from what makes their sexual reality, and often unwillingly. Confronted
with impotence, frigidity, the intrusion of uncomfortable *jouissances*,
sardonic repetitions of their choice of object, insurmountable disgust,
uncontrollable appetite, automatic escape, even indifference or insensitivity, and equally—Oh surprise!—unexpected happy encounters, in all
these cases there is nothing they can do about it. They are far from seeing themselves as the secret agents of their symptoms. The symptoms
of *jouissance* are certainly sexed, but not sexuating.

I would conclude that if they authorise themselves, this "themselves"
is not a subject: or at least, not the subject supposed by the enunciations
of the complaint and the suffering to which it attests.

Lacan's thesis is unintelligible without the conception of the division
of the speaking being and who, despite being divided, is still just one
individual, since he has a body and only one of them. He is divided
between what he is as represented by the signifier, and what he is as
affected in his *jouissance* by language. The gap between the two is irreducible. A subject does not have much to do with *jouissance*, Lacan says
in *Encore*, but the corporeal individual who underlies it does, for he is
himself the subject of the furrowing effects of the Other. Contrary to
what he said before, Lacan notes in 1977 that the unconscious does not
make a chain: between the word which represents the subject, the one
who speaks to us on the couch, and the signifiers of knowledge from
lalangue that mark the *jouissance* of the living body, there is a gap. In
other words: *jouissance* is subject to language and more exactly, to the
lalangue that colonises it, but the subject remains separated from his
jouissance. We call it "his" because it is his body that is affected. With

all due respect to the Freudian Oedipus and to the identifications it governs, Freud would have wished that they ordered everything, but the *jouissance* of sexuated beings doesn't authorise itself from the Other, no more from the Other than from their anatomy.

The formulas of 1964 that I evoked do not give any translation of the real difference of the sexes in the field of the *parlêtre*. If Lacan had remained at that point, then yes, we would have had a sexuated identity purely "Otherfied", if I can say it in that way: between the semblants on one side and the partial drives, in themselves asexual, on the other, there is no place for real sex. It is this that Lacan corrects, starting with the formulas of sexuation. The difference between the sexes has nothing to do with semblants; it is well and truly inscribed in the Real by the two modes of enjoying that I have discussed already. Obviously the confusion—or at least, the complication—emphasised in *Encore*, is that these two modes, as real as they are, are in no way natural and belong only to the being of language.

The choice of sex is the choice of *jouissance*, but in the subjective sense, to the point that one could almost say that it is *jouissance* that chooses, where it responds and in the forms in which it will respond: all or not all. It rules ... the sexual. Would I say epiphanies (in the plural) of the Real in the space of the subject? Lacan's thesis was only apparently paradoxical, but it is definitely sardonic.

Indeed, if these subjects authorise themselves, it is a "themselves" which is certainly very close to them, as close as what they are as body, but a "themselves" which is neither ego nor subject, strictly speaking. Without any free will, no liberty of indifference, no question of choosing this so extimate an intimacy. It has already chosen you, and far from it speaking, it makes you speak. The Real governs the saying of truth (Lacan, 1973, p. 9). It is thus in what you say, more precisely it is in your saying—in the way Lacan defines it—that we will recognise it. This means—by the way—that it is useless to expect anything from testimonies, which are so much in fashion today. Such is the generic curse evoked by the formula of the sexuated who authorise themselves. When I say "generic" I mean that it is for all *parlêtres*. You see that we are far, far away from the Foucauldian illusion. What margin of choice remains for the one who says "I"? It is that of the position he takes with regard to what chooses him: rejection, consent, patience, enthusiasm, there are many of them. That would be another chapter, and the notion of identification with the symptom starts there.

CHAPTER FOURTEEN

Symptom of the real unconscious

The status of the *jouissance* that does not write the sexual relation changes the function of what we call the symptom. If all *jouissance* could be said to be perverse—and this applies to everyone—we must not say "all perverts" for that would add nothing except complacency. But if, on the other hand, this *jouissance* is displaced everywhere in the series of signs which carry it and where we decipher it, constituting reality and even social bonds, it is a matter of extricating both the specificity of the symptom in so far as it is a formation of *jouissance* and that which of the two unconsciouses determines it.

The symptom, indeed, is not just any decipherable formation of the unconscious. The dream, the lapsus, and the bungled action, although sometimes repeated, are punctual but the symptom, by its constancy and fixity, both enjoyable and uncomfortable, is different from these ephemeral manifestations. It is different from the coding of the unconscious and from the metonymic drift of speech that never stops displacing castrated *jouissance* and surplus *jouissance*. On the contrary, where language displaces in the series of signs, the symptom anchors, fixes, makes "*fixion*".

Remember that in *RSI* Lacan wrote the structure of this symptomatic exception as a function of the letter: $f(x)$, f being the *jouissance* function, x any element of the unconscious that has become the enjoyed letter, which, in contrast to the signifier, is characterised by self-identity. This is what led Lacan to say that the symptom is "the way in which each enjoys his unconscious" (Lacan, 1974–1975, lesson of February 18th 1975). But there are several of these ways, and they can be ordered. The generalised perversion of *jouissance* calls for a clinic of variety—"*varité*", said Lacan playing with the equivocation between "*variété*" and "*verité*" [variety and truth]—the "*varité*" of these arrangements: in other words, there are diverse versions of the symptom according to whether its *jouissance* will be knotted or not to the two other dimensions. This will determine whether it will include the truth of the phantasy or not.

Autistic or socialising

Lacan's distinction between symptom and *sinthome*—he writes the latter in a different place in the Borromean knot—echoes, but in a different way, the Freudian distinction between auto and hetero-erotism, the latter beginning, according to Freud, before the distinction between the sexes, at the level of the aggressive drive. The *jouissance* of the linguistic element, of the *moterialité* of the unconscious, does not need a partner. Configurations of *jouissance* that may be so diverse phenomenologically—the lonely jubilation of Joyce squeezing out *lalangue* when he writes *Finnegan's Wake*, the satisfaction of Freud the smoker, or some corporeal compulsion of the schizophrenic—have this in common: they ask nothing of another body. This is what I have called autistic symptoms, to be written between the Real and the Symbolic, as a direct effect of *lalangue* on *jouissance*. In themselves they exclude the social bond, withdrawing to a *jouissance* that I would readily call autoerotic if Lacan did not contest this term on the grounds that for the *parlêtre*, there is no *jouissance*—at any rate not that of the phallic organ—that does not suppose the heterity (*hétérité*) of language.

These autistic symptoms are to be distinguished from those that I call socialising, in which *jouissance*, although not very social, is lodged in a bond by virtue of the fact of being knotted to the Imaginary and the Symbolic of the partner. These deserve to be called Borromean symptoms. Lacan went from the generalisation of *jouissance* "deemed perverse", equivalent to the sexual non-relation, to the affirmation of the partner-symptom which makes up for the foreclosure of the relation. There is no sexual relation but for everyone there is the fundamental symptom that comes in its place, as I said earlier. The thesis is explicit for the hetero couple in the famous lesson of January 1975: "For a man, what is a woman? She is a symptom. In other words, a body to enjoy." (Lacan, 1974–1975, lesson of January 21st 1975). And to say "body to enjoy" is to say more than object cause of desire.

A body to enjoy, but not just any body. It is not just any woman that is symptom for a man, in spite of the feminine dream of Don Juan. So, it is a body that is chosen via the unconscious. In other words, for a man, a woman is a formation of his unconscious. Isn't it the case for every partner? Isn't it demonstrated by the example of the Rat Man's obsession? Although it holds the secret of his loneliness and haunts his most intimate depths, it is not autistic: that rat is certainly metonymised in the forms that Freud details, but the obsession only invokes it as knotted to the signifiers of the father and the lady, and to the representations of the body in the torture scene.

From one perspective, we can say about this obsession what Lacan says of all symptoms, that it "savagely" ensures the *jouissance* of a letter of the RUCS, a letter it makes manifest in this case; from another, that which includes phantasy and truth, it knots this *jouissance* of the letter to meaning or rather, to *joui-sens*.

Obviously, in the course of this elaboration, the meaning of the symptom has changed. Classically, it is the sign of something that is a problem, whether it is called an illness or not; for psychoanalysis it is a sign as well, but of a generic illness of sex, of the disturbing side of sexuality that Freud observed right to the end, and for which Lacan gives the formula. As a result, as well as being a sign, as I have emphasised, it is also an answer and a solution, always singular, to a failure, which is, on the contrary, general. And as a consequence, just as the unconscious is not reduced by analysis, the symptom is found again at the end of an analysis, transformed without doubt (the therapeutic effect) but as that which does not stop writing itself for each person, as guarantor of the *jouissance* that his castration has left him.

A psychotic unconscious?

In all cases, the lettrified (*lettrifié*) One of the symptom, which may be holophrastic, applies only to a given subject, depending on the *jouissance* value that words have for that subject. It is *jouissance* of the real unconscious, outside meaning. In other words, it is neologistic, if the neologism is indeed a word or an expression that can carry the weight of an ineffable and personal *jouissance*. Hence the term "autism" that I have applied to it. It is the psychotic kernel of those who are not psychotic, and which makes of each subject "scattered, odd" (Lacan, 1981a, p. ix, [trans.mod.]) according to Lacan's beautiful expression in the "Preface to the English-language edition". The letter outside meaning is homologous to the basic schizophrenic phenomenon where words are treated like things, according to Freud; for the schizophrenic "all the symbolic is real", outside the chain and outside meaning.

Lacan engaged in much polemic against those who held to the idea of a psychotic kernel, introduced by Melanie Klein, but this is because she makes it homologous with the phantasy of the maternal body, which supposes a relation to the Other. We must bring the thesis up to date with the real unconscious: it comes from *lalangue* outside meaning and is not necessarily linked to the phantasy.

With the Borromean knot, Lacan retranslated the "outside discourse" of psychosis, which implied being outside the social bond, in terms of not knotting. The RUCS—the core of the symptom—combines an element of language with *jouissance*, thus it is between Symbolic and Real, but it is not necessarily knotted with the Imaginary in a Borromean way to make a social bond.

From now on, the clinical field is divided between subjects whose symptoms are *all* in the real unconscious—let's say those of pure schizophrenia if it exists, outside the bond, outside meaning and where the Imaginary is unknotted—and those who are *not all* in it, since they have what Lacan called a *sinthome*, a knotting of this Real to the unconscious as phantasy, between the Imaginary and Symbolic.

But then there is the case of Joyce.

Joyce, a father of deo-logue

I said all or not all in the real unconscious, but Joyce is both all and not all in it, as I tried to show in the year when I dealt with the "The quarrel of diagnoses".

His symptomatology

He is all in it in so far as he gathers, at the start, the real scraps of the heard that are his epiphanies, and at the end, in as much as he enjoys the pulverised ciphers of *lalangue* in writing *Finnegan's Wake*.

This literary manipulation of the letter "not to be read" is produced without passing through the body, the phantasies of the body, which goes well with the absence of imaginary passions in Joyce in relation to the counterpart (Soler, 2001) that Lacan made such a big deal of. Nevertheless, he is finally not all in it to the extent that, through publication, which has a different function, he established himself ultimately as "The artist" he wanted to be. He thus restored a social bond with his audience that corrected the autistic symptom of his real unconscious by inserting it into this specific bond with the public, even making use of it there. We know, and I have emphasised this, that he sought this bond in a frenzied and precocious way. Certainly, for Joyce, this social bond is atypical, without a link to sex, but it is very effective, since it allows him to rename himself. *Sinthome*, says Lacan in order to designate what must be added to the three consistencies of the Imaginary, Symbolic, and Real so that they are knotted. Generally, this knotting most often relies on the nominating saying of the father, but for Joyce, it was a self-nominating saying that he succeeded in establishing.

It is a very singular saying that links the real unconscious to the imaginary of the relation to his counterparts, without passing by way of the body. Joyce, in contrast, let's say, with the man in the street, was more idolatrous of his text—the "Book of himself"—than of his own body, and if one is to believe Lacan, as I do, it is through this special Ego that he was maintained as The Artist, with the definite article and the capital. The knot that it produces, effective enough to rename him, does not pass by way of the father. This "non-dupe" of the father only wanted to know about masterly saying. Ignoring the "hystoriole"—both that of Christ and of Oedipus—and a stranger to every Oedipal solution, Joyce did not even take himself for the redeemer, for if he saves himself, he has done so alone. And yet he will have compensated for the paternal deficit, and will have done this without the father by using his letter symptoms for his self-institution.

That is why Lacan can affirm that Joyce has made "a tour of the reserve" of the unconscious. Indeed, he illustrates alternately and sometimes conjointly the symptom of the word in the real of *jouissance* outside meaning and outside any social bond—despite the link to his *jouissance* (Σ)—and the subject that I call Borromean whose RUCS is caught in the social bond, his artist's Ego having made up for the paternal deficit. That is why Lacan made of him a father of deo-logue (*dio-logy*).

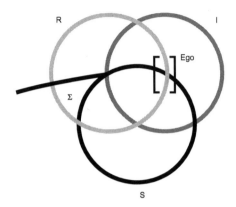

Joyce's *sinthome*. The failed knot corrected by the artist's ego

It is clear that this fundamental symptom, constituting a social bond, in contrast to what is usually the case, does not involve for him the difference between the sexes, or his link to the woman. In other words, it does not supplement the sexual non-relation, but only the outside-discourse of his relation to *lalangue*, produced by the paternal deficit from which he suffered. Joyce teaches us something here about the function of the father. I will come back to this. It no longer surprises me that since 1967, in "The mistake of the subject supposed to know", Lacan situated him among the Fathers of deo-logue, with Moses and Meister Eckhart—in other words, with those who knew how to mark the place of God-the-Father—and that in 1975 he called him "necessary son". But we are also left with the question of Joyce's relation to the Other sex.

His "odd relation"

We can thus ask what Nora the woman was for Joyce the man, in his singularity. Lacan could say of Joyce that he was "unsubscribed from the unconscious". But how can he also say that with his writing of *Finnegan's Wake* he goes directly to the best one can expect from an analysis? Certainly he is unsubscribed from the unconscious as truth organised by the phantasy but not from the real unconscious disconnected from the Imaginary where the letter and *jouissance* are joined without mediation. Except that for Joyce, this copulation of *lalangue* with *jouissance* does not involve the enjoying substance of the body: he enjoys *lalangue* as a thing.

Freud tried to define various types of object choice: narcissistic or anaclitic. As for Lacan, in his seminar *RSI*, he defined the typical partner of the man as pertaining to the father version of the symptom. But Nora is other as Joyce himself is other.

It is clear that Nora his wife, Giorgio his son, and Lucia his daughter, are not placed in the constitutive social bond of which I have just spoken. Nora was not even his muse, the common name for designating the fetish of the artist's desire. However, Joyce cared for them in an almost fanatical way. This is an opportunity for us to verify once more that there are several ways to cherish one or more beings, and in addition, that the question cannot be resolved at the level of observable social reality. A wife and children: what could be more conventional? But it tells us nothing about heterosexuality or about the paternal position of Joyce. How then can we situate the indubitable strength of his relation to Nora and his children? I am approaching things at the surface level, the most visible level.

Exiled, but not without luggage

I say all alone, but not without his luggage. In a first approximation, I think that Nora and his children almost had the status of "luggage". This is an image, obviously, and I have developed it elsewhere. We know very well that a partner to whom one is attached can be valued on very diverse grounds. Analytic theory has listed a number of them. For example, the partner can have the value of a cash register when it is the rich woman or the wealthy man; a pantry (we see couples like this), a domestic animal that is almost a transitional object and—why not?—a piece of furniture. Lacan evokes such a case in one of his seminars.

Luggage is another thing, a little variation. Luggage accompanies you on your travels, and God knows that Joyce, exiled and homeless, knew a lot about travelling, some more or less necessary, some more or less capricious. Luggage accompanies you, you put it down occasionally, sometimes it encumbers you, often it is too heavy, but you don't abandon it, and you know that if you do not want it stolen, you must guard it possessively.

In Richard Ellman's biography of Joyce there is an anecdote that struck me at the time I read it because it pointed to a certain subjective singularity in Nora. But that is not what interests me today. Richard Ellman notes that at the time of their first departure, on their arrival in London and then in Paris, the same thing happened: each time he deposited Nora and the luggage in a park and set off in search of acquaintances in order to find money and a place to stay. And Nora waits with the luggage for the time that it takes him to find them. We have testimony to this in one of her letters. The first time she thought he would not come back but, despite this she did not move: she continued to wait for the man who did not come back and who, as night fell, finally found her there waiting. Obviously, the subjective impact of this episode must be relativised in terms of its context. This was Ireland at the beginning of the century; according to the figures that I have been able to find, 17,500 Irish people left in the same year, but even so. Then, when it is she who wishes to leave him, it is he who goes to find her and bring her back. Finally, through an obscure agreement, I would say from unconscious to unconscious, she never became a lost object. This place of the absolute condition cannot but evoke for the psychoanalyst the transitional object; the "it does not matter what" that in itself has no value, but that is required unconditionally.

I say "luggage" in order to characterise a bond that I would qualify as the bond of "adjoiningness", a sort of extension of the subject himself.

There is no doubt however, that for Joyce, Nora was a chosen woman, unique in spite of two or three transitory flings. Lacan says: "She was the only one for him". Indeed, and this is rather rare. So for him she was acquired, absolutely—everything points to that—but as what?

Since Freud, we know about the narcissistic relation to the partner; however, there is nothing like that with Nora. Those close to Joyce were very surprised by this disparate choice of a woman who was clearly uncultivated—it was exactly as those close to Jean-Jacques Rousseau responded to his choice of Thérèse. She was not acquired on the grounds of intellectual affinity. Nor was she a mother according to the Freudian schema. She never took care of her body, of her corporeal comfort, of their meals (completely broke, they still ate everyday at a restaurant), etc. This is neither a narcissistic nor an anaclitic choice. Can we assume then that erotic benefits were central here? It seems not. This is even the hypothesis emphasised by Lacan: "He wore her as a glove but only with repugnance". Repugnance is a strong word. There are certainly erotic letters from Joyce to Nora. But erotic letters precisely do not involve body to body; on the contrary, they involve the separation of bodies, and it is exactly this that clears the field for the letter. Scatological and masturbatory erotism is evident here, but Nora's place is not particularly readable. It seems, moreover, that according to what people have said, that after these passionate letters, when Joyce returned home everything changed. Nor was she acquired in order to make children for him—as in the "father version" of the man—for each time a child was born there was a great drama. We know that Giorgio was only registered one year after his birth, Joyce having been charged to do it. He was given the name, moreover, of a dead brother …

Contrary to the case of the father as symptom, "the children were not part of the plan". That is, not planned in the scripted programme of the symptom that was not tied in any way to Nora; nor was it foreseen in the specific bond that tied him to her. Perhaps it is not without an obscure relation to their future destiny: the schizophrenia of Lucia and the serious alcoholism of Giorgio. Everything indicates that their births were a problem and that Joyce could not bear the change produced in Nora by becoming a mother. The theme is classic, but there is a letter Joyce wrote to his aunt after the birth of Giorgio, the eldest son, where he complains of the change in their relations and the abandonment he suffers and where he says: "After all I am not a domestic animal, I am supposed to be an artist". He complains bitterly about the birth of his children but he did not abandon them. He tried to encourage and protect them, moving heaven and earth so that Giorgio could become a tenor, since there was a tradition of singing in his family. As for Lucia, he did all he could to protect her against the psychiatrists right up to the end.

"She doesn't serve any purpose"

To the question "What was this woman then for this man?" Lacan replies: "She doesn't serve any purpose. It is only through the greatest of depreciations that he made of Nora the chosen woman" (Lacan, 2005, p. 84).

The term "depreciation" deserves an explanation. It would appear to contradict all the evidence we have of the esteem in which Joyce held Nora, and also with the patent fact that he used her all his life. But according to Lacan, "depreciation", when it concerns a woman, does not designate a narcissistic minimising of the characteristic qualities of the person. The term refers to her function as a woman, at a time when Lacan produced the thesis of a woman as symptom for a man, that is, a body involved in the *jouissance* of another body, a point he elaborates with great precision in the second lecture on Joyce. And isn't it precisely the symptom that serves *jouissance* which everyone is the most interested in, even if this is to their cost, the cost of their ego? We could put it in a different way—Nora didn't serve as Joyce's phallic armour: it was provided not by her but by his writing.

What is implicit in Lacan's affirmation, his postulate, is that the appreciation of a woman consists in raising her to the rank of symptom: in other words, to make use of her for the purpose of *jouissance*. This thesis may appear out of line in a time where the narcissistic claim for recognition and equality is at its peak. Here is the question: men and women can be equal in many ways, even in all ways pertaining to social reality, but does equality mean anything at the erotic level? Today, some people would like to believe it does and campaign for it, as we know, but it is always at the price of the denial of the unconscious. Curiously, on this point Lacan, who was always so syntonic with his times, does not pander to the epoch at all, and maintains the incommensurability of the sexes in the matter of *jouissance*, not their equality.

Joyce, who was beyond all the prejudices of his time, knew how to value Nora, her simplicity, her good qualities, her honesty, her imaginativeness, her flexibility in life, but he did not make use of her as the symptom of *jouissance*, which would have been to appreciate her as a woman. His own symptom is his writing, and in order to enjoy the letter and make a name out of it he does not pass through the body of Nora. It was enough that Nora accompanied him, that's all.

The exile from the sexual relation takes a particular form in Joyce, one that Lacan diagnosed in the seminar of January 13th, 1976. Commenting on the text *Exiles* written, he says "during the reign of Nora", he asserts that "the way to approach Joyce's central symptom [...] is that there is no reason for him to take one woman, among others, for his woman". And in fact, right from the beginning Joyce said to Nora that she would never be his woman, in the sense that he would never marry her. In other words, he would never utter an implicit "you are my wife". And if he did not consider himself a man like other men, how could he consider this unique, chosen woman to be his, for that would be the standard solution of the Oedipal man: that is to say, the *père-version*.

She fits him like a glove ...

This is indeed why Lacan could add correlatively that she fits him like a glove. For him, the symptom, whatever its benefits of *jouissance*, never fits like a glove: it puts us at odds, always including the uncomfortable and irrepressible dimension of the unconscious. And furthermore, it is not a mystery to anyone that the valorisation of a woman as symptom is not at all propitious for the peace of the household.

With this expression, Lacan stressed the function of the Imaginary, while his definition of the symptom accentuates rather the knotting of the Real and the Symbolic. Lacan often referred to the glove that you need to turn inside out in order for the right hand glove to be the same as that of the left. It is a reference he borrows from Immanuel Kant. This reversal has the advantage of both annulling and revealing the asymmetry included in the specular relation itself, which is manifested through the inversion of right and left in the mirror. This has the consequence that, in spite of appearances, the reflected image is not identical to its model. The turning inside out of the glove annuls this difference (the right-hand glove then looks the same as the left) unless, Lacan notes, the glove has a button, something that Kant disregarded, for then the button which was on the exterior would be found on the interior of the glove that is turned inside out. There is thus a return to the difference between the subject and his specular object! We should not be surprised that Lacan makes a parallel between this button and the clitoris, and hence the phallic disparity.

On the 10th of February 1976, Lacan notes that all that "remains of the sexual relation is this geometry to which we have alluded with the glove. That is all that remains for the human species to support the relation". So this is not only for Joyce but for all of us. This development is important for it completes the thesis of the symptom as a function of the letter, $f(x)$. The *jouissance* of the letter of the unconscious, between the Symbolic and the Real, allows Lacan to assert: "We make love with our unconscious". The geometry of the glove reintroduces the consideration of the imaginary of bodies. But there tends to be a button.

As a result, we grasp the meaning of "she fits him like a glove" which, assuming that there is no button, means the annulment of the heterogeneity between the subject and the object—the image being the first object—a heterogeneity that the mirror itself preserved. The expression designates a relation in which not only the *hetero*—what we now call the "not all"—is absent, but in which imaginary disparity itself is overcome: no button on the glove. This is why I spoke of "adjoiningness". I will evoke a sort of object transitivism—not reciprocal perhaps, as we do not know what Joyce was for Nora—which obviously created for her some hefty obligations, once she consented to them. Not only was there the obligation to put up with his riotous life, the obligation to bear *him*, to bend to his caprices, to his decisions to move house, for example, but the additional obligation of looking to him exclusively, and to look at him with the eye with which he looked at himself, annulling the split between the eye and the gaze. It is this that we notice in the letter that I evoked where, at the birth of Giorgio, he complains about the eye that does not see him as an artist.

Exiled from the standard symptomatic relation to a woman, did Joyce make of Nora the god of his life? Not in the least. It is very clear that Nora was not for Joyce what God was for Schreber. If there is something obvious in their bond, it is that she does not have speech. Not that she is gagged but that she says nothing of importance. There is nothing in Joyce that looks like "my wife says that ..." Why? Here is my hypothesis: if there is no phallic objection that would classically block the sexual relation, there is what I will call the egotistic [*égotique*] objection, to equivocate between ego symptom [*ego-symptôme*] and the meaning of the word *égotique* [egotistic] in French. This is what prevented him from taking himself for the redeemer, as I said earlier, and that prevented him from instituting Nora in a position that I could call deified: Nora is not the god of Joyce.

Let's say what Joyce's particularity consists of: the non-relation, which is structural, is revealed to him, while it is generally veiled for each of us by the symptomatic relation, so veiled moreover that it requires the whole of psychoanalytic elaboration in order to produce the thesis, for it is not learned from books. You have to be the *Egotistic* Joyce in order for the reign of the adored one to unveil the non-relation instead of covering it, as is generally the case, at least for a time.

What then remains of the relation if this woman is neither the one of the symptom nor the god of his life? The answer, and I will conclude here, is a glove that annuls disparity. Indeed it makes an odd relation, barely sexual, reduced to the geometry of the imaginary envelope, a geometry that is normally knotted to the symptom of *jouissance*. An envelope in the form of a glove, Nora will have been the imaginary supplement to the a-corporeal ego of Joyce.

It is in this way that Joyce illustrates, inversely, the true function of the father as condition and "model" of the fundamental sexual symptom.

CHAPTER FIFTEEN

The father and the Real

Lacan introduced the Name-of-the-Father as a metaphoric function. Hence a question: for a clinic that includes the real outside meaning, what becomes of the function of the Father? It remains. The beyond of the Oedipus is not the beyond of its function. I have been able to show (Soler, 2003–2004) I believe, that it was necessary for Lacan to give the two seminars, "RSI" and "Joyce the symptom" in order to conclude, after tentative steps and hesitations, that the triadic knotting of the three consistencies represented by the three circles of string that make the knot, supposed a fourth element, represented by a fourth circle that he calls *sinthome*, inscribing the function that is the condition of knotting. The Father, not his signifier but his saying— more precisely, his nominating saying that makes the *sinthome*—is the existential condition of Borromean knotting. And it is from here that Lacan drew his conclusion about the "symptomatology" of Joyce and the particularity of his *sinthome* of suppletion.

If it is the condition of knotting, we can conclude that the Father as *sinthome* is necessary in order for the *dit-mension* of meaning to be limited by the Real, and for the Real not to be disconnected. It is an effect of this knotting to suppose that the Real does have a meaning, but a limited one. As a result, we can attribute to foreclosure, on the one hand the real signifier, the too real of the schizophrenic, and on the other, the untethered meaning that occurs when mentality goes as far as psychosis. The one who speaks "thinks feeble-mindedly", he has a mentality, dreams while wide awake, does not come out of his linguistic envelope and the representations over which it presides. The glue of meaning does not let him go, but in so far as meaning is without the ballast of the Real it is the "illness of mentality" as I have illustrated in the case of Pessoa.

However, this raises the question of what this new framework of the Borromean knot—with all the revisions that follow from it—changes or complements regarding the first ideas on the paternal function.

What precedes it implies that the avatars of the Father function are not without effects on the type of symptom for each subject—whether it is autistic or socialising—that is, what we call in classical terms, clinical structures. Moreover, Lacan finishes by situating the Father function as a function of the symptom.

Castration without the father

I will review the steps taken in this elaboration. I recalled Freud's discoveries on the partial drive and castration that led Lacan to the formula "there is no sexual relation", which entails that *jouissance* does not make a social bond. From then on, the sexuated bonds of the couple are symptoms that make up for the foreclosure of the relation by knotting the *jouissance* of the real unconscious to the bonds of the phantasy. However, the fundamental symptom of the couple is not for every subject, as I have just shown in relation to Joyce, and nor is it necessarily the heterosexual symptom, which poses the question of what makes it possible. It is at this point that Lacan invokes the father.

Castration and the specific anxiety attached to it are at the root of all the symptomatic constructions thinkable in the analytic sense. This thesis is Freudian, and we can date it precisely and explicitly to the 1926 text *Inhibitions, Symptoms and Anxiety* (Freud, 1926d). In a categorical fashion, and reversing all that he had said up until then, Freud now claims that the genealogy of the symptom—if I can use this term—goes from primary anxiety to the symptom. In other words, it goes from castration to the symptom.

The fact is that perverse *jouissance*, which is the lot of the *parlêtre*, makes do with very diverse symptom-partners. This mode of *jouissance*, as I said earlier, is that of the individual fallen under the blow of the effect of language, the effect of mortification: primary castration. This says nothing about what has been called in the history of psychoanalysis since Freud, object choice, or about sexual identity. I will not give an account of the detail of the Freudian constructions here but the fact is that they always invoke the castration complex in its link to the Oedipal father. Lacan takes a sideways step here that is fundamental. This begins with the seminar *L'angoisse* and, despite appearances, goes right up to the so-called formulas of sexuation.

It is striking to note that, beginning in the 1960s, Lacan constructs his theory of the object *a* and of castration without recourse to the father. This step is particularly clear in the seminar *L'angoisse*, where he elaborates a deduction of the object *a* from the Other, from the effect of language, and takes an approach which is almost naturalistic, with the phallus as the "default organ" which short-circuits all reference to the father in conceptualising castration as real. We find the same feature in "Position of the unconscious". The father is not evoked there, and to the myths of the forbidden fruit and the Oedipus, Lacan adds one of his own, that of the lamella which mythifies the part of life that is lost, without the father or even the Other, since here, the enigmas of life and of the link between sexed reproduction and individual death are evoked, even before there is any intervention of the Other. All Lacan's effort will have been to detach the cause from castration, which is not a myth of the father, from both *Totem and Taboo* and the Oedipus complex.

Lacan stressed his disagreement with Freud on this point, and throughout his seminar we can follow the recurrence of his virulent critiques of the Oedipal father, supposed instigator of castration anxiety. We will read successively that the prohibition, the threat and the murder are lures, a secondary comedy (Oedipus has no use in analysis), and worse, the worst that we can say of an analytic theory, that it is contrary to experience. However, each time, Lacan tries to recuperate what justified Freud in sustaining the unsustainable and attempts to put it in other words, to the point of making that year culminate in considerations about the father and the necessary passage towards The Names of the Father that he announces for the following year.

The first subtraction that cuts out object *a* is an effect of language which owes nothing to the father and everything to the entry of the natural subject into language and to the functioning of its unary traits. Limited *jouissance*, that we could already call the castration of the one who speaks, is not the effect of any prohibition. At the phallic level, castration itself is not the threat to the organ that Freud believed. It bears on the disjunction of desire and *jouissance* and on the properties of the organ of copulation that make of the phallus "the default organ", which can be put in a series with the objects *a*. We will read in *L'angoisse* the lengthy elaborations devoted to the sexual act and to the impossibility of desire acceding to the Other of *jouissance*. Castration, thus, is not a myth but a bone, said Lacan; that is, a real that owes nothing to the father as Bogeyman. The father is not the agent of castration.

In Lacan's work we can find many texts that would appear to contest this, in particular, his analyses of the father of little Hans who, he says in the seminar *Object Relations*, is insufficiently castrating, although the "Question prior" does not take this up; and also the formula in *L'angoisse*, "the desire of the father is the law", if one does not read it correctly by omitting the commentary that he made on it; and above all, "the saying that no of the father" [*le dire que non du père*] in "L'étourdit". Some believed they recognised the Freudian father of *Totem and Taboo* there, uncastrated, enjoying all the women. This is an error, I believe. It would be strange and above all illogical that, in order to translate the father of the Oedipus anew, Lacan would make an appeal to the primal father, a notion which he never stopped denouncing, one that he attributed to Freud's neurosis, and which he mocked again in "L'étourdit", joking about the "*père orant*", the "*pérorant outang*" imagined by Freud. Moreover, how would this reading fit with what Lacan said so clearly: that the "saying that no" of the father—taking care to distinguish it from the saying no—offers no hope of access to the sexual relation. In other words, it does not offer the possibility of an exit from the castration of *jouissance*. Can we ignore the fact that all the texts that follow on the father, notably *RSI* and "Joyce the symptom", situate the father, a father, as a solution symptom to castration?

Hence the question that Lacan never stopped working on: what use is the father? The question is all the more justified in that he ended up asserting that as far as the father is concerned, we can go beyond him on the condition that "we make use of him".

As for the father solution, the thesis is constructed in two stages: at the end of *L'angoisse, a* father is thought of as a model of a "completed" desire, and in 1975, as the "model" of the symptom.

From the object cause to the father

Neither the construction of the object *a* as cause of desire, nor the inscription of subjects in phallic *jouissance*, resolves the question of object choice, of the mystery of "elective affinities", and of the strange and rare conjunction of the object of desire and the object of *jouissance*.

It is a fact that the partner of sexed love is not just anyone, he is chosen: it is the ABC of love life. And everyone asks him or herself about the one he or she finds: is it this one or that one? We know the response of Montaigne: "Because it was him, because it was me". Lacan at first objected to this through a reference to a masked ball, well known within the genre of light comedy, and he liked to repeat that at the end of the masked ball, it was neither him nor her. This is of course because it is the object *a* that causes desire, the object that is no partner in particular, only the counterpart of the subject in the phantasy.

The object *a* lies to the partner. Hence the comments at the end of the seminar *Le transfert* (Lacan, 2001e), asserting that there is no object that is worth more than any other. This is true if all objects take on their value from the anonymity of the object *a*, to which they are ultimately reduced. As a result, the "I do not love him" that Freud reserved for psychosis is for everyone, neurosis and perversion included (Lacan, 1990b, p. 10). The comedy of love makes me believe that my life is entirely with one unique, irreplaceable object only, the man or woman of my life, as we say. And the humourist that Lacan cites in *L'angoisse* says, in reference to the film *Hiroshima mon amour*, that Resnais shows that "no matter how irreplaceable the German, he can immediately find a perfectly worthy substitute in the first Japanese person he meets at the corner of the street" (Lacan, 2004, p. 387). Lacan does not leave it there though, and we understand why.

Certainly, it is the object *a*, as the object that has fallen, that has been subtracted through the primary operation of language, the object "that one no longer has," which is the principle of all eruptions of appetite, all extensions of libido. But this original "separtition" (*sépartition*) makes of it an "unsubjectifiable" secret as Lacan says in *L'angoisse* from which a subject remains divided enough never to know whence he desires if it were not for the index of anxiety which alone signals the *a*-phenomenal object in experience. The object *a*, which has no more a name than an image, is certainly a cause of desire, but a cause that is indeterminate and anonymous. There is a gap between the cause and the chosen object that would fix desire and give it its finite forms, liveable within a social bond. We can represent this structure of the gap of indeterminate desire without a specific end:

$$a \rightarrow d \rightarrow (\dots ? \dots).$$

In other words, the cause creates desire, a vector, but leaves the target blank. It does not say what the desirable is. Certainly there are types of desire linked to corporeal cuts, and one can speak of desire as oral, anal, scopic, or invocatory in order to specify the surplus *jouissance* aimed for, but that says nothing about a chosen partner from which the surplus *jouissance* can be taken, and which, through the relation to the object cause, always appears as a "lure". Lacan enumerated some of the forms of indeterminate desire which dominate the desire for something else: boredom, prayer, watching, waiting. There are others, depression some-times when it is like an anorexia of all objects, and why not vagrancy which re-establishes indetermination in the place of the chosen object.

This structure of the gap of the cause allows us to grasp that the fixa-tion of desire on specific objects, notably sexual ones, requires a com-plementary condition. Which one? We can easily see that discourses use the structure of the gap of the cause in order to commercialise desire, and to make desiring the objects that they offer "a command-ment". Today, these imperatives of discourse take the specific form of the market of capitalist consumption, using images and publicity slo-gans to direct aspirations towards industrialised surplus *jouissances*, but this operation is not new. There have always been suggestions, arising from discourse, that are offered in order to fill the empty brackets of our diagram and to designate the desirable. Obviously, there need to be a lot of images in order to captivate interest by imaginary induc-tion and a lot of words to suggest value. It is in this way that forms of desire are subject to historical variation—Freud would have said, "to civilisation"—even though the cause, an effect of structure, sticks to the subject a-historically.

It is thus necessary to distinguish the object *a* as pure cause of desire from the object *a* that has "passed into the space of the Other"—according

to the eloquent formula in *L'angoisse*—when its *quantum* of investment
is transferred to historicised objects, dressed up in the images and signifiers of discourse. The phantasy is nothing other than the product of
this transfusion of *a* into the field of the Other. It is, moreover, from
there that Lacan defines his conception of mourning as the time of sustained attachment to the details of the specular and historical indices of
the object, which only ends by its reduction to the object *a* as pure cause,
at the moment when the first Japanese person comes ...

It is the same passage to the Other which makes transference possible, if we agree that the subject supposed to know, where the object
is "latent", is another name for what Lacan called in 1963 the space of
the Other. I could call this object that has become the target of desire
the symptom object, in implicit reference to the subsequent texts, and
write it: a^Σ.

$$a \rightarrow d \rightarrow (a^\Sigma).$$

This is the level at which we meet the model of the father: he presents
the example of a solution to the indetermination of desire, which, at
the same time, makes it the condition of going beyond anxiety, for let's
not forget that Lacan's aim was to go beyond the Freudian endpoint of
castration anxiety. It is this that the last lesson of the seminar asserts.
He says it in a precise way: "the desire of the father, desire hooked
to a determined object" is a finite desire which "has reintegrated its
cause", and which moves forward in what he calls the "realisation"
of his desire. In other words, it is what moves towards a sexual object
invoked as a response to castration. What is exceptional about this is
that in spite of the (-φ) there is an *a* that is guaranteed for him, that is
fixed. Thus a father is not a problematic figure but a solution, a symptomatic solution.

Lacan still saw a problem here: if it is like this, why does the function of the father remain so indissolubly linked to the prohibition of
incest? I will pause at the formulas of *L'angoisse*. "The desire of the
father and the Law are one and the same thing". This sentence does
not mean—he is specific—that we must submit to the desire of the
father, but rather, that he shows the path of desire: desire, he says, is
the Law: "Desire, as desire for the mother is identical to the function
of the law. [...] In short, we desire the commandment. The Oedipus
myth means that the desire of the father made the law" (Lacan, 2004,

p. 126). What is there to say if not that it prescribes the feminine object in subtracting the first object? Thus, it seems to do for the sexual relation what language does, without prohibition, for the drive: to ensure a subtraction of *jouissance* that generates appetite.[1] Nevertheless, this father as subtractor is only ever the rationalisation of the impossible. It is not the Father who prevents us from enjoying the Other, it is rather that the *jouissance* of the Other is impossible: castration of the relation, if I can put it like that. The father, through his object, or as Lacan will go on to say, through his symptom, indicates a path of suppletion.

The father as symptom

Some fifteen years later, *RSI*, including the Real, goes further. Lacan refers less to the desire of the father than to his symptom, namely a woman/mother who gives him his children. This is a symptom that makes the social bond in two ways: between the sexes and between the generations, as I have already developed—thus making up for the foreclosure of the sexual relation in language. It does not operate openly but rather has its effects only through a "true half-saying". Still at the stage of trial and error, Lacan could say in *L'angoisse* (Lacan, 2004, p. 389) that the father *knows* to what object his desire is bound. In fact, no subject *can know* from where he desires but he can half-say, that is, leave his truth to be heard by the interpretive ears of his descendants. This shows that a father is invoked here as a subject, falling as all subjects do under the sway of the not whole truth, and that he operates through his saying.

It is a major turning point, for saying is not a signifying function but a function of existence. If the function Name-of-the-Father is conveyed through a singular existence, and Lacan never went back on this thesis, there are "so very many" existences that the plural is justified in order to designate the supports of the function. With this plural, announced at the end of *L'angoisse*, contingency appears, as I have shown, although the function is very necessary in order for the subject to be able to exist "appended from finite desires" (Lacan, 2004, p. 389), without which it does not have an authentic realisation.

We see that a father presents a version of the fundamental symptom: if it is not nature that speaks—there is no doubt on that point—and if the object *a* does not determine the singularity of choice, castration does not decide on the chosen partner. All that's left is the sexual symptom to make up for the foreclosure of the sexual relation. It fills the gap of the "there is not" by a "there is", establishing a substitute, a suppletion. And one can then say that the subject, besides being subject to the great law of lack, is married to a constant of specific *jouissance* via the words of the RUCS. A father only transmits his function because he has *the* symptom of the father, a version of generalised perversion. This is the case for masculine libido, a case amongst others, for there are also the hetero non-fathers and those that Lacan called the bachelors, to designate those who are not linked to the Other sex. A father is specified firstly by a heterosexual desire that "makes a woman the cause of his desire" and then by a desire that links the woman partner to the mother partner to the child partner, thus a triple partner in some ways. His symptom is Borromean: it knots the RUCS to the truth of the phantasy. He can have other symptoms, but it is through this one that he transmits his function. Hence the question of its link with the conjugal family. I will come back to this point.

Note

1. Already in the text "Kant with Sade", written just prior to this, he posited an identity of the desire of the father and the law, concluding with a "verdict" on Sade: Sade remained stuck to prohibition, subject to the Law, "raped and sewn shut, the mother stays forbidden". This is the negative side of desire, but as for a real treatise on desire, in its positive aspect, Sade gives us nothing.

CHAPTER SIXTEEN

Towards the father of the name

If a father is only a Father, if he incarnates his function only by the half-saying of his symptom, the question is raised of knowing how this saying operates in order to ensure what Lacan calls the *sinthome* function of knotting the three dimensions together. Lacan ends up by asserting that this knotting takes place via the nominating saying, thus sliding from the Name-of-the-Father to the Father of the name.

Before this thesis crystallizes, Lacan had marked the link of the function of the father with nomination several times. Notably, this occurs at the end of the seminar *L'angoisse*, where the father is invoked in the link with his object as the principle of overcoming anxiety. These are brief but very precious indications after some remarks about the transference transposing the object into the field of the Other: "Anxiety is only surmounted when the Other is named. Of love, there is nothing more than the name, as each of us knows from experience. The moment when the name of the one to whom our love is addressed is uttered, we know very well that it is a threshold of the greatest importance" (Lacan, 2004, p. 390).

The name is that which founds "a desire which is not anonymous" according to the expression in *Notes à Jenny Aubry* [Notes on the child] (1990c, pp. 7–8). This refers to a chosen, particularised desire for an object distinguished from all others, in which one can recognise oneself, in contrast to the unknown object of anxiety. Love is a great inventor of names, at all levels, even in the relation to the child—from pet names to great names—and the names that we give to our beloved. Claudel, with his Ysé, knew that already.

The object, the true object, the one written *a*, does not have a name. It is the cause of anxiety precisely because it is anonymous and unknown. It is worthwhile here to juxtapose the endings of the seminars *Le transfert* (Lacan, 2001e) and *L'angoisse*. In the first, we read: "There is no object that is worth more than another", "here is the mourning around which is centred the desire of the analyst". That allowed some people to think that to become an analyst necessitated a transformation of the subject so that at the end of analysis he would enter into cynical indifference. But it actually referred to the extraction of object *a*, destituting the partner that it annuls, that it "a-nuls" ["*a-nise*"], Lacan goes so far as to say. And the whole movement of the seminar goes from love, from its brilliance, from its "miracle"—in brief, from its metaphor—towards another metaphor that is completely opposed to it, that of desire, that substitutes the object for the *agalma* of the idealised Other that falls. Lacan evoked "the perfect destructiveness of desire" caused by this object summoned to be the complement of life, which has no name and which we find also in anxiety.

The seminar *L'angoisse* starts with the object that marks the endpoint of *Le transfert*. It goes from the anxiety of a subject confronted with the enigmatic desire of the Other and the imminence of his reduction to the object that is not chosen, to the last lesson which turns to the father as the principle of overcoming anxiety, through his object, not only finite, but also named. In the terms of the times, we see the function given to nomination: it is a shield against anxiety in that it makes the anonymous *a* pass into narrative and history: in other words, it transfers the unknown cause of desire towards the nameable object.

Kno(t)mination

The Father of the name is a major conceptual leap. We could imagine that with this naming father, Lacan saves the father, and simply perpetuates both the old biblical refrain and the Freudian Oedipus. However, this would be very surprising at a time when we see the expressions of debasement of the father multiply: it's a name to get rid of, to do without, have no recourse to etc. In fact, it is the opposite of a salvaging: Lacan's definition maintains the function of the Name-of-the-Father but disconnects it, in effect, from the fathers of the traditional family, the fathers of the Oedipal triad. This is what I would like to show. It is a crucial thesis for us at a time where the failure of the father of the family manifests in an efflorescence of clinical phenomena.

Clearly, I am not ignoring what all assiduous readers of *RSI* have in their heads, and that I evoked above: the famous passage from the lesson of January 21st 1975 on what is a father worthy of this name— and when I say "famous", it means that it has already become a Lacanian slogan. This passage specifies under what conditions a particular father—a father as subject—can convey the father function, can be what I am going to call a father-Name-of-the-Father. However, that a father can do it does not imply that he is the only one who can.

To say that the father names is already to say that his function is not the function of metaphor. Nor is it a function of the letter connecting an element of the Symbolic to real *jouissance*. Strictly speaking, nomination is not a signifying function although it is the privilege of the *parlêtre*. It is the function of saying, and saying, as Lacan says, "is event". It is neither true nor false, it just is or is not. Exactly like the act, I would add. Event implies contingency. A "that which does not stop saying itself". Unlike signifiers that are in the Other, "to be taken up", the "naming" of the father is a fact of ex-sistence.

This leaves the question of the relation of the Father to semblants, these semblants that the English translate so precisely as "make believe". Concerning the signifier of the Father, we could say that it was itself a semblant, but what about "saying"? Its event ex-sists in relation to semblants and, because of this, it can put them in their place, allowing the subject to avail himself of discourse, to be its dupe, to consent to the semblant that grounds this discourse, which is always a discourse of "the semblant". However, as I have had the opportunity to demonstrate, the discourses themselves are always appended to a saying, incarnated for each one by a historical figure. Lacan named them: Lycurgus for the discourse of the master, Charlemagne for that of the university, Socrates for that of the hysteric and, of course, Freud for the analyst. Without the saying that puts the semblant in its place, we would not understand the assertions of the seminar *Encore*, those that posit that with each change of discourse a new love arises, and even an emergence of analytic discourse. A new saying makes a promise, a promise of another solution, and a new knowledge—which will lead to another barrier.

Another way of formulating this is in terms of the Borromean knot: the efficacy of the Father is to knot the three consistencies, to hook the unthinkable Real of the symptom to semblants, between the Imaginary and the Symbolic. The *sinthome* as saying presides over the consistency of the semblants, which does not go without the Real, without the symptoms of the RUCS.

But in what way, and how, does a nominating saying make a knot?

Nomination fans out (*s'éventaille*), if I can put it this way, from the attribution of the common noun to that of the Name that we call "proper" because it belongs to one and no other. The Bible attributes the naming of things to God. But God only gave things their common name. The proper Name has a greater claim and more import.

The function of the proper name responds to what is unthinkable in being, to what cannot be qualified. The unqualifiable is a problem with which each psychoanalysis confronts us every day, for although he is represented by his speech or his signifiers, the subject who speaks is none the less unqualifiable. Put in more familiar terms, in speech [*la parole*]—chatter [*"la parlotte"*], as Lacan says—only primary repression responds to the subject's question, to his *"Che vuoi?"*. To say this in another way: the "Symbolic makes a hole", an irreducible hole. This hole has a name outside psychoanalysis: it is God, the God of "I am that I am", an assertion about the unqualifiable. In psychoanalysis, the name of the hole is the thing itself.

What recourse is there against this hole? Outside analysis, it is identification that covers the hole in the subject, but without reducing it; and it is a psychoanalysis that allows an uncovering of this hole. The proper name is precisely what tries to make up for the impotence of identification. How it gets there is another question.

Names come from the hole of the unconscious. The hole, says Lacan, spits out the Names of the Father. Actually, it spits out some names and, indeed, each subject or rather each unconscious, produces some names, and when it is in an analysis, it does so via interpreted chatter. But what is named? Everything that does not pass into the signifier: the object, and most of all, the Real. This is clearly visible with the saying of a father-Name-of-the-Father. I have noted that his saying names his objects, his woman as symptom and his children, and in so doing, knots the *jouissance* which constitutes him to the Symbolic and to the

Imaginary: let's say, the Real to the semblants. It is in this way that the saying of the name is knotting. "By *naming*, chatter is knotted to something of the Real". The Real is holed by the signifier but knotted by the name. To the point, as I said earlier, that we should write with a calculated neologism: kno(t)mination. Nomination knots the chatter that represents the subject with the real of enjoying: let's say, with its symptom name. It is this that justifies Lacan's saying that the names that respond to the unqualifiable are the Names of the Father. They might not have anything to do with any actual father: what matters is that they have a function of Borromean knotting.

There is more: the knotting of chatter with the Real cannot be dissociated from the social bond. It is neither self-production nor self-attribution of the name. The name, whether it is a common name or, more radically, a proper name, must be ratified in order to exist. Of course we might wish for a name, some people are renowned/renamed [*se renomment*] through their works, good or bad, but no one assigns himself his own name. Joyce proves this: he "delusioned" [*il a déliré*] his name, if I can put it like that, before having it, but there would be no Joyce without Joyceans, without the magisterial saying of the Joyceans. A more general example: the patronymic name Mr Poubelle has become a common noun for an everyday object ["*une poubelle*" is a rubbish bin], but not without the public who recognised its usefulness. The hetero-attribution of the name is important even for the name as "symptom". See for example—I've mentioned them already—Jack the Ripper, M. the Accursed, Zorro the Avenger, and even the Rat Man. The name that indexes identity is sanctioned within the social bond.

QED: nomination knots the three consistencies, it makes the *sinthome* (to be distinguished from the symptom as a function of the letter), and that is why Lacan suggests adding the letter "*h*", the "*h*" of *homme* [man], between the *n* and the *o*" "*n'hommer*". Nomination makes the One of the man, thus correcting the always equivocal "from them/two" ["*d'eux*"] of the subject. Naming is Father. From now on I will write: Nomination-Name-of-the-Father. Fathers are now reduced to being only particular and contingent instances of a more general function.

This point was already implied in the pluralisation of the Names of the Father. We did not understand it, perhaps because it was not decipherable then. It led Lacan to say that the father has so many names that he does not have a proper Name. A father, who has the father version of the symptom, has a proper name, but not the function. Lacan gave some examples of these multiple names of the function, as I have mentioned.

Without the family

The first consequence is considerable: the function Name-of-the-Father is not necessarily dependent on the family. In 1969, Lacan spoke of the conjugal family as the final remainder of the fragmenting of social bonds. We know today that it's not the final remainder: he saw himself that the final remainder was the individual. Today, it is from the outside, from current mores and from the family, that psychoanalysts receive a merciless questioning in the media that they could have taken up forty years earlier, since it was already there in Lacan's work. *Rethinking Kinship and Marriage* is not new. In 1977, it was already the title of a book by Rodney Needham (1971), which Lacan quotes in his lesson of April 18th of that year. After all this time, it is urgent, I think, to extract the responses that Lacan gave to questions that aimed at analysts and to evaluate their possible use for our clinic.

The hard core of these responses is the questioning of the Freudian Oedipus, a "show that cannot run indefinitely" (Lacan, [1960b] 2006, p. 688) and, over the decades, a constant redefining of the paternal function that led to the function of nomination. Now the family is not the condition of nomination. It refers to an existential saying that has nothing to do with the establishment of any conformist conjugal household.

It is through the name that he gives to his symptom-objects—woman, mother, and children—that a father makes the kno(t)mination [*nou(e) mination*], and even an 'us' "*nous*" [us]. This has nothing to do with the family, for we know from experience that even in its most conformist configurations it is far from warding off foreclosure.

There is a topical question here. We no longer live in a time when it is possible to raise the cry: "Families, I hate you". Today, there is only one great inverse cry: "Families, we miss you". Is it that the function of the existential saying of the Father does not imply his presence in the family, nor even the stability of the couple, nor heterosexuality as such? The same question was raised when Lacan spoke of a father of desire.

Indeed, when we speak of the desire of the father—or of the saying of the father—it is not only a matter of a signifier as Lacan had at first claimed, but apparently of a libidinal presence. In his "On a question prior to any possible treatment of psychosis", Lacan specified that the signifier Name-of-the-Father could very well be compatible with the absence of the actual father (Lacan, [1957–1958] 2006, p. 557), which not only disconnected the paternal function from the progenitor, but also from the avatars of the conjugal family, to the point where we can identify this signifier with an abstraction.

What about the Father of the saying? Can he only be conveyed by discourse, without requiring his presence, or is the "father one meets at breakfast" necessary, as Winnicott said? The English *breakfast* is quite different from the French breakfast: *"petit dejeune"*. It is a metonymy, this father at breakfast, which goes back to what preceded breakfast, the father in the marital bed from which the child is excluded. With this metonymy, we run the same risk as with Lacan's first metaphor. This did not imply the father at breakfast, as I just said, but it does seem to suggest, in a hasty reading, a mother accountable for the presence of the signifier. And the risk, largely already realised, is to interpret it in a conformist family-oriented way, and consequently, with the success of Lacan's thesis, to move directly, particularly in services dealing with children, to appeals to the father that destitute him more than they sustain him, since they signify, whether we want this or not, that he is not doing his job. This is also to confuse the desire of the father and the educational advice of the father: let's say, the *magister* father, which Lacan always fought against.

We are on an ideological frontier here that Lacan evoked at the end of "Proposition of 9 October 1967 on the psychoanalyst of the school", especially in its first version. There he denounces "the Oedipal ideology" as "the attachment specified for analysis to the coordinates of the family, [...] bound to a mode of questioning of sexuality that carries the high risk of missing a sexual conversion that is taking place beneath our very eyes" (Lacan, 2001c, *Annexes*, p. 587). He had thus perceived how analysts were out of touch with their times, and if there is conversion, it can only be tied to the "ascent to the social zenith" of the a-sexed object *a*.

However, the same question returns in the texts of January 1975, from *RSI*. Lacan again approaches the question of the relation between the logical function of the exception and the individuals who incarnate this exception. It is not the mother who is in the hot seat here, but the father. According to Lacan, the paternal exception should be able to be found in anyone, but this anyone cannot be just anyone for he must fulfil two conditions. The first is that he has desire for a woman, the father's wife; the second, which Lacan now adds, and it is crucial, is that he takes care, *paternal* care of the children that she has given him.

We are far from the metaphor which would substitute the desired woman for the primordial mother. Here it is the opposite: the perspective given by the desire of the Father, that is, the desire of a man who is not just anyone, the desire of a heterosexual man not just anyone, who makes his woman become a mother, the mother of his children. In other words, hetero desire is not enough.

But what is paternal care? It is certainly not maternal care. With these notions of maternal and paternal care, we advance into an ideologically thorny terrain. Indeed, today, the ideals of equality between the sexes lead to the increasing separation of social and familial roles—along with the respective responsibilities—from their sexed anchoring. And we see women claim the right for aid with care of the body, with survival and with the family economy in which they were so long confined. I see only one way of understanding this specific paternal care at the moment Lacan evoked it: it is the care of nomination, the care, that distinguishing its objects—here the children as products of the couple—takes them out of the generic anonymity of being simply what bodies reproduce. For the child it promises, it makes possible, what Lacan called at one time the humanisation of desire. Indeed, what purpose does nomination serve, for it does serve a purpose? It guards against the proletarian status of the corporeal individual, who has nothing to make a social bond. It is the association of signifiers which allows the creation of bonds, and it is this that gives us the naming father, or the naming that is Father: the signifiers of the original bond which produced the child. The whole clinic shows how crucial this is.

The only presence required of the father—the only one which protects against psychosis, for the question is not whether the amenities of daily life depend on whether the father is there or not—the only required presence is that of the saying which names. In evoking a specific paternal care, Lacan does not situate himself on the wave of equality, that's for sure, nor does he, I believe, situate himself on the wave of patriarchal chauvinism either which, indeed, has not lasted around here.

The question remains: does not the Father as saying require that the father of the family is there at breakfast? Certainly not. The founding event of saying implies contingency, and can therefore be disconnected from the circumstances of generation, of the care of the body and of the arrangements of everyday life.

I have already emphasised that when Lacan introduces this function of nomination, the Father of the name, it is to be read in two ways: the Father, a father-Father names, but also that which names is Father, or *sinthome*. Without this contingency, we cannot grasp the complexity of our current times.

This means that it is not the family that makes the father-Name-of-the-Father. It is, on the contrary, the saying that names, when it is there, that holds bodies together, without necessarily going through the Registry Office, the ring on the finger, and the cohabitation of various objects that the family was supposed to gather under the same roof. The nomination-Name-of-the-Father can do without fathers and can make do with the names of any other *sinthomes*. The extreme proof is in Joyce.

Thus psychoanalysts should themselves be able to do without their attachment to the coordinates of the traditional family that Lacan stigmatised since 1967. That would allow them to face up to the current situation rather than deploring it.

The question of its link to sex remains. Can the nomination-Name-of-the-Father, always with the hyphens, also be disconnected from sex? Saying that a father makes a woman the cause of his desire, doesn't it signify a necessary adhesion of the function to a hetero man? However, on closer inspection—I mean, taking into account the set of texts—I note that in the writings of Lacan, the names of Name-of-the-Father are not sexed. This is quite another moment, one that catches in an impressive way the evolutions of the time. Evoking sexual subversion in 1967 was visionary: now, we see it every day. The subversion in question is linked to what we now know, thanks to capitalism and without doubt also to psychoanalysis, that our *jouissance* is only situated in surplus *jouissance*: in other words, it does not make a relation. But this regime of *jouissance* changes the place of heterosexuality in discourse, and correlatively relativises the figure of the hetero father.

That the father is not the biological parent, although the biological parent can also be a father, is Lacan's original thesis and one that contemporary science realises. The nomination-Name-of-the-Father generalises this disjunction by adding to it the disjunction with the copulation of bodies. The consequences of *naming*, says Lacan, reach as far as enjoyment, but if all the names of the Name-of-the-Father refer to *jouissance*, not all refer to sex, as we see very clearly in the example of the "the masked man" of "Spring Awakening" whose sex is unclear and whom Lacan makes one of the Names of the Father, and even more so with "The Artist", the asexual *sinthome* that gives Joyce his name, the one without a body.

Indeed, today we can see that the configurations of what is transmitted in the form of "you are my symptom", or "you are my son, or my daughter", you are the name of one of my *jouissances*, are much more varied in social reality than they used to be. The thesis of the nomination-Name-of-the-Father as disconnected from the family and from sex—that it can, however, include—allows us to reflect on these evolutions, at the very moment when science is putting into question the transmission of life by means of sex at the level of the reproduction of bodies.

I conclude with a very concrete and current consequence: the contingency of *naming* in the social bond, a contingency, I insist, which opens onto the encounter—*a priori* objection to prediction—and with it, all the projects of prevention with regard to children. I am obviously distinguishing the protection of children that is a response to actual facts from prevention which claims to anticipate effects and which, postulating a false causality, seeks to guard against supposed damage, with results that are generally closer to discrimination than to real care.

That the nominating saying is, as I have qualified it, epiphanic, an event, belies the prediction so dear to the politics of health and education. The theme is current since, if we believe a recent report from INSERM, children with problematic futures can be detected from the age of 36 months! The whole question for analysts would be to finally drop the reference to the Oedipal and familial norm in order to look for and recognise the clinical variety of nominating sayings, where they present themselves.

CHAPTER SEVENTEEN

Love and the Real

The question of knowing if psychoanalysis can promise a new love, beyond the symptoms of love life that are addressed to it, has been there from the start. Today, given the preceding elaborations, it is more precisely a matter of knowing what new light is brought to this question by taking the real unconscious into account.

From the beginning, Freud postulated that the bonds of the passions of love, incomprehensible as they are, escape neither rationality nor logic. He succeeded in showing the workings of repetition. One love repeats another. In other words, the object carries the traits, the marks of the primary object. As Freud said, the first is thus always the second. In Lacan's terms, the object bears the marks of the first Other encountered in the first demand for love, what Freud called the Oedipal objects. We are at the level of family stories here. Now, according to Freud, these are always stories of despair. There is no happy childhood, despite people's amnesia. One should read *Beyond the Pleasure Principle* on this theme, where there is an astonishing page, penned with an unusual animation, on the unhappiness of childhood (Freud, 1920g, p. 20).

At the erotic level, however, the object inherits something else, not the marks of the Other, but the traits where the first encounters with *jouissance* were inscribed, something seen, heard or felt: always

163

traumatic, says Freud. Here we are at the level of a story of the body, more precisely, of what Lacan called the "events of the body". For Freud, both despair and trauma are condensed in the term "castration" and are the two sources of repetition. From this we can understand that love, even when called reparation, fails to avoid the repetitions that ruin love life.

In addition, for Freud, the transference is also repetition and will thus reiterate the worst of the past without the possibility of pleasure. This risks making it basically a reiterated experience of castration: lack of love, of knowledge, and of sexual satisfaction. And hence an impasse.

Love on trial

Lacan followed the same axis that bound love to castration, in itself the effect of language, as I have already pointed out. The famous formula, "Love is to give what you haven't got", is situated at this level. And the seminar *Le transfert* often evoked the effect of being that is obtained when the beloved loves in his turn, an illusory effect, however, when it comes to desire.

It is not excessive to say that there is in the teaching of Lacan something like a trial of love where the prosecutor concludes: first of all, on the baseness of love (Lacan, [1964b] 2006, p. 723). "To love is to want to be loved" (Lacan, [1964b] 2006, p. 723) and it is true that the question of a possibly disinterested love has travelled the centuries before psychoanalysis. In Christian theology, it gave rise—notably in one of its last articulations with Madame Guyon—to the debate on pure love that would not call for any reward, not even that of salvation. He then concludes on the cowardice of love that does not want to know the irreducible real of castration that founds desire and marks *jouissance*. But there is also love's deception, for love lies about the true partner; Lacan indeed generalises the "I do not love him" that Freud applied to psychosis to all the clinical structures. At the end of the ball, it was not her, and it was not him, as I reminded you. There is more besides: the speech of love itself is rival to the beloved, for to speak of love is itself a *jouissance* that demands nothing from anyone. On this point, Lacan is justified in evoking Saint Thomas, who, after a life of discourse consecrated to the love of God and for God, concludes at the end with a "*sicut palea*", which connotes both the lie and the *jouissance* of the drive. Finally, Lacan refers to the comic illusion that an object is one's life. All these developments affirm the antinomy between the stage where love produces its colourful effects and the real where it runs aground.

It is not simply a matter of a making a survey here: we are dealing with ethical judgements. There are many such judgements in Freud's writing and the notion of defence itself involves them. When Lacan says that the neurotic is a coward, that his sadness is a fault, not against God as in Christianity, but against the analytic imperative, it is a judgment relative to the ethics of psychoanalysis. For there are several types of courage—that of the master is not that of the analyst—and the neurotic can also be a hero in other situations, for example in wartime, while he recoils in front of the real of the unconscious. There are judgements that recognise in love and in the taste that we have for it, a figure of defence against the Real, friend of the passion for ignorance that wants to know nothing about it. Obviously it is not a question of any real here, but of that which is at stake in analysis.

Is this the last word, however? Transference love already required a reservation. For Freud, this unexpected love was a surprising discovery, unforeseen in his procedure, and its demands embarrassed him. But he perceived quickly enough that it was the condition of analysis.

As long as the partner operates in the analyst, that love which, contrary to any other, arises almost automatically in the Freudian procedure is already according to Lacan a "new" love, although no less illusory. Love is blind, says the proverb, but perhaps not that of the transference. Contrary to any other, because "it is addressed to knowledge" (Lacan, 1975c, p. 16), to unconscious knowledge. It therefore seems to be excepted from the three passions of being, already distinguished in Buddhism—love, hate, and ignorance—from the moment that it awaits not so much an effect of being as an interpretation. It is a love that would have an epistemic import except that, as we know from Freud, it also resists analytic revelation. Lacan did not disagree. As necessary as the transference is with its love of knowledge, its postulation of a subject supposed to know, indeed to a supposed knowledge which would give meaning to the symptom, the transference is in fact a denial of the real unconscious. There is a divergence of the supposition from the transference to the unconscious, as already indicated in "The mistake of the supposed subject of knowledge" (Lacan, 2001d, p. 329).

A love that knows

Lacan took one further step when he brought to light the real unconscious. The generalised foreclosure of the sexual relation, which creates the "curse on sex" specific to humans, is connected with the thesis of the symptom as partner, whether this takes the form of a *jouissance* partner civilised by *lalangue* or of the human partner who sometimes houses it and who is chosen by the signifiers and the representations of the phantasy. *Jouissance* "is not the sign of love" (Lacan, 1998, p. 4) but it can happen that they are knotted together. To make love is poetry, said Lacan, for the sexual act is nothing other than "the polymorphous perversion of the male". Thus, no sexual relation, but a possible relation of love that, this time, recognises the other.

At the end of seminar *Encore*, Lacan introduces this as an affect, an *effect* of the real unconscious. I have already indicated that beginning with the RUCS, Lacan had given a new function to affects, or rather to the enigmatic character of affects. He did the same with love, recognising it as a sign there: the sign of a perception of the unconscious and its effects. Love is an obscure recognition, in "always enigmatic signs" (Lacan, 1998, p. 144) of the way in which the other is affected by the destiny that the unconscious has made for him. The mystery of love is not reduced, but linked to its unconscious foundation. It is a step beyond the Freudian attempts that looked instead for the determining factors, something like the laws of production, which would remove its mystery. The term "recognition" suggests that this love has the new function of revealing the presence and the effects of the unconscious.

The text seems to hesitate on the nature of this recognition. It considers the idea that this is a recognition of the "courage" of a being in bearing its fate as *parlêtre*, its relation to the real of the non-relation and the symptom that makes up for it. Love would then be like an ethical detector of a subject affected by solitude and by a *jouissance* which he cannot master. But perhaps this is too much to claim and perhaps it is necessary—and more probable—to say that it involves a recognition between two unconscious knowledges, two *lalangues*, which do not necessarily engage the ethics of the subject who is affected. In both cases, the enigma of love, as has always been recognised, appears like the revelatory sign of the perception of a knowledge which is there, unknown, but obscurely apprehended: an index not of intersubjectivity, but of an inter-recognition between two *parlêtres*, made of two *lalangues*.

It follows that to make of love—this very mischievous god—a revelation, is to imply that the signifier is no longer the only indicator of knowledge. This is a considerable change of perspective, and we see the difference with the famous formula "you are my wife". This full speech was an act instituting the other, the partner. Love that is obscure recognition is not primarily an act, it is a sensitivity which registers something like an affinity—this does not mean an identity—between two unknown and thus incommensurable unconsciouses.

Obviously there is a snag here, at least on the epistemic level: what is recognised cannot be transmitted, and only recognition itself is shown or staged in some way.

This thesis of love as recognition of the unconscious has some major consequences, which do not seem to me to have been entirely noticed. Yet it allows us to throw a new light on a variety of well-known phenomena.

For example, the fact that love is so talkative. That it speaks and even sings is well known. The unspeakable object is made word, and it is very difficult to believe in a silent love. History shows that even if the god of love is silent, he has his interpreters and they are always very prolix. We denounce this blah-blah as deceptive, the lie of seduction, sweet talk, and indeed, as self-reflexive due to its enjoyment, as love letters are. This is not false, but one can also observe that if love loosens one's tongue, it is perhaps because it is precisely based on the meeting between two *lalangues*. And if *lalangue* is an obscenity where *jouissance* has been deposited, we must say then that the epithalamium, the duet between lovers, is a specific relation between two obscenities, between two enjoyed *lalangues* which, while not necessarily having anything to do with the sexual act, guarantees the verbal copulation of two *parlêtres*. Thus we understand why the private dialogue of lovers reverts so irresistibly to baby talk, as if talking nonsense is aimed at a return to the lallation of the start of life.

Likewise, we could rethink object choice here. The choice marked by repetition that Freud perceived is in fact sustained from two sides: on one side, the programme of *jouissance*, and on the other that of narcissism. On the narcissistic side is the ego ideal, which, according to Lacan, is in fact an ideal of the Other, I(A). It is at stake in what Freud saw as the idealisation of the object. For him, our particular loves are bound to the values of a particular time, to what is esteemed at each moment of civilisation according to its semblants. Thus, love as repetitive works in the direction of conformity.

We cannot ignore love's surprises, however, those choices that are discordant with the subject's world, which surprisingly bring together individuals who are perfectly mismatched relative to the semblants that govern them. It is difficult to explain this discordance with the phantasy as one's only reference, that is to say, with the object *a*. The involvement of the object—it too—determines typical choices, not from the point of view of semblants but from that of the drive: oral partner, scopic partner, etc., and, far from implying the exclusivity of the partner as object, it suggests instead the secret equivalence of all one's chosen objects.

The meeting of the two obscenities allows us, on the contrary, to better understand these discordant choices, for *lalangue* obeys neither the ideal nor the phantasy. It is the last mainspring of singularity—alas, of a singularity resistant to being grasped conceptually.

We can add some developments here on the question of speech under transference. What part is taken by the enjoyment of *lalangue* when the analysand speaks without saying anything? What Freud situated as a moment of the closing of the unconscious—and Lacan as empty speech—was at first formalised in the structure of language beginning with the object coming into the position of the shutter. But we can rethink this starting with this other unconscious that is the unconscious as *lalangue*, which is given a much freer rein once the constraints of everyday speech are suspended in free association. Empty speech, chewing over wearisome repetitions, turns out to be not so empty, as it is saturated with the enjoyed signs of *lalangue*, and it imposes on the analyst the specific task not of revealing meaning but of approaching the specific value that the subject gives to words, this opaque *jouissance* raising the question of knowing if the handling of these moments is not more important in an analysis than those in which the pearls of a subject's truth are gathered.

The analytic promise

Finally, a crucial question: is the analytic promise modified? Everything that has been elaborated up until now explains the obstacles, the curse on sex. Dante obtained from Beatrice only the fluttering of an eyelash, a look, the object of his phantasy. The Other remains the partner for between man and woman there is a wall. In other words, the partner of the couple is never other than the place holder of the true partner, of the object *a*, aimed at by desire, and of the *jouissance* of the unconscious, when it is the symptom of another body. However, neither the object *a* nor the *jouissance* of the unconscious dissipates the mystery of elective choice.

They tell us what value a Beatrice might have, but they do not tell us why it is Beatrice and not someone else. Why not a Juliet? From now on, one could ascribe the elective and even exclusive encounters of love—which certainly exist—to contingency, good fortune (*l'heur bon*) and say, as Lacan does in *Television*, "the subject is happy (*heureux*)". Happy because he can only repeat himself in his relation to the partner, but more essentially because he is subjected to fortune in terms of the encounter. I translate thus: like the rose, the elective object of love is without reason. The contingency of the encounter is the mystery of love reintroduced into Freudianism. Would this be a way of giving in? It is rather an indispensible way of situating the analytic promise, by placing the mystery of love within the logic of the treatment.

The analytic promise, if it does not lie, depends on what of the speech of the analysand can be inscribed. Now the elaboration of the unconscious only inscribes the One, not the two of love: One of *jouissance*, letter or sign, and One saying of the speaker that only relates to solitude. We know the historical avatars of the analytic promise, especially at the time when a certain current did not hesitate to promise, even to demand from an end of analysis, what is called genital love, precisely the love that would constitute an encounter. Lacan fought against this fallacious offer, yet strangely it has known some pseudo-Lacanian variants, with the quasi-imperative "desire the woman you love", and vice-versa. It is not that this doesn't happen, but that the *tuché* cannot be programmed. Analysis can certainly promise change, even substantial change, starting from what is inscribed of the speech of the analysand, but the happy encounter is contingent and cannot be promised; only the conditions of its possibility can be created.

To say that love is a recognition from unconscious to unconscious does not change anything. We can no longer really say about it that it is a rose, without a why. The unconscious affects have a why: Lacan takes a further step here, but one that cannot be absorbed into knowledge and does not reduce the contingency of the encounter.

Is this at least the promise to remedy "the no dialogue" which Lacan emphasised? This "no dialogue" is not a novelty, everyone is aware of it, but psychoanalysis explains it. The non-relation of *jouissance* has repercussions at the level of exchange, producing a non-relation of speech. Metonymised perverse *jouissance* drifts in the chain of speech, especially in the speech of seduction, and even, scandalously, in the words of love. The anti-cognitivist postulate of Lacanian psychoanalysis, which recognises in language the unique apparatus of access to reality and to *jouissance*, implies that "to each his truth" is founded on "to each his *jouissance*". There is no dialogue, a drawback even within each sex, and ultimately, to speak of love is in itself a *jouissance*. The partner of speech is perverse *jouissance*. The word makes a sign, certainly, but not to anyone. *Jouissance* of the blah blah, says Lacan. It has no more access to the Other partner than does orgasm itself. Today, moreover, the non-relation of speech is out in the open, denied sometimes, but there all the same, and it feeds the two main themes of contemporary complaint: the precariousness of couples and loneliness.

Women demand that they be spoken to. This is a hopeless request that the unconscious as *lalangue* intensifies with words outside its meaning, unsuited to exchange. It is true that the lovers' epithalamium that I evoked might seem to contradict this: with its verbal duets, it would seem to be an exception, but do two voices in unison playing opposite each other really make a dialogue? This is not so sure. The great duets of opera must give us a hint at least.

"Love more worthy"

We cannot imagine, however, that analysis has no effect on love and experience, indeed, proves that this is not the case.

In his "Italian note" of 1975, Lacan referred to a "more worthy" love (Lacan, 2001b, p. 307) to qualify this change: that is, more worthy than the proliferation of chatter that it generally consists of. Thus a love which has perceived its real kernel, outside meaning, that has thus become the symptom in which we no longer believe. We believe in the symptom, Lacan said, and that signifies that we believe it can say something. This is the very definition of the symptom of transference: we expect that it can say something, since we suppose unconscious knowledge to it. When the symptom is a woman, the distinction between believing her and believing in her is imposed as soon as she speaks. To believe in her, is to believe that she can say something about you. I have had the opportunity to emphasise how certain subjects receive their message in an inverted form, in the style of "my wife says that". Believing her is another thing: that makes her equivalent to the voice of "mental autom-atism", speaking of you in the Real. Certain subjects sustain themselves for a whole lifetime provided that she consents to take this role.

Love more worthy is a love that neither believes in the partner, nor believes her—and so it is not mad. Having recognised the real uncon-scious and the contingency of the encounter that goes with it, love does not question it on its meaning, for it has grasped at least a little bit the *jouissance* outside meaning which is localised there. I have called this atheistic and not transferential love, no less solid than other forms of love, but certainly less verbose.

Psychoanalysis, however, does not prescribe this love, and rightly so, for it is only one of the diverse forms of socialising symptoms, the essential dividing line being between autistic symptoms that are out-side social bonds and the socialising symptoms that create these bonds. Between these there is no hierarchy, as there is no Other who could say what their value is. At most, there are some more or less convenient consequences for subjects. But who can decide about this if not them-selves? Common discourse prescribes modalities of acceptable satisfac-tion, not Lacanian psychoanalysis. Its only imperative, if there is one, is to recognise the Real, or that which functions as Real. Hence the suspi-cion that I evoked re the truth which can only lie about the Real outside meaning.

Neither science, nor the capitalism that it conditions, work for Eros, the god of the bond. Thus it is up to psychoanalysis to make an ally of Eros, but to the extent that is possible for each subject in terms of the symptomatic real which defines him, and without passing through the norm, whether hetero or not. It thus returns to the evolutions that, in the reorganisation of social groups, troubles—for better or worse—the traditional norms of sex and the family.

This is a different program for psychoanalysis, it must be said, than that of its beginnings, which sought to base the unconscious on reason, in order to give to psychoanalytic knowledge a dignity equal to that of science. With the change of paradigm introduced by the RUCS, it is a rather a question of configurations of *jouissance*, the satisfactions/ dissatisfactions of subjects and the consequences of these for social bonds.

PART IV

POLITICAL PERSPECTIVES

CHAPTER EIGHTEEN

Dissidence of the symptom?

All of Lacan's rethinking of the regulations of *jouissance*, sex, the Father, clinical structures, love, and the correlative ends of analysis, has political implications and consequences. As well as revising them in the light of these developments, they should also to be adjusted to the changes of our times and to the social reorganisation produced by the triumph of globalised capitalism.

That the symptom has a political import is a Freudian thesis; a simple title like *Civilization and its Discontents* indicates this.

Announcing, as Lacan did, a final identification with the symptom—construed as the product of a double "event" of the body and of saying—no doubt adds something to this.

The implication of *jouissance* is clear in the conversion symptoms of hysteria and in the perversions, which both involve scenarios with the body. It is also visible enough in schizophrenia, with its anomalous phenomena of the body. But what of obsession and paranoia? Obsession is certainly a mental phenomenon that interferes with thought, yet obsessions are always thoughts of *jouissance*. The same goes for paranoia. The paranoiac is also a thinker, but what does he think of if not the *jouissance* of the other, of the persecutor?

The civilised body

These symptom events of the body are to be situated in relation to the body we deal with: the civilised body—that is, socialised. We must gauge the extent to which there is a body factory for our socialised bodies. The body is not a product of nature, it is rather a product of art. And it is certain that what we call education is first an attempt—which succeeds what's more—to tame the body, to make it enter into the collectivising practices of the body. We teach the child how to eat, how to regulate its excretions, at what time, in what form, how to present himself, etc. We transmit social conventions to the child. And in order for the child to observe good manners, we bend him to *habitus*, to use an often-appropriated term of Pierre Bourdieu's. If we ask how we manage this, it is first by the operation of master signifiers functioning as imperatives, by the breviaries of good conduct, but also by imaginary contagion, by the induction of models, for the fact is that little children are transitivists, they have a tendency to "do as". In this sense, the socialised body is not only for "good society". Children of the street, of shantytowns, from under-developed countries fall in the same way under the induction of corporeal models.

We verify here how the human body assimilates symbolic and imaginary relations. Lacan formulated this right at the beginning of his teaching in saying that "Habit and forgetting are the sign of the integration of symbolic relations into the organism", and that are translated later as the folds of the body and which become identical to the feeling that everyone has of himself. Indeed, a body that I am calling civilised is always connected with the state of mentalities, with all they imply of the Symbolic and Imaginary.

If we wish to gauge the degree of this profound socialisation of the body, we can turn to the differences between civilisations where body practices are not the same. In eighteenth century France there was a great discovery: Man was believed to be universal. Well, there were others as well, those whom Montesquieu called the "Persians". It was a shock at that time to discover the heterogeneous manners of other civilisations. It must be said that between the different practices of the body of different civilisations, there is not always much understanding because, fundamentally, other practices of the body are always perceived to be barbarian and indeed, this question is very delicate. Today, globalisation of the capitalist market is homogenising to the point of including practices of the body, but we see that the signs of antipathy between discourses become even more controversial. When we hear talk of female genital mutilation, we, in our part of the world, shudder; when we think about the atrophied feet of Chinese women over the centuries (that is no longer practised) or of the neck or the lips of certain African women, all these practices of the body which had, and which still have sometimes, the aim of distinguishing the body according to sex—man/woman—then in the name of the hegemonic discourse of the universal rights of man and of the individual, we raise our eyebrows. But this ultimately shows that there is a sort of competition between regulations of the body according to places and times, rather than an antipathy. This is what Lacan said in a very striking formula: he spoke of the "racism of discourses in action".

A small parenthesis here. We see clearly the offer made by the discourse that we call capitalist. It consists in trying to make all *jouissances* enter into the mad machine of production-consumption. We always say, and with good reason, that for psychoanalysis there is no collective unconscious, it is true, but there are collectivised modes of *jouissance*. And it is these collectivised modes that are transposed onto all cultural productions. It starts with the songs that are sung in one culture and extends to the most elevated productions of art—what we call sublimations, which are sublimations of *jouissance*. These are the collectivised modes of *jouissance* that ground the feeling of belonging to a nation, to a place, to a people: there are many names to designate that to which we belong. This is a critical question in Europe today. It grounds the feeling of belonging as well as the feeling of exile.

Thus discourse gives us our bodies. The body that we must say we "have". The subject, the one who speaks, in contrast to the animal, is not his body. We see this in the fact that he precedes it in the discourse of the Other, and survives it for a time in memory, whereas his body is returned, as we say in a certain tradition, to dust. Hence the insistence that we must say, "the subject has a body", because to have a body is to say what? All subjects indeed have an organism, but perhaps all do not have a body, if to have a body is decided, according to Lacan, at the level of the use we can make of it.

We use and we abuse our bodies. First, we treat it like an object, beginning with the image that we have of it, the image that is our first object. We love or hate this image, or both, but above all we apply ourselves to transforming it, to improving it, to distinguishing it. In addition to fashion, we should mention here all the surgical uses, which go from sex change in the operations on transsexuals to all the practices of piercing and of tattooing which multiply today: a whole industry to accommodate the body to the tastes of the subjects of our times.

Use is not only at the level of the image. There are also uses for performance, for example in sport, which is a good example to illustrate the body instrument, the body that we make use of. And then, certainly, the erotic use of the body that can be sold, loaned, refused etc.

Subjects who do not have a body, as Lacan says of Joyce, for example, but also of a young woman in a clinical presentation, these subjects obviously have an organism and an image, but they cannot make use of them, or in any case, not the standard use. The use of the body applies to the socialised body, and this use has a limit, for we effectively make use of something over which we have a certain mastery.

The limit of "to do something with" is at the sexual level, or more precisely at the level of the response of the *jouissance* of the body, of which the subject is not master. That is, the use of the body, which supposes a certain degree of instrumentalisation of the body, stops as soon as we approach the *jouissance* called sexual. I could add "with due respect to Michel Foucault", because Michel Foucault, who has much merit otherwise, insisted on what he calls the choice of pleasures, the choice of practices which govern the type of sexual pleasure that we choose. It is certain that we can in a voluntary way choose body-to-body scenarios. What is also certain is that we can never choose the response of *jouissance*. This is very true at the level of the sexual orgasm as all the failures of this register show us, but not only there. In the sado-masochistic practices which are so fashionable today, you can completely programme the scenarios, but the effect of *jouissance* cannot be programmed; you encounter it or you don't.

So it is the symptom of sexual *jouissance* that marks the limit point of this use of the socialised body. The schizophrenic, outside discourse—but not outside *langue*—copes with his organs without the help of an established discourse. By homology, we could say: each of us copes with the sexual body-to-body without the help of an established discourse. Discourse says a great deal about sex, it constructs semblants of it and even organises the scenarios of erotic practices that we know are subject to the influences of culture. In this sense it touches even what happens in bed, but it has no hold over what I have called the response of *jouissance*.

Body outside discourse

We could illustrate the socialised body *a contrario* by comparing it to autism, which seems to me very demonstrative. I am speaking here about the little autistic subjects, not in the expanded sense of the term that is often used today. What is it that characterises these autistic subjects? They are not delusional; they have trouble with language, with the relation to the counterpart and then above all, trouble at the level of the drive. Now, for anyone who refers to the teaching of Lacan, trouble with the drive is a translation of trouble with the relation to the Other of language. It is the Other's saying that determines the order of the drives, the passage of the oral drive to the anal drive by an inflection of demand, and the setting in motion of the scopic and invocatory drives through the emergence of its desire.

What is striking, for example, for anyone reading the works of Margaret Mahler or Melzer on autism, is to note the degree to which it is a major theoretical problem for them. How can one understand that a six-year-old child manifests the same oral eroticism as a baby of six months? They do not have any other framework than to assume an organic disorder. And Meltzer imagines that perhaps the child was born with a dominant sense amongst the five senses that we recognise.

We can refer to two famous cases in order to get an idea of a way of tackling the problem: Bruno Bettelheim's case of Joey and Margaret Mahler's case of Stanley.

For Little Joey, none of his bodily functions work by themselves. He can neither eat, nor defecate, nor sleep, without being connected to his machine—he had a machine. And, fundamentally, that is understandable enough for us: it is because the machine of discourse has not been incorporated—the condition through which the body is socialised—and hence functions outside, or rather, finds a suppletion in the Real.

The case of little Stanley is even more demonstrative. Margaret Mahler is very insistent on saying that this child has two states: in one, he presents himself like a rag, an inanimate package; in other words, as totally de-libidinised and even de-functionalised, and she describes very precisely how he comes to life, and that she could not have invented, she has observed it. He has two modes: either to touch the body of an adult, the therapist here, or else to utter certain words. That is to say, it is a case where we can see that another body, homologous to Joey's machine, as well as some words from *langue*, have the same effect. They work as separated in the Real because of the failure of incorporation that would produce a dynamic subtraction.

So, it is not only that not all bodies are socialised, but that in order that they might be there has to be a knotting of the three dimensions, of semblants and the Real. But when they are not outside discourse—that is, when they are civilised—there is still a *jouissance* that does not walk in step with the discourse of the norm. Not all of *jouissance* can be absorbed in the offerings of discourse, and this is very noticeable at the level of sexual symptoms. Moreover, how many times does the subject who comes to ask for an analysis not ask himself why he is not "like others" in making a couple like all his mates, having a child at the same age as his friends, finding a woman *ad hoc* like most of them, etc.? The sexual symptom is the point of exception from the established social bond.

That is perhaps one of the reasons why in the Anglo-Saxon world the word "symptom" has disappeared in favour of "disorder". They do not say "obsession", but "obsessional disorder". And effectively, the term "disorder" indicates that the order of established discourse that regulates the body is thwarted. That leads me to what I would call the dissidence of the symptom, to mark its political import.

The symptom as objector

I'll take two main examples. The first occurs very early in psychoanalysis. At the time of the 1914–1918 war, Freud was confronted with the appearance of what were then called "war neuroses". The war neuroses presented descriptively as very close to hysterical symptomology: subjects terrified by the murderous body-to-body combat—it was still a war of body-to-body combat, with bayonets—terrified subjects who were seized with fainting, vomiting, trembling, and the impossibility of going to the front. You know, no doubt, that the military authorities consulted Freud—the times have certainly changed—in order to know if they were simulating illness or were ill. They were right to pose this question because at the same time there were subjects who refused to go to the front, not because of war neurosis but because of antimilitarism. The only two alternatives for the military authorities were to shoot them—as they had shot a number of conscientious objectors in order to set an example—or to care for them, the care envisaged being electric shock treatment [sic]. There is a marvellous letter from Freud to the military authorities, where we are struck by the courage of Freud the man: obviously he was against electric shock treatment. However, at a theoretical level, independent of his response to the authorities, what does he say? The war neurotic is an objector who does not know himself, an objector in the unconscious, and thus a subject divided between the unconscious that objects and his conscious that wants to go to war. In other words, war neurosis has a political significance: it objects to the discourse of the military master.

The other example is hysteria—more exactly, the conversion symptom of the hysteric. The functional disturbance without organic foundation can affect walking (paralysis), sight (blindness), the stomach (digestion), sleep. They are disturbances of a functional order without being an illness of the organism: according to Freud, they are an out of place erogenisation. The civilised, socialised body has its designated sites for erogenisation that Freud called the erogenous zones, mapped on the surface of the body by speech, by the saying of the Other. In this sense, the conversion symptom manifests the "refusal of the body" specific to hysteria: it objects to the erotic norm in eroticising the zones that are silent with respect to eroticism.

Here we see the ambiguity of hysteria. The hysterical subject—I am not speaking of the hysterical symptom—the hysterical subject is not an objector at all. Besides, Lacan always calls them, both men and women, the lovers [les amoureuses], or the lover [l'amoureux] (Soler, 2007). We know that as subject, the hysterical subject is rather a supporter of the master, a fan, but there is the "but" of his symptom that does not march in step but objects. Charcot, with his prescription of the male norm "repeated application of the penis" as a treatment for hysteria, was completely mistaken. Each hysteria, whether of man or woman, is divided between these two poles, and at the level of the body symptom we can understand the expression that Lacan used: "She goes on strike with her body". What could be more political! Strike against the corporeal norm in the conversion symptom, strike also and above all against the genital relation where, whatever might be the behavioural liberties that are so conducive to confusing the issue today, she refuses to be the symptom of another body. The expression "strike with her body" is designed to convey its political import.

The political value of the dissident symptom in relation to the social-ised body was noticed very early, as I mentioned above, but we have seen it change over time. When the master signifier is still powerful, the symptom appears clearly as a political dissident. Think of the Marxist slogan "Psychoanalysis is bourgeois science", indicating that treatment was intended to make people stay in line, that therapy is a collabora-tion with the dominant discourse. Lacan said that, indeed, about the psychotherapies. Think also of Russian psychiatry, of the Stalinist *"belle époque"* which forged the notion of "white psychosis" thereby justifying the incarceration of a number of opponents of the regime on the basis of their supposed mental illness.

At this level something has changed. It is linked no doubt with what Foucault has called bio-power, in order to designate the fact that now the State takes charge of life, it aims to sustain life, as is indeed dem-onstrated in all the politics of birth, of health, and now in the protec-tion of the planet, compensation, etc. In relation to this bio-power, what we should call bio-symptoms, the symptoms of the body, are evaluated differently. But our bio-power is not just any power—it belongs to the time of capitalism where the imperative of discourse is competition in production and consumption, and the symptoms that concern us are not those of sexual malaise, but on the contrary those that challenge life and put competitiveness into question. Anorexia, which can be fatal, depression, that prevents working and costs dearly, everything that can lead to suicide—drugs, obviously, and also, certainly, destructive vio-lence. Now capitalist bio-power is allied with the ideology of science and with the performance values it supports, so basically, it no longer considers bio-symptoms as political dissidents, even if they have politi-cal consequences. Capitalist bio-power thinks of them as dysfunction-alities or as breakdowns of a human machine—neurological, hormonal, social, etc.—which goes haywire just as any machine could go haywire. This is a huge change that forecloses the value of the truth of the symp-tom that Freud revealed.

As a result, what do these bio-powers say today about sexual symp-toms? Very little. They are indifferent enough to sex as is clear in the fact that sado-masochistic lobbies are well established; this is the permis-siveness of our time, and in the name of what could we object? There is then only one barrier to the discourse of capitalist individualism united with the rights of man: everything is permitted sexually within the limits of mutual consent. I have had the opportunity to develop this point elsewhere. As a result, besides murder, there remains essentially only one big sexual taboo: paedophilia, where reciprocal consent does not apply.

An emergency discourse

All of this changes the place of psychoanalysis: it is in direct conflict with the operation of capitalist bio-power. The latter has two sides: on one, keeping alive the instruments of the market—that is, individuals—maintaining what is now called human material, by constructing the standard symptoms of the normalised producer-consumer by means of images and slogans. On the other, reducing the atypical symptoms that don't fit and make things stall by reducing them to dysfunctions that have led to the breakdown of the cognitive behavioural machine. It is a whole programme: make the anorexic eat, make the mute person speak, make the depressive smile, tranquillise the stressed person, calm the agitated and all will be well. It is clear that we live in the age of psychotropic drugs. And in the age of "psy", certainly less bad, but which "leads back to the worst". The symptoms that we sometimes call new, which affect orality, action and mood, are almost all symptoms outside the social bond, bearers of autistic *jouissance*.

What can psychoanalysis do in this situation, a psychoanalysis that does not reject the therapeutic aim? More precisely, does the real unconscious, the notion forged and founded by Lacan, change the way things are here? The notion implies, as I said earlier, a division of the unconscious between a decipherable unconscious as language to which the phantasy gives its meaning, or its truth value, even its *joui-sens*, and the real unconscious which fixes *jouissance* to a linguistic element outside meaning, in itself disconnected from the Imaginary. Neologic or holophrastic, coming from the effects of *lalangue*, it is not a product of discourse—and it does not walk in step with collective injunctions. Nor does it lend itself to any form of exchange: it is autistic, even if not always resistant to the perception of obscure affinities. It constitutes, whether it is knotted or not to the Imaginary, the most real kernel of the singularity of each *parlêtre*.

From where does it come if not from our first encounters? In spite of the distance between the formulas, it is also Freud's thesis—the Freud of

Inhibitions, Symptoms and Anxiety—which asserts that for all subjects, the symptom comes from the anxiety produced by the encounter, deemed traumatic, the surprise encounter with the emergence of an unexpected *jouissance*, seen or heard, or felt. Events of the body. It is why, I believe, Freud never incriminated the Other in explaining symptomatic *jouissances*, despite all of his Oedipal construction. Lacan defines the RUCS in establishing the link between these first events of the body and the encounter with the first *lalangue*, also contingent in its modalities. Thus, to the contingency of Freud's traumatic encounters, he adds the contingency of the first saying; it is also traumatic. That does not incriminate the Other either. History certainly starts at the very beginning of infancy where the two heterities—the first *jouissances* and the first saying—are linked, but this does not make a destiny.

I note that the symptomatic manifestations of the real unconscious that Lacan brought to light—whether they are isolated or whether they can be included in a Borromean link with the phantasmatic partner—share at least one trait with the so-called "new symptoms": that of an autistic *jouissance* outside the social bond and outside exchange. Except—and this is the crucial difference—they are not, like these symptoms, the reverse side of the pressures of a triumphant capitalism. Who would hesitate to choose between a symptom of real singularity which gives an anchoring to identity and separation, and others, just as autistic, but which have repercussions in that they invert the alienation to the injunctions of discourse and do not subtract the subject from the common clamour?

Psychoanalysis treats, certainly, it even wants to treat but without lying about either the relation that lacks, or about the Real and the symptoms that both make up for and make each subject's destiny as a *parlêtre*. Contrary to what some imagine, it could be that the multiplication of victims of global capitalism—always producing more subjects outside the social bond—is enlarging the psychoanalyst's field of action rather than reducing it. That is, in fact, what the notion of the Lacanian field that Lacan introduced in 1970 is about.

Yet it must be understood that psychoanalysis does not reduce the sexual deficit. It just brings to light its foundation in the linguistic "curse", the untreatable fact that language does not direct us to any other partner than those objects detached from the body by language—the oral object, the anal object, etc.—and that the social bond is only installed by discursive artifices. In this sense, the bonds organised by each discourse, and specifically the models of the couple that they construct via their semblants, make up for the lacking relation in constructing the implicit norms of love.

However, not everyone has yet understood this. Those who would doubt it can read Otto Kernberg's 1995 book—it is not so old—*Love Relations* (Kernberg, 1995). He explains the characteristics of mature sexual love, the result of a successful analysis. It is the return—how anachronistic—to the genital oblativity of the 1950s, which was, moreover, nothing other than the pseudo-psychoanalytic version of the edifying ideology that is Christian love that has already had a history of some centuries in the master's discourse. Psychoanalysis in the service of the old norms here. The psychoanalysis, on the contrary, that aims at the Real has another aim: not of re-establishing the status quo but of revealing the fundamental symptom of the subject's unconscious, that which creates his singularity.

Thus the first question for each subject is to know what his suppleting symptom is, and what level of humanisation it allows in a liveable social bond. If it is socialising, the aim will go from the phantasmatic novel of a life towards the misrecognised real of the autistic unary letter, in bringing to light the original contingencies that repetition elevated to the level of the necessary and which, from then on, never stop writing themselves as a programme of *jouissance*. In the contrary case, it would aim to go from a Real that is too free, outside the social bond, towards a linguistic mooring. In both cases, it aims at what Lacan called at one time "absolute difference" (Lacan, 1981b, p. 276); this is very far from making the subject bear the weight of not being completely within the norm, or of inducing him to make himself its clone.

This means that the malaise in capitalism is more than ever the concern of the psychoanalyst, since its programme of *jouissance* does not undermine sexuality as such but the socialising libido, in aid of the great aggregates of the proletarian body, which no longer have anything "from which to make the social bond." I have said that these social bonds are the discourses that make up for the bond of the relation that lacks, all of them, except the capitalist discourse that forecloses the "business of love" and does not construct any standard couple. From this point on, there remains only the precariousness of love-symptoms, arising according to particular unconsciouses and the contingencies of the encounter.

Yet it is not capitalism alone that is to blame here, but what has made it possible through the technological developments due to science. The wonders of science, with all their apparent progress, cannot make us forget that science works for what Freud called the death drive. With the leap forward in biology at the beginning of the twenty-first century, and the devitalisation that it makes possible, this is indeed no longer a secret. In the previous century, some scholars in physics were alerted to the lethal consequences of their discoveries. That stopped nothing. Today, from ethics committee to ethics committee, we are alert to the fact that biology, the only science that Lacan inscribed at the level of the Real, traffics in life: its reproduction, its selection, its longevity, etc. Probably, that will not stop anything either, but it raises psychoanalysis to the status of the emergency discourse in civilisation.

A discourse of resistance, which privileges a Real different from that of science, that of the *parlêtre*, a Real that works to knot it to the Eros of a possible, liveable bond. It must be said that this offer corresponds to a perceptible change in social demand. Now, life is thought of as an object to manage. "What should one make of one's life?" has not always been a question, but is more and more a question today, linked obviously to the multiplication of possibilities that leave choice to the responsibility of each subject. In these circumstances, symptoms of sex are far from being the most invoked, while a number of people deplore their difficulty in "constructing" personal relationships, as they put it, whether this be at work, in love, with the family or with friendship. The aspiration to be integrated is everywhere. There's nothing to add here: it is the disruptive effect of capitalism that motivates this.

With Lacan, the analysis of the malaise in sexuality has revealed that the non-relation of the sexed *jouissances*, connected in our reality to the generalised cynicism of perverse *jouissance*, is at the root of the difficulties in the social bond: no dialogue between the sexes, but no longer dialogue between real symptoms either. Psychoanalysis cannot therefore promise fusion, but as long as it leads the subject to recognise himself in his fundamental symptom and not in membership of the groups that are prescribed for him, it allows, one by one, this "exit" from the capitalist discourse that Lacan evoked in *Television*.

I said psychoanalysis, to be understood as defined by the act constituting its discourse, not psychoanalysts. As for them, they are notorious for their insensitivity to their times. How many of them are nostalgic for a tradition that they confuse, incorrectly, with the efficacy of the father, who moan about our times, and who denounce subjects prey to the deleterious values of capitalism when they should receive them in their discourse. How many who, not having grasped the subversion that is properly Lacanian, lack the power to use the resources that it has produced with this real unconscious and which would still allow them to meet "the subjectivity of their times" (Lacan, [1953] 2006, p. 264), that of the beginning of this century which is Freud's no longer.

CHAPTER NINETEEN

Psychoanalysis and capitalism

Psychoanalysts today have got into the habit of incriminating capitalism. Their grievances deserve to be scrutinised.

Both Freud and Lacan exalted analytic action as one of the highest and most subversive forms of action. They speak in these terms: plague, atopia, ex-sistence, other desire, subversion. We are no longer exactly at that moment; the tone has changed. Yet there is no way to erase the opposition of aims here: the one who analyses is in a battle. And yet the distance of a century allows us better to perceive that psychoanalysis is also connected to what it fights against, and that psychoanalysis and capitalism cannot be contrasted in such a binary way. If psychoanalysis is indeed the other side of the discourse of the master, as Lacan has shown, it is not the other side of the capitalist discourse.

Eye opening

We should recognise that a part of what psychoanalysis produces in the individual, capitalism seems to obtain on a grand scale in the Real. Does not each psychoanalysis aim, at both the disidentification of the subject (the fall of the semblants introjected from the Other)—which is also disalienation—and the bringing to light of the object of *jouissance* that governs him? "Cynical remainder" of analysis, said Lacan. Now, doesn't capitalism also produce, by other means, the fall of the great semblants—God, the father, the woman, etc.—in favour of the imperatives of merchandise, of the push-to-consumption that homogenises without passing through the universal of the ideals of tradition and which breaks up even the Freudian crowd suspended from the paternal exception?

What psychoanalysis has revealed at great cost about sex is now in the open: that the demand of the drive is one of the major mainsprings of the libido, as if a century later the secret was uncovered. I have pointed out that Freud's *Three Essays on the Theory of Sexuality* are nothing compared with what appears on our screens. Human rights now extend to the right to *jouissance*, that we can thereby display and claim, and it is even possible to make a private cause of it. In fact, we can see that interpreting with the drive occurs everywhere outside psychoanalysis, in politics as well as in love. How could the formulations of demand, along with the conditions of analytic interpretation, not be changed? It is difficult to imagine that psychoanalysis could be exempted from any responsibility for this development.

Indeed, the misfortunes of sex can no longer be blamed on capitalism. It has often been thought that if we don't enjoy well, it is due to the effects of a defective social organisation. Hence the dreams of a better world and a new man which preoccupied the preceding century, with the results that we know. They didn't last, it's true, and today all that remains is the lamentation of the victims seeking those responsible to incriminate them.

Concerning the problems of survival and of the meeting of needs, we could legitimately incriminate the flawed social order: monopolisation, dispossession, exploitation, and I could go on, are certainly not empty words. But as for Eros, the mischievous god from whom we expect the union of souls and bodies, it is not the fault of society if it goes wrong. The "no sexual relation" to which Lacanian psychoanalysis attests, is not the doing of capitalism. It is rather that the arrangements that the discourses propose are, in every case, incapable of preventing a "curse on sex" which comes from somewhere else.

Is this to say that all social orders have the same value? Surely not, and how could the psychoanalyst not be actively involved here? The first symptomatic sufferings that are presented to him always testify to the inadequacies of the standard solution, and today he receives a clamour as globalised, as I said earlier, as the capitalist discourse itself. Depression, morosity, impotent rebellions, the sudden collapse of soldiers, abulias, distractions, violence, different excesses, repeated traumas, and I could go on, speak of the non-sense of striving for some sham surplus *jouissance*, without any transcendence, and the ineptitude of scraping a living within the balance of producer-consumer, moreless. This clamour protests against the pre-treatment of subjects by the norms of desire and *jouissance* of a discourse which no longer masks the curse on sex which destroys all the semblants that cover it in the other discourses. Another affinity with psychoanalysis. The malaise is going to increase, like the dark shadow of the well-being that capitalism claims to bring.

Each discourse—what Freud called civilisation—constructs a type of social bond, a sort of standard couple: master and slave, teacher and student, hysteric and master, and then psychoanalyst and psychoanalysand. They do not have the same value, of course, and they can be denounced, but all make a bond, and can be used as recourse against the programmed misfortunes of the sexual couple. But there is no such possibility in the scientificised capitalist discourse. It is not a variant of the discourse of the master, and can only constitute a single, barely social bond between the individual and products. Indifferent as it is to "the business of love", it moves towards an increasing fragmentation and instability of social bonds, and leaves individuals always more exposed to insecurity and loneliness (Soler, 2000).

The result has something paradoxical about it: in a market of generalised lack of enjoyment, the satisfactions obtained are, at the same time, dissatisfactions. Indeed, all the offers which this discourse makes in terms of consumption and "narcynical" success, as I have put it—with all that implies of fanatical individualism, of competition and of the generalised instability of the bonds of work, the state of the world, etc.—even this offer is the object itself of dissatisfactions and complaints.

But this discourse needs the satisfaction of contemporary subjects in order for the machine to keep working. This was not always the case; there were times, for example, when religion allowed the treatment, even the idealisation, of the concrete dissatisfaction of the masses. This time is no more, for bio-politics is supposed to take charge of the well-being of subjects, at the very moment when the victims are ever more numerous.

Regarding the equivalence between satisfaction and dissatisfaction, the most significant aspect, to my eyes, is not the dissatisfaction of the losers, as they say, it is that of the winners. Witness all these phenomena of sudden collapse, of which, some ten years ago, there was an epidemic in the United States of America among top executives, and today, all those in the top echelons of business, the arts, show-biz who, feeling overwhelmed, run to religions, sects, "psys" of various sorts, and many other things as well. And the cherry on the cake is that, given that the values of combativeness and optimism that our whole culture tries to instil do not succeed in masking the other side of the coin, there is someone to promote the value of resilience for everyone by making it each person's duty to bear the real and subjective failings of our times without letting himself be defeated!

But the multiplication of victims, with the correlative increase in the ideology of victimisation, does not prevail only because the capitalist universe is hard, making satisfaction and dissatisfaction twin sisters. There were times that were much harder in Western history. I have had the opportunity to develop this point (Soler, 2005). There is no horror that a consistent discourse cannot surmount—just look at fundamentalisms today.

Capitalism is not only hard, but it fails at another point. It destroys what Pierre Bourdieu called symbolic capital. Symbolic capital cannot be reduced to the stock of transmitted knowledges, those knowledges that are the weapons, the instruments of success. It includes the ways of the world and with them, what we call values, whether they are aesthetic, moral or religious. They allow meaning to be given to the tribulations of subjects or act as compensations for them; thus, they offer them support in organising their innermost defences.

Bourdieu denounced the unequal distribution of symbolic capital along class lines. He was right, but I believe that the phenomenon goes beyond the differentiation of classes. In rereading whatever great literary work of the nineteenth century or of the beginning of the twentieth century, or even watching the films of the 1950s again, we can see what has been lost of symbolic capital. Stefan Zweig, the contemporary and friend of Freud, was one of those who was perhaps most aware of it and this makes him sometimes seem very dated. It is not that there are no longer values, but in contrast to the market, they are not globalised; on the contrary, they are fragmented, local, the least shared things in the world. And human rights try in vain to maintain a final barrier against the generalised commodification of individuals.

The derision of speech

But even so, can't we credit our times with the fact of accepting the articulation of complaint, recognising it enough to allow a good listener, someone who is not simply an instrument of the social order there to redress a symptomatic deviance? There is no doubt that this condition is not always a given in history and we can easily see that it is one that totalitarianisms as well as fundamentalisms exclude. We understand why and how: in the framework of an absolute political or religious order, individual voices are only acceptable if that they are in unison with the one and only message. From that point on, all truth-value is automatically refused to the symptom's deviance. Such a discourse eventually makes way for the psychiatrist or to various judges, but never to the psychoanalyst-interpreter.

It would appear that we are not at that point yet. Completely to the contrary, the capitalist discourse, united with the political forms of democracy, seems to give the freedom of the city to the most diverse individual voices. Even more so, it encourages speaking, recognises the benefits of speech and produces endless "psys" for all varieties of trauma. The one by one has become the rule and we participate in phenomena of speech without precedent. Take the practice of testimony, for example. Today it is pushed to the point of mania, independent of all content. You have nothing to say? All the more reason for you to express yourself. A woman was interviewed on the radio: "I am nothing, I have no particular information, but that is no reason for me to be silent". What a great comment.

The processes of monopolisation of speech have certainly not disappeared, but the ideology of the right to expression has triumphed so much today that, aside from anecdote, there is perhaps no longer anything to hear but the universal clamour of human misfortune, that is proclaimed or denied. This is the other side of the phenomenon. Say what you like, it will be completely without consequence. "You chatter, you chatter ...". A supreme derision of speech reduced to its role as cathartic outlet, expected only to stifle the sufferings of the consumer-voter. And what was in the seventeenth century the fine art of conversation is no more, for chatter and silence are now one. The gag has not been lifted: it has only changed its terms. I also see here one of the reasons for the unprecedented development of techniques of listening targeting solitary voices in distress rather than really finding help for them. They have a compensatory social function. Besides, and without it being recognised, this new regime of speech probably sustains itself due to the fact that to speak, and even to speak in vain, is in itself a *jouissance*, and one which comes at no extra cost!

What could we expect from this for psychoanalysis? Contrary to what we might imagine, this culture of speech without consequence is hardly favourable, and we can see that it is more than compatible with the reduction of the symptom to an organic disorder that I was criticising earlier. For psychoanalysis, it is a considerable obstacle to the institution of the subject supposed to know without which the mainspring of the symptom cannot be put in question. We meet this difficulty in the majority of first consultations where the wish to confide, to say what is known and to be understood, is in conflict with free association and with the expectation of an interpretation of what one did not know.

At a more collective level, we might fear some boomerang effect. If there are only media ratings intended to supplement the big Other— and that number represents no one—is not the path open for a "return in the Real" of the voices of exception? The multiplication of sects points in this direction. All of them attach themselves to the prophetic voice of a One who is out of the ordinary, and they bank on the promise of some transcendence, which goes beyond and sweeps up subjects. To boast of generalised cynicism is fashionable everywhere today, and for some Lacanians too. We go on repeating that the time of great collective causes, the prerogative of the twentieth century, is behind us, that ideas and values are going downhill, etc. It's true. Nevertheless, it is also obvious that other causes are sought which seem indeed to come from the side of religion, as Lacan had indeed predicted.

Yet Freud, who didn't have any illusions about the speaking "thing", had already perceived how the being who knows himself to be mortal aspires to something that goes beyond him. He stressed, in the 1920s, that men are not only more "immoral" than they believe themselves to be, they are also more "moral" and aim, in spite of their wishes to the contrary, at what I would call at least a little "dose" of ideal. Clearly, this vocabulary is no longer ours, but Lacan engaged with this thesis, although in different terms: left to themselves, subjects sublimate with a vengeance, he said in *Encore*. Governed by their drives, yes, doubtless, but what the effect of language leaves them with regard to satisfaction—which is nothing if not limited, fragmented, and certainly unable to create the fusion of which Eros dreams—makes them dream of something else. Yet this Other thing itself, depending on the circumstances, could well prove lethal. The famous death drive, if one wishes to use the term for anything which threatens the homeostasis of discourse, is not only on the side of cynical *jouissance*, but it also takes sustenance from expectations of despair. To be continued, then, in the new century.

What is already sure is that they also reinforce segregations. I am not speaking only of segregations imposed by various ostracisms, but segregations that inspire affinities, those we choose spontaneously to find a place once more amongst those who are like us, our brothers and sisters in the symptom. Most notably: alcoholics anonymous, the obese, gays, but also the "Sloane Rangers" of the posh districts. All of these are groupings upon which subjects now base identifications, and they are given even more weight by their number.

I come back to the psychoanalyst. He receives the malaise, but he cannot dream of eliminating it. It is another score that interests him, the one which produces the always individual unconscious, and which inscribes a barrier between the satisfactions/dissatisfactions, the standard ups and downs of life on one side and the truth of *jouissance* on the other—this truth that responds in each of us through fictions, or *"fixions"*, that are always particular, which separate us from the herd, and which are only revealed in an analysis.

The bond between the analyst and the analysand, a very singular social bond, is organised entirely by the "question of *jouissance*". When I say question, I am not simply saying treatment, adjustment or therapy of *jouissance*. A question is not in the register of care, it refers to knowledge, this knowledge that the analysand lacks from the start, since he knows so little about where his symptomatic suffering comes from that he expects interpretation to reveal it to him. This polarisation of analytic action towards the most real does not short-circuit Freudian truth—free association is still obligatory—but it is not happy with its half-saying either, and it takes issue with the aims of common discourse. Let's not be lured by a possible dialogue between the various discursive orders of *jouissance*: between the first discourse and that of psychoanalysis, there is an opposition of aims.

This is so true that there is a question of knowing what made the emergence and success of Freud possible. Freud's success is that a century later there are still psychoanalysts and psychoanalysands, subjects who continue to make the offer of an analysis and others who take up this offer in order to do an analysis with them.

Freud masked

How could the capitalism of the end of the nineteenth century have received the new practice? Not without resisting, it is true. I see only one answer: it did not know. Like Descartes, Freud advanced masked.[1] We know, indeed, his remark: they do not know that we are bringing them the plague. The affinities between Freud's works and the humanist tradition, which has since fizzled out, are frequently evoked. Freud was, indeed, a scholar in this tradition, and the scope of his invention goes far beyond therapeutic problems. The notion of the unconscious introduced something new to the subject of this tradition, a true subversion, which had its enthusiasts. But can it seriously be argued that this is what granted him the indulgence of the capitalist master of the time? The discovery was philosophically and ethically subversive, but Freud did not proceed as a subversive.

At a time that was, at least in Europe, a fertile period for psychiatry, psychoanalysis was born as a derivation of mental health practices confronted with the symptom of a growing *nervousness*. The impetus came to Freud from the enigmas of neurosis, for neither psychosis nor perversion were the muses of the inventor of psychoanalysis. Between the damage caused by neurosis and registered by the social body on one side, and the impotence of the offers of the medical body to respond to them on the other, the new technique advanced by asserting its therapeutic efficacy and the scientificity of its method. Novelty, efficacy, scientificity: there's nothing there to challenge the ideals of capitalism, far from it. Freud could believe in his plague, he who had taken the measure of the unconscious, and imagined that it sounded the death knell for the classical master. But what he had not foreseen was that capitalism had no interest in the subject and the truth of his *jouissance*. Appropriating the foreclosure of the subject that characterises science, it knows only the management of individuals—I mean, of proletarian bodies—to which it gives an industrial dimension today. This is what we are now dealing with, for to manage *jouissance* and to question it are two very different operations. Hence the question: what weapons does psychoanalysis have at its disposal?

Note

1. I'm alluding here to Descrates' remark "At the moment of stepping onto the world's stage, I advance masked".

CHAPTER TWENTY

Malaise in psychoanalysis

There is a palpable anxiety here. This was no doubt always the case, for the concern for the survival of psychoanalysis was there since the time of Freud. The difference, however, is that it was then translated into a fighting stance—the texts and correspondence generally attest to this and it was also the case with Lacan. Today, something has changed in civilisation, and no less with psychoanalysts.

Yet everywhere psychoanalysts are consumed. That is a sign, there is no doubt about it. On the radio one morning a psychoanalyst, with a pleasant voice and a delivery suited to a very large audience, dispenses plain common sense, never going beyond conventional banalities on the trivial social phenomena submitted to her for comment. Why make them come from the mouth of a psychoanalyst? Must we suppose that a statement by a psychoanalyst has a special aura, whether anyone knows it or not? Here is something that would indicate the presence of a collective transference. Or could it be exactly the opposite? Because once the psychoanalyst is put in a series with all the other experts on sport, medicine, current catastrophes, aggressors and victims, festivals, national fairs, men of the moment etc, what's left of him?

On the other hand, how many forecasts have there been about the future of psychoanalysis over the last thirty years saying that it does not have one! The novelty in recent years is that there are still psychoanalysts who perpetuate this, and they themselves sign the anticipated funeral oration. There is every reason to suppose that psychoanalysis, the product of civilisation, remains at the mercy of its evolutions, but there is still a malaise in psychoanalysis. It takes the form, as I said earlier, of a nostalgia for the humanism of the past, accompanied by a denunciation of contemporary culture and of the modern subjects that it produces with their new symptoms. This phenomenon is recent. It has nothing to do with what Freud and then Lacan articulated. The first diagnosed the malaise, as we know; the second repeatedly put into question "the growing impasses of our civilisation", and even envisaged that it could "lay down its arms", in order to give psychoanalysis its objectives corresponding to that moment in its history.

And indeed, have there ever been subjects pre-adapted to the Freudian subversion? We should consider anew the degree of will required by the inventors—I am thinking of Freud, of Melanie Klein, of Lacan—to go as far as they did, to invent or renew the practice in circumstances that were always adverse. We can reread Freud's texts to see how he described how the technique of free association started, like a forced association, imposed by Freud, aided by placing his hands on the forehead of the patient (!) in order that the secret thoughts linked to the symptom could be formulated. And Melanie Klein: how was she able to recognise the transference in the child that no one else saw? Her own phantasy must have played a part, but isn't it because, above all, she dared to carry interpretation to the point where it had not yet gone, to the language of play and the behaviour of the child—the point where Anna Freud and all the others saw nothing other than a subject to educate. In her act, she refuted the existence of the first unanalysable element supposed by psychoanalysis: the child. Fortunately, the certainty of Melanie Klein nevertheless spread like wildfire and later on, Anna Freud herself would inflect her positions. As for Lacan! I like to imagine where psychoanalysis would be today if he had waited for the subjects of capitalism to ask him to adjust the time of the treatment and of the session to the time of the *parlêtre*.

So, a suspicion: if psychoanalysis is losing its fighting stance today, would it not be due to the fact that psychoanalysts themselves are also among the subjects we are speaking about, subjects modified by capitalism? The potential candidates for an analysis are perhaps not the only ones whose desire is imbued with the values of capitalism.

Precariousness of institutions

It is a fact that the social position of psychoanalysts has changed over the last few decades. What has happened for the "at least me" of each one, as Lacan said, to take such a media-friendly form today?

With the passing of time, I sometimes say to myself that the great mutes of psychoanalysis had their merit. I am not speaking of the fact that with psychoanalysts, as with others, there are diverse tastes and aptitudes: some are tenors and some do not say a word. I am speaking of the collective position of the analytic group.

There was a time when these hyper-discreet analysts existed. It is true that this was before the time of the generalised "*loft*", where everyone has to sing his little song. The IPA had even made a doctrine of it via the necessity of neutrality, of a colourless analyst who kept any possible comments for the inner circle of his colleagues. Lacan gave them ironic homage in a pamphlet "The situation of psychoanalysis in 1956" (Lacan, [1956b] 2006, p. 384) stigmatising their air of self-importance and their parodic church. And yet his School, the Freudian School of Paris, did not hinder their spontaneous generation. So he mocked both equally, in the name of the ideal of Enlightenment reason, and knowing full well, as he says, that "noise does not suit the name psychoanalyst"—as doubtless he knew from experience.

I am by no means pleading for a return to the complacency of silence. I think, on the contrary, that it is all the more necessary that psychoanalysts address today's subjects, but on condition that they speak to them about what psychoanalysis is, that they explain, that they confront the specific difficulties of transmission in their field. This is something different from devoting themselves to media chatter.

And yet, if there is a domain in which the rigours of the Bourbakian ambition for complete transmission has always met obstacles, it is certainly psychoanalysis. Lacan himself ended up by admitting this, saying, "The analytic thing will not be mathematical". Not because of any ill will, but just because the unconscious, which is rational, and the *jouissance* it programs, do not allow the elision of singularity that science does. This is so crucial in practice that it runs counter to the analyst being reduced to his common name of analyst.

Has an analyst ever once received a single subject who, in demanding an analysis, does not arrive equipped with a word, with a sentence he has heard, with a reading that indexes the one he is addressing? That it will usually be with the greatest misunderstanding and without any relation to the true criteria of competence, it is certain. But this imaginary hook indicates the impossibility of the anonymous analyst. Lacan could speak of the "any signifier whatever" of the analytic address, but he also added that the analyst must be someone, even if his signifier can be any one whatever. To be pinned down to the name of the function psychoanalyst is never enough: a little extra sign is needed—however illusory it may be—which says to the candidate that it concerns some One who is worth something.

This clinical fact indicates two things. First, with his initial step, the candidate for an analysis never authorises from himself. Then, and above all, that the transference love that accompanies the institution of the subject supposed to know is addressed, at its horizon, as with all love, to a proper name, at least potentially.

This is the cross that psychoanalytic associations have to bear! They would like the one who does not authorise from himself, in addressing his demand for analysis, to put his trust in their authority rather than in what circulates by word of mouth and from one person to another according to whom he meets. In other words, they would like a preliminary transference to the institution to orient individual transferences. This wish is not unfounded—we can never say it enough, for the guarantee for an analyst can only come from those who know him and who recognise him. When that happens, when the analytic institution is raised to the status of subject supposed to know, this transference reflects on each one of its members, and then each one can be very discreet also, for his membership is a guarantee for him.

This was the case for decades, as long as the International Association created in Freud's time was supposed to be the only repository of analytic knowledge. But now the good old days of the single institution have ended. A strange history, in fact: the contingencies of its adventures concur so well with the spirit of these times of free enterprise that we could suspect them to have been contrived.

Take an association stemming directly from Freud, wanted by him, with many members, international, that watches over the formation and the guarantee of analysts, and that even succeeded in making diverse currents converge, for example, keeping Melanie Klein and Anna Freud together. What a performance! So, seen from the outside—that is the indicator of respectability—all seems in order until the teaching of Lacan emerges. I'll skip over the accidents in this history in order to go straight to the result: a discreet expurgation. *Exit* the troublemaker.

No good riddance though: it is from this point that everything starts, that the subject supposed to know is divided irremediably with the renewal of analytic theory, and the splitting of the field is fixed. This will go to the point of a centrifugal dispersion after the dissolution of the School of Lacan. How could this attack, against a unique subject supposed to know in psychoanalysis, not have reverberations in the form of a very perceptible anxiety? From now on, unfettered competition has spread in the psychoanalytic associations, the transferential rivalries which were at first internal being transposed to the inter-associative level; it is the struggle for public recognition that is culminating now, with an ultimate appeal to the State. That quackery finds comfort here is something that each of us can see. I note moreover that it is not surprising, logic never losing its rights, that some people start dreaming of a reunification and—why not say it?—of a "merger" in order to stay in tune with the logic of the large corporations of capitalism.

I said malaise, but this is a euphemism when it is the whole of institutional logic that runs counter to analytic subversion. It does not spare anyone, dominates everyone, for the solitary way is not a more promising alternative due to the fact that the analyst connot establish himself on his own. He certainly authorises from himself in his act, and not from his institution—Lacan will have at least passed on this truth—but this act requires an elaboration of discourse which cannot be undertaken alone, and which places each person under the supervision of his peers. It is from this fact that Lacan argued for the necessity of a School of psychoanalysis.

The institution reinvented

The question is controversial, but it is certain that the concept of the School, far from being an addition that could be subtracted, is central to the Lacanian path. We know that the practitioners of analysis find both a social inscription and a guarantee in the comfort and the discomfort of associative groups, and perhaps today, a shelter against the inquisitions of the State as well. But the logic of these groupings is not that of the analytic discourse.

The term "School" is designed to bring us back to it. It seems to indicate that essentially it is a question of knowledge. This is not false, but it is only partially true. It is indeed a question of what psychoanalysis teaches, of what each has learned from his analysis that may possibly be valuable for all; about what it changed in each case and can be reproduced for others; of what the analyst himself knows about it and how he acts in relation to it. From the beginning, the old notion of didactic analysis implied that an analysand was schooled by his own psychoanalysis. Yet it is necessary that what he believes he has learned be put to the test of transmission, since it concerns an experience that is always singular and never repeatable, contrary to what happens in science. Ideally at least, the question of the project of the School is not to find a shelter, but rather a place to question both the experience of the unconscious and what analysts make of it. This cannot be solitary work, for it is necessary that there are multiple presences in order to think psychoanalysis, even for innovators like Freud and Lacan. So the School does indeed have an aim of epistemic transmission, but I believe that this is in fact secondary.

Here, as elsewhere, we work on knowledge through rectifying ethics. Moreover, can twenty years of seminars be without effects of a School, without effects on the desire of the analyst? Beyond the elaboration of doctrine, a saying is affirmed and a desire is transmitted.

In contrast with science, in psychoanalysis we are dealing with the horror of the knowledge at play, which, for everyone, is nothing other than knowledge—acquired with great difficulty—about his own unconscious, as real, and its consequences. Since Freud, the main consequence has a name: castration. This name is as suggestive as it is deceptive with its connotations of mutilation, which says—though not very well and invoking too much imaginary—that for the analysand this knowledge can only be approached at the price of passing through anxiety.

That the latter can lead to a retreat is only too obvious and it touches psychoanalysts to the extent that they shy away from it more than they should. Psychoanalysis is thus at the mercy of the psychoanalyst, who, Lacan did not hesitate to say, is "responsible" for the unconscious. Responsible for its articulation in so far as the analysand can only question it to the point of producing a response if it is caused by the desire in act of the analyst. A School is made to sustain this desire. Indeed, there is a homology between the analysis of the analyst and the School: that there be a psychoanalyst is the stake in both cases. Of the first we expect the development of a desire which allows the analysand to bear the analytic act—it can never be sufficiently remembered that this is not simply a therapeutic act—while with regard to a School of psychoanalysis with its pass, we expect that the analysts, without whom the unconscious could not be questioned, put themselves in question, not so much in terms of what they know but in terms of the rectification of their ethics.

A rectification without a rectifier, obviously, and never acquired once and for all, not only because psychoanalysts have a horror of what has been revealed to them, but also because the conditions of the invocation of the unconscious via the transference change according to the evolutions of civilisation. If the unconscious is indeed what Freud and then Lacan and a few others have said it is, psychoanalysts have this curious destiny of only being able to become integrated—God knows that the theme is current—as "extimate". Assimilated, they join the mass of psychotherapists; excluded, it is no better, they disappear. If the only politics possible is to make their discourse *ex-sist*, to maintain its status as the exception, they have both to get rid of the models that were adjusted to previous decades, and never depart from the ethics of well-saying. How could they not have to permanently reinvent their strategy when dealing with subjects who address them from the other discourse? Imitation and repetition are fatal to them, but no less fatal is forgetting the Freudian subversion that stirred things up at the beginning of the twentieth century.

The procedure of the pass is thus consubstantial with the School. In 1976, ten years after having conceived the pass, Lacan returned to it as a *leitmotif* in the preface that I commented upon, but one that had been rethought. He puts the analyst in the hot seat so that he testify to his relation to the subject supposed to know, to the truth and to the Real. It is a test, there is no doubt about that, and this is indeed what its detractors held against this pass. We have already heard everything on this theme: a time bomb for the institution, even an indication of Lacan's malice; an anthropophagous procedure which devours the *passant* if it does not vomit him up; a useless one which produced nothing new; for already, the idea of finished analyses had been questioned, or there's no need to question anyway, etc. Arguments that come from the pressure cooker are always a sign of confusion, but it is true that there is a test and not only for the *passant*.

But is it so serious? And isn't it also the case in the treatment itself? In both there is the same stake: that of well-saying, because of the inconsistency of the Other. It's amazing that analysts already established in the profession could collectively refuse the test.

Beyond its aims of guarantee and selection, isn't the procedure of the pass also the most propitious way for everyone—the *passant* in particular—to measure what his relation to the subject supposed to know has become, to see just where he has really gone in his exploration of the Other, and this insight is sometimes the occasion for taking up analysis again, and it is a rather good sign—and, above all, to see what use he makes of what he has learned? For there are several possibilities here, the most obvious being forgetting, flight, cynical exploitation, etc.

There could very well be some "returns in the Real" of what analytic practice imposes on the person of the analyst. The fact is not new, but perhaps our times offer new ways. For more than half a century, it was the analytic institution that absorbed these phenomena of compensatory returns. Now they have passed into collective space and interfere in the public discourse of analysts. There is more, however. The analytic function, as we know, presupposes a long and difficult formation, the outcome of which is never guaranteed. I offer the preliminary hypothesis that this function has become even more gruelling in the current climate of capitalism.

Very early on, and without doubt because of the limits of his own analysis, Sándor Ferenczi was the first to really see the price that had to be paid by the one who offers himself as support for the analysand's transference. Several terms have been produced to say what this is: "abstinence" and "neutrality" said Freud in order to designate a suspension of the person's prejudices, tastes and essential choices—in brief, all of his own options—with the aim of maintaining an even interest in all the statements of the subject and aiming only at their interpretation. All analytic currents agree on this point: the analytic function supposes that the analyst will put into suspense what there is of himself. On this condition, the analyst can embody for each analysand the object that causes him. Indeed, the term "counter-transference", of which so much is made in both theory and practice in Ego psychology, is indicative of the difficulty of this abnegation and the ever-present temptation to give voice to the person of the analyst in the treatment itself.

No doubt the analyst suffers from having to efface his person—in other words, to put his phantasy and his symptom in parentheses—in order to make himself, for the length of the treatment, the cause of the analysand's work. This is the price of the analytic act. It is true that this methodical subtraction of the personal factor costs more or less according to the exigencies of the analyst's own narcissism, and it is necessary to establish a specific desire here, called the "desire of the analyst". This is never completely accomplished, and there is always a remainder, but, in all cases, this elision which defines the psychic economy of the analyst at work produces return phenomena which would need to be studied, since what is renounced on one side always risks making itself felt on the other.

There is more. Lacan recognised that with analysts there was what he designated as a "horror of their act". The term is strong and goes much further than merely signifying the transferential responsibility perceived by Ferenczi. It involves the end of analysis, what it aims for.

The unconscious is certainly a very complex thing: indestructible unconscious desire, said Freud, or essential primary repression. Lacan reformulates this as the subject of the unconscious supposed to the unconscious as language, primordially and irreducibly repressed. Then, as I said earlier, he reinvented the RUCS, the embodied unconscious, which becomes corporeal in order to fix the *jouissance* of the symptom. The concept was not elaborated all at once, and remains open to re-workings, but in all cases the unconscious is seen as indestructible, impossible to reduce, for it is inherent to the speaking being. In contrast, what is not indestructible and what has emerged historically is the procedure that allows us to explore it. Freud invented the procedure specific to the revelation of the unconscious, with the real that it involves, and this procedure includes the analyst. Thus psychoanalysis remains partly at the mercy of psychoanalysts.

Now, to reveal the unconscious is to make an effect of irreducible division appear. For example, to follow the path of deciphering the formations of the unconscious—dreams but above all the lapsus—would already reveal to the subject that language works in him, without him and indeed at his expense. Freud made this the first objective of the analysis of the analyst: that he experience this effect enough, he said, for him to "believe" in the unconscious. That doesn't seem much, but it is a lot and it is perhaps the maximum, if it shows him the effect of division that annuls introspection and renders all self-analysis impossible. A true "subversion of the subject" said Lacan in designating this challenge to unity and the supposed autonomy of the classical subject with his aims for mastery. Lapsus of intentions, counter-will of unconscious desire, sardonic injunctions of repetition all signal the distance between the prescriptions of collective discourse and the scheming of an unconscious that works *jouissance* and that moves "beyond the pleasure principle", rather than towards the equilibriums of what is called happiness. Who would wish for, or wish to know, this unconscious that is so unlovable? Someone like a new age saint?

All the more so since at the end, the analyst is the refuse of his experience. What does this mean? We must not let ourselves be deceived by the pathetic resonances of the term. It does not simply mean that the analyst is an object destined to be left, a very common fate, but that he can be such only on the condition of being deposed from his position as object of the transference, and hence the term "disbeing" (*"désêtre"*): I will add though, and this is the essential point, deposed without the benefits of the operation returning to him.

An act without reward

The analytic act, when it operates, produces transformation in the analysis, but it is forgotten in proportion to its efficacy, as all the benefit accrues to the analysand, and rightly so. It is in this sense that the analyst is the waste product or refuse of the operation. He undertakes an eminent and difficult task, the effects of which do not return to his name. This is a unique fate: the analytic act operates, but it does not have a signature. That does not stop analysts from being very different: the personal factor cannot be reduced to zero, but the analysand does not bear its mark—and when he does, it is, rather, the indication of the limits of a practice. The obscure hero of an act that dispossesses him, the analyst must bear being responsible for the failures of the analyses that he directs, while any successes must be given to the credit of the analysand. He is responsible, but not the beneficiary: we understand why he must be paid! To put it in other words: the act and the genealogical tree are incompatible. The analyst does not have descendants:

the transformed analysand is neither the descendent nor the heir and even less the work of the analyst. Which means that it is impossible to identify with the analyst defined by his act. We might as well say that psychoanalysis is perpetuated but not transmitted.

This is why, I believe, Lacan could evoke the enigma of the choice of this position. How can one sustain an act that is so anti-capitalist when the big question resounds: what is the return and where is the advantage? In a world that works only in terms of accountable remuneration, how can one bear this act without the Other, both solitary in its essence and non-capitalisable in one's proper name? Earning one's livelihood doesn't require that much!

To put it another way, can one be a saint in a capitalist regime? I'm formulating it like this in order to echo the celebrated page in *Television* where Lacan compared the analyst with what was, in former times, the saint: someone who had a singular and contagious desire and was driven to the margins of every canonical path, outside the sign-posted routes of the discourse of his time. This is why, indeed, he was rather suspect while living and could only be canonised after his death. The analogy has its coherence: no canonical path for the act that aims at an exit from capitalist discourse (Lacan, 1990b, pp. 15–16).

Yet there is a difference from the classical saint. The saint was not alone. He lived in a time that made the Other exist, which assured him of the divine presence and promised him infinite beatitude. Thus his tribulations and his sacrifices never left him alone, even if he were an anchorite in the desert. No doubt authorising from himself rather than from the precepts of his Church, but not without the Other, even an Other of reward. The condemnation of Madame Guyon is exemplary here: to question the God of reward with his "pure love" was to threaten the whole edifice (see Le Brun, 2002).

Obviously no such thing applies to the analyst. The refuse of his discourse, he can expect nothing from the capitalist discourse, except objection. That discourse can promise him nothing: its path turns in a closed circuit. Lacan described this in 1970 in terms of an infernal cycle in which surplus *jouissance* governs the subject; that subject governs the chain of language which governs the production of surplus *jouissance* which governs the subject, etc. When the Other is consistent, the most marginal pathways can be made desirable, even sanctified according to the moment. But when the Other is no longer there and social bonds come undone, it is, on the contrary, the desire for integration that rages in proportion to the sense of dereliction. We see this everywhere today, and analysts escape even less from this logic that now dominates their institutional life since they cannot count on any return for their act.

Not even that of the proper name. The artist, the politician, the sportsman even, and all those who become established through some exploit whatever it might be, make a name through their action. This is not the case for the analyst who never makes a name for himself through the daily round of his practice. This is verified by the simple fact that all that remains in the history of psychoanalysis are the names of those who have done more than practise, those who have tried to think psychoanalysis and produce knowledge, Freud being the very first. To make himself the creator of discursivity is still an act, no doubt, but not exactly the same one. It indicates at any rate that the connection between the desire of the analyst and desire for knowledge cannot be erased. Take away what is elaborated of a possible transmission of knowledge and the analyst is reduced to the "practitioner". And how would one practitioner be distinguished from any other without all the doctrine that has been laid down, starting with Freud's desire to know, starting with the concept of the unconscious.

Indeed, this is why Lacan wanted a School, a place that sustains the desire that is necessary to resist the adverse seductions of contemporary discourse and to maintain the specific aims of psychoanalysis in the new epoch.

CHAPTER TWENTY-ONE

What does the psychoanalyst want?

The fact remains that putting psychoanalysis in the singular is becoming more and more of a problem, in the singular, with the fragmentation of associations and doctrines. Could we really say that it has only one politics, inherent to the relational procedure invented by Freud? Indeed, we can consider, as did Lacan, that this procedure is even more important than the discovery of the unconscious and, and that the constraints it establishes and the rules that it promotes prevail over the diversity of players involved.

Thus, from the free association required of the analysand and the duty of interpretation demanded of the analyst, we could conclude that there is one central politics: that of the revelation of the unconscious. Similarly, on the basis of the rules of evenly suspended attention and benevolent neutrality laid down by Freud, we can conclude that to analyse is not to direct the patient and that the desire of the analyst excludes the desire to be the master, etc.

The majority of analysts would no doubt agree with these very general formulas, but it would be an agreement without consequence if they do not ask of the unconscious: "What is it?" and from there, "what can happen to it in a psychoanalysis?"

If you say, for example, as was the case in a certain current, that there is certainly a diabolical unconscious, fomenter of trouble and anomalies—that is, symptoms—but this Freudian plague isn't the only thing, there is also a healthy, rational part of the ego with which we can reason, and which makes use of mechanisms of consciousness independent of the drives and can contribute to the reinforcement of its autonomy, well, then what![1] Theoretically, before the term was used as it is today, you have brought cognitivism into psychoanalysis. And it is to the filial piety of Anna Freud that we owe this Trojan horse, tailored to ensure the defeat of the Freudian unconscious!

Politically, could it be said that you're acting as master? This would be too simple. You would only be introducing the master into the psychic apparatus; it is an epistemic question that involves the conception of the subject. From there you can argue that far from acting as master, you have only made yourself the ally of what was already in place in the form of the ego, as an apparatus of reality, the agent of mastery and of consciousness. Thus you become the re-educator of a shackled ego. But why, if the unconscious were indestructible as the inventor of psychoanalysis believed, why would this CBP [cognitive behaviouralist psychoanalysis] be more successful than the pressures of early education, combined with those of the social superego that weighs on the shoulders of poor subjects. It is not surprising, in fact, that there where this Ego-psychology passed, it succeeded in bringing to an end not people's symptoms—which still flourished, even more so—but Freudianism itself.

Similarly, if you claim that the sexual impasse is resolved at the end of an analysis, and that the libido that had first gone astray in the symptom can be made to return to the norm of genital love, you apparently do not take a position on the psychical apparatus, but nonetheless postulate that the operativity of the unconscious—which forges these "formations of *jouissance*"[2] that are symptoms—can be put out of action. In doing this, how could you avoid pushing subjects towards the heterosexual norm, out of step with our times, and above all, completely contrary to the analytic discourse which is there precisely to offer the other side of the discourse of the norm.

Can it be said, then, that the way in which we think psychoanalysis will determine not just the modalities of its action but its actual ends?

A text like Lacan's "The direction of the treatment and the principles of its power" (Lacan, [1958] 2006) might make us think that this is the case. Indeed, he subordinates what he calls precisely the politics of the analyst, its ends, to the instrument used—speech in the field of language—and its potentialities. He thus suggests an order that goes from understanding to analytic action and from knowledge to political orientation. Take for example an imperative such as "Desire must be taken literally" ("*Il faut prendre le désir à la letter*"), the title of the fifth section of the text. Does it not suggest a political purpose subordinated to knowledge of structure—that of speech—where the desire that Freud called unconscious comes into the place of the signified? And how indeed could a signified be approached if not literally, that is, by the chain that signifies it? Epistemo-politics, perhaps? Not quite. In fact, this imperative only concerns the how—so, epistemo-strategy—not the purpose itself that remains implicit and which stems from a choice that knowledge does not determine: to target the desire that Freud called unconscious rather than that which could contain it. And referring to my two preceding examples, surely it is something other than aiming to reinforce the defences that the ego is able to oppose to desire, or trying to make conform to the sexual norm. Thinking and doing psychoanalysis well are interdependent for the psychoanalyst, although we can't say that one governs the other, for if doctrine and practice are knotted, both derive from the same third path.

The aims attached to a discourse, whatever it may be, always remain suspended from contingency, always borne by historical figures and susceptible to inflection by a new saying. They are at the mercy of the act, the act of those who come into the position of agent: the master, the teacher, the divided subject or the psychoanalyst. If we can do no less than say "Freudian psychoanalysis" or "Lacan psychoanalysis", it is not only to designate the differences between doctrines, but it is precisely because the procedure installs the place of saying from where the order of discourse can be renewed or, on the contrary, repudiated. This is not the level of the *automaton* of the rule, but existential, that of the choice—contingent, indestructible and, occasionally, founding.

In 1962, at the beginning of his "Kant with Sade", Lacan wrote: "[...] one paves the way for science by rectifying the position of ethics" (Lacan, [1963] 2006, p. 745) and elsewhere, "Thinking only proceeds by the ethical path" (Lacan, 1975d, p. 9). This was to say that ethical choice prevails over the epistemic register—which, as I have just mentioned, is itself knotted to the political. The thesis holds for all cases, since the comment applies as much to the circumstances that have made the emergence of modern science possible as to those that opened Freud's path, and it seems to me to be even more certain today than yesterday.

The other side of cognitivism

The catch here is that once this effect of division is recognised, we must also recognise that it spares nothing, not even thought, which we would like to think [*sic*] could be spared. But no, the desire on which thought lives is no less subject to the effect of division than any other desire. In this sense, we cannot really think the division of the subject; at best we can think "in division".[3] The discourse on the unconscious is a condemned discourse, for there is no coherence of discourse which the unconscious does not undermine. Given that, how can one have a conversation with those who do not have the experience of psychoanalysis or elaborate its epistemology?

In the end we can conclude, as Lacan did in *Encore*, that "reality is approached with the apparatuses of *jouissance*" (Lacan, 1998, p. 55). A sole apparatus, language, organises access to perception, thought and *jouissance*, at the same time. This means that thought itself only proceeds on an ethical path, that "judgement, similarly, up to the 'last', is only phantasy [...]" (Lacan, 1973, p. 44) and that there is no "universal that cannot be reduced to the possible" (Lacan, 1973, p. 7). Such is the radically anti-cognitivist postulate of psychoanalysis in the version that I would gladly call Freudo-Lacanian, rather than Lacanian only, although the formulas are Lacan's.

Indeed I do not share the thesis of Freud the scientist. Certainly, in Freud's work there are formulations that have a touch of the scientist about them, but no scientific inspiration could ever have given birth to psychoanalysis. As for the postulate that I have called anti-cognitivist, it has nothing to do with a return to any kind of pre-rationalism which would be to completely ignore the demonstration specific to the scientific spirit itself which Freud, like Lacan, always considered to be crucial. It is the opposite: we should rather see that cognitivism itself, far from being able to give an account of science—so unequal is it to the epistemology that science requires—is rather a debasement of it. But that is not my intention here.

Three theses are knotted: there is no politics of psychoanalysis without a conception of psychoanalysis and of the subject that it treats. This is why Lacan could evoke his own "efforts to undo the arrest of psychoanalytic thought" (Lacan, 1968b, p. 50) and to restore its scientific aim. But, on the other hand, there is no thought at all that escapes the effects of division: the "I think" is divided, and for each assertion there is a world between the reasons that justify it and the cause that produces it. Thought, far from being able to think its own cause, is divided from it; as a result, it is ethical choice that dominates knowledge and politics. Moreover, we should consider here the indifference to doctrinal material—current discourse tends to make a virtue of being open [sic]—to the point of reproaching all creators of discursivity for their sectarianism, without seeing that in giving up thought they are giving up the ethics of their discourse. Today the term "ethics" is, alas, well and truly overused by analysts, who sometimes don't hesitate to cloak themselves in it, but nevertheless, it retains its value. The ethics of psychoanalysis are situated, like all others, in relation to the Real, but they are distinguished from all others by aiming at this Real through "well-saying". What, then, can a politics oriented by the sole duty of well-saying be at the level of each treatment and the level of analytic institutions?

A non-prescriptive therapeutics

It is not surprising that psychoanalysis is questioned about its objectives, since well-saying [le bien-dire] is not well-caring [le bien-soigner]. It does not set therapeutic results at the level of ends. It does not neglect for all that but it makes something like a secondary benefit, coming "in addition", as Freud said. Some people can then imagine that this well-saying is a luxury in relation to the well-curing (le bien-guérir). As for the psychoanalysts of today, caught up in the politics of control and of standardised care, they have a tendency to become confused, even to fall out with each other: we saw this with regard to the law on mental health, finally voted on in 2004. Some even claimed not to be therapists, contrary to what opinion attributed to them, and attributed to them so well that, in order to denigrate them, they were reproached for not curing as fast and as efficaciously as other therapies! But let's leave that, for the essential problem is elsewhere.

What is it to care for, since we are not in the field of physical medicine, but in that of the divided subject? We can already note that well-saying is not opposed to well-doing. It is niether the beautiful-saying, nor the saying of one person, but the saying that is inferred from all the statements that the analytic work registers, it is a saying that satisfies. It satisfies in the sense of satisfaction, but also in the sense of operation: it *satis-fies* [*satis-fait*], enough for the one who enters the procedure. The alternative between analysing and curing is too simplistic to be pertinent and would benefit from being reformulated.

What's more, we can see that a century of psychoanalysis, right up to Lacan's last elaborations, have led to a rethinking of the definition of the symptom itself. In the common approximation today, we are happy with vague ideas and there is a tendency to treat any of the various ills of contemporary subjects as symptoms to be cured. Now, there is certainly a market for suffering. But not all pain is a symptom, and to administer to the misery of the world and its clamour, assuming that the intention is laudable, is not to treat the *parlêtre*.

As I said earlier, as soon as the symptom that the unconscious creates makes up for the deficit of generic sex for the *parlêtre*, as soon as it governs each person's choice of partner or partners of *jouissance*, and sometimes even this relation of subject to subject that is called love, then there is only a symptomatic partner determined by the unconscious, and the heterosexual norm itself, realised solely by the paths of the private discourse of the unconscious, becomes a symptom.

Obviously, these theses have repercussions for therapeutic aims. We can no longer think of reducing the symptom to zero and if there is no subject without a symptom, then what does the therapeutic effect of analysis become? It certainly exists, experience proves it, but it is only a change in the symptom. To put it without irony, an obsession can decrease because a man or a woman, or any other partner, can come and replace it! An assumed homosexuality can be substituted for a heterosexuality that was only a facade, and the other way around etc. That a symptom that is more liveable for a subject is substituted for one that was intolerable for him is a great success! And yet, it is a success that only the subject himself can evaluate for only he experiences the benefit of satisfaction. That's the catch, because nothing says that a symptom that is more liveable for him conforms more readily to the expectations of his entourage and, more generally, to social prejudices. Thus we must expect the continuation of the familiar protests from those who do not find the analysed to their taste.

Today, who would dare to say, and in what name, what the symptom of exiting an analysis must be? Would it necessarily, for example, be hetero rather than homo, peaceful to keep the neighbours happy, maternal when one is a woman, etc.? I say today, for something has already changed in discourse. It can be seen in the fact that a century ago, homosexuality was treated as an offence and a perversion of nature while today it is generally accepted. Psychoanalysis has without doubt played a role in this evolution, and a part of what it teaches us has, in fact, passed into common discourse.

How would the psychoanalyst find fault with this evolution in taste? At the most he could observe that once puritanical repression is undone and the *jouissances* "deemed perverse" (Lacan, 1984b, p. 22) are permitted, subjects are hardly more cheerful, that is a fact. He will not be surprised, for he is paid to know that the *jouissances* of the *parlê-tre* meet obstacles that are not accidental. He could even anticipate the superegoic process of the escalation towards excess that a permissive regime does not fail to induce. He will not conclude from this that there is increasing perversion, but rather an enforced capture of subjects in the effect of discourse.

On the other hand, the psychoanalyst cannot preach about the discourse of his time without leaving his own: the analyst's discourse does not aim to rectify morals, but to analyse the symptoms of each person who asks him and to reduce them to the point of his fundamental symptom. The ethics of well-saying are relative to the analytic discourse. Hence the problem arises for analysts of knowing how to situate themselves in the politics of their time, without going back on, and without exceeding, the knowledge that their experience produces. How could this dilemma be resolved? The pitfalls are legion: demagoguery and coquetry on one side, and an anachronistic purism on the other. They constitute two opposed poles, generators of this professional stupidity that is growing at the same rate as psychoanalysts' wish to authorise themselves on the basis of public opinion. We can see this case by case: it is unforgivable. And yet, we can't doubt that the politics of psychoanalysis forces it to continue to "be at a premium on the market" (2001b, p. 310), as Lacan formulated it in 1974, since its practice is dependent on the transference of subjects. It is impossible for psychoanalysis to disassociate itself from the politics of the discourse of its time. Once again, psychoanalysis must make itself heard.

Fortunately, most of the time, psychoanalysts today are so conformist that the more we hear them, the more we suspect that analytic subversion must be taking place somewhere else! Perhaps with those who still dare to attempt the adventure of an analysis, even if they cannot know in advance where it will lead them.

Notes

1. See the three "lines of development" that Anna Freud distinguished, that of the ego, that of object relations, and that of the drives.
2. I use this expression in reference to the "formations of the unconscious" introduced by Lacan, to indicate that the symptom is also *jouissance*.
3. Hence Lacan's appeal to topology and set theory.

REFERENCES

Claudel, P. (1967). *Partage de midi*. Paris: Gallimard, Èditions de La Pléiade.

Freud, S. (1920g). *Beyond the Pleasure Principle*. *S. E., 18* (pp. 3–64). London: Hogarth.

Freud, S. (1926d). *Inhibitions, Symptoms, and Anxiety*. *S. E., 20* (pp. 77–175). London: Hogarth.

Kernberg, O. (1995). *Love Relations: Normality and Pathology*. New Haven: Yale University Press.

Lacan, J. (1968b). La psychanalyse. Raison d'un échec. *Scilicet, 1*. Paris: Éditions du Seuil.

Lacan, J. (1970a). Discours à l'École freudienne de Paris. *Scilicet, 2/3*, Paris: Éditions du Seuil. (Also in: *Autres Écrits*. Paris: Éditions du Seuil, 2001.)

Lacan, J. (1970b). Radiophonie. *Scilicet, 2/3*, Paris: Éditions du Seuil. (Also in: *Autres Écrits*. Paris: Éditions du Seuil, 2001.)

Lacan, J. The Seminar of Jacques Lacan, The Knowledge of the Psychoanalyst 1971–1972. (Trans. C. Gallagher from unedited French manuscripts, unpublished manuscript).

Lacan, J. (1973). L'étourdit. *Scilicet, 4*, Paris: Éditions du Seuil. (Also in: *Autres écrits*. Paris: Éditions du Seuil, 2001.)

Lacan, J. (1974–1975). *RSI* (Unpublished manuscript).

Lacan, J. (1975a). La troisième: Intervention au congress de Rome, *Lettres de l'École freudienne, 16*: 177–203.

Lacan, J. (1975b). Joyce le symptôme 1. In: J. Aubert (Ed.), *Joyce avec Lacan*. Paris: Navarin, 1987.

Lacan, J. (1975c). Introduction à l'édition allemande d'un premier volume des *Écrits*. *Scilicet*, 5, Paris: Éditions du Seuil. (Also in: *Autres Écrits*. Paris: Éditions du Seuil, 2001.)

Lacan, J. (1975d). ... ou Pire. Compte rendu du Séminaire 1971–1972. *Scilicet*, 5, Paris: Éditions du Seuil. (Also in: *Autres Écrits*. Paris : Éditions du Seuil.)

Lacan, J. (1979). Joyce le symptôme 11. In: *Joyce avec Lacan*. Paris: Navarin, 1987.

Lacan, J. (1981a [1977]). Preface to the English-language edition. In: *The Four Fundamental Concepts of Psychoanalysis, The Seminar of Jacques Lacan, Book XI*. New York: W. W. Norton.

Lacan, J. (1981b). *The Four Fundamental Concepts of Psychoanalysis*. Trans. A. Sheridan. New York: W. W. Norton.

Lacan, J. (1984a). Compte rendu du Séminaire 1966–1967: La logique du fantasme. *Ornicar? 29*. Paris: Navarin. (Also in: *Autres Écrits*. Paris, Éditions du Seuil, 2001.)

Lacan, J. (1984b). Compte rendu du Séminaire 1967–1968: L'acte analytique. *Ornicar? 29*. Paris: Navarin. (Also in: *Autres Écrits*. Paris, Éditions du Seuil, 2001.)

Lacan, J. (1987). *Joyce avec Lacan*. Paris: Navarin.

Lacan, J. (1989). Geneva lecture on the symptom. *Analysis*, 1: 7–26.

Lacan, J. (1990a [1964]). Founding act. In: *Television: A Challenge to the Psychoanalytic Establishment*. Trans. D. Hollier, R. Krauss, A. Michelson. New York: W. W. Norton.

Lacan, J. (1990b). *Television: A Challenge to the Psychoanalytic Establishment* [1973]. Trans. D. Hollier, R. Krauss, A. Michelson. New York: W. W. Norton.

Lacan, J. (1990c [1969]). Notes on the child. *Analysis*, 2: 7–8.

Lacan, J. (1992). *The Ethics of Psychoanalysis 1959–1960, The Seminar of Jacques Lacan, Book VII*. Trans. D. Porter. London: Tavistock/Routledge.

Lacan, J. (1995). Proposition of 9 October 1967 on the psychoanalyst of the school. Trans. R. Grigg. *Analysis*, 6: 1–13.

Lacan, J. (1998). *The Seminar of Jacques Lacan, On Feminine Sexuality, The Limits of Love and Knowledge, Book XX Encore 1972–1973*. Trans. B. Fink. New York: W. W. Norton.

Lacan, J. (2001a [1975]). Peut-être à Vincennes. In: *Autres Écrits*. Paris: Éditions du Seuil.

Lacan, J. (2001b [1973]). Note italienne. In: *Autres Écrits*. Paris: Éditions du Seuil.

Lacan, J. (2001c). Annexes. *Autres Écrits*. Paris: Éditions du Seuil.

Lacan, J. (2001d [1968]). La méprise du sujet supposé savoir. In: *Autres Écrits*. Paris: Éditions du Seuil.

Lacan, J. (2001e). *Le Séminaire de Jacques Lacan, Livre VIII, Le Transfert 1960–1961*. Paris: Éditions du Seuil.

Lacan, J. (2004 [1962–1963]). *L'angoisse*. Paris: Éditions du Seuil.

Lacan, J. (2005). *Le Séminaire de Jacques Lacan, Livre XXIII, Le Sinthome 1975–1976*. Paris: Éditions du Seuil.

Lacan, J. (2006 [1946]). Presentation on psychical causality. In: *Écrits: The First Complete Edition in English*. Trans. B. Fink. New York: W. W. Norton.

Lacan, J. (2006 [1948]). Aggressiveness in psychoanalysis. In: *Écrits: The First Complete Edition in English*. Trans. B. Fink. New York: W. W. Norton.

Lacan, J. (2006 [1949]). The mirror stage as formative of the *I* function, as revealed in the psychoanalytic experience. In: *Écrits: The First Complete Edition in English*. Trans. B. Fink. New York: W. W. Norton.

Lacan, J. (2006 [1953]). The function and field of speech and language in psychoanalysis. In: *Écrits: The First Complete Edition in English*. Trans. B. Fink. New York: W. W. Norton.

Lacan, J. (2006 [1955]). The Freudian Thing, or the meaning of the return to Freud in psychoanalysis. In: *Écrits: The First Complete Edition in English*. Trans. B. Fink. New York: W. W. Norton.

Lacan, J. (2006 [1956a]). Seminar on "The Purloined Letter". In: *Écrits: The First Complete Edition in English*. Trans. B. Fink. New York: W. W. Norton.

Lacan, J. (2006 [1956b]). The situation of psychoanalysis and the training of psychoanalysts in 1956. In: *Écrits: The First Complete Edition in English*. Trans. B. Fink. New York: W. W. Norton.

Lacan, J. (2006 [1957–1958]). On a question prior to any possible treatment of psychosis. In: *Écrits: The First Complete Edition in English*. Trans. B. Fink. New York: W. W. Norton.

Lacan, J. (2006 [1958]). The direction of the treatment and the principles of its power. In: *Écrits: The First Complete Edition in English*. Trans. B. Fink. New York: W. W. Norton.

Lacan, J. (2006 [1960a]). Remarks on Daniel Lagache's presentation: "Psychoanalysis and personality structure". In: *Écrits: The First Complete Edition in English*. Trans. B. Fink. New York: W. W. Norton.

Lacan, J. (2006 [1960b]). Subversion of the subject and the dialectic of desire in the Freudian unconscious. In: *Écrits: The First Complete Edition in English*. Trans. B. Fink. New York: W. W. Norton.

Lacan, J. (2006 [1963]). Kant with Sade. In: *Écrits: The First Complete Edition in English*. Trans. B. Fink. New York: W. W. Norton.

Lacan, J. (2006 [1964a]). Position of the unconscious. In: *Écrits: The First Complete Edition in English*. Trans. B. Fink. New York: W. W. Norton.

Lacan, J. (2006 [1964b]). On Freud's "Trieb" and the psychoanalyst's desire. In: *Écrits: The First Complete Edition in English*. Trans. B. Fink. New York: W. W. Norton.

Lacan, J. (2006 [1966]). Science and Truth. In: *Écrits: The First Complete Edition in English*. Trans. B. Fink. New York: W. W. Norton.

Lacan, J. (2006). *Le Séminaire de Jacques Lacan, Livre XVI, D'un Autre à l'autre 1968–1969*. Paris: Éditions du Seuil.

Le Brun, J. (2002). *Le pur amour de Platon à Lacan*. Paris: Éditions du Seuil.

Lombardi, G. (2005). *L'aventure mathématique. Liberté et rigueur psychotique (Cantor, Gödel, Turing)*. Paris: Le Champ lacanien.

Milner, J. -C. (2006). *Le juif de savoir*. Paris: Grasset.

Needham, R. (Ed.) (1971). *Rethinking Kinship and Marriage*. London: Tavistock Publications.

Soler, C. (1992). Otherness today. Colloquium of the EEP, *Limits of Gender*. London, 22 March 1992.

Soler, C. (1994). Leçon clinique de la passe I. *Comment finissent les analyses?* Paris: Éditions du Seuil.

Soler, C. (1998). The commandments of jouissance. *Analysis, 8*: 15–25.

Soler, C. (1999). Les deux amours. Journées des Forums du Champ lacanien (FCL).

Soler, C. (2000 [1989]). Une par une. *Retour à la passe*, Publication des FCL, 2000.

Soler, C. (2000). Le discours capitaliste. Opening address of conference, la découverte freudienne. Université de Mirail, Toulouse.

Soler, C. (2001). *L'aventure littérraire, ou la psychose inspirée. Rousseau, Joyce, Pessoa*. Paris: Le Champ lacanien.

Soler, C. (2003–2004). La querelle des diagnostics. *Documents du Champ lacanien*.

Soler, C. (2004). Les invariants de l'analyse finie. *Hetérité, Revue de psychanalyse: La psychanalyse et ses interprétations II, IF-EPCL, 5*: 113–121.

Soler, C. (2005). *L'époque des traumatismes/The Era of Traumatism*. Rome: Biblink.

Soler, C. (2006). *What Lacan Said about Women: A Psychoanalytic Study*. Trans. J. Holland. New York: Other Press.

Soler, C. (2007). Conférence à Rennes.

Soler, C. (2007a). L'hystérie, les hystériques. *L'Évolution psychiatrique, 72.1*: 43–53.

Soler, C. (2007b). Une pratique sans bavardage (Nov. 2003). Colloque de la Fondation européenne de psychanalyse. In: A. Didier-Weill & M. Safouan (Eds.), *Travailler avec Lacan*. Paris: Aubier.

Soler, C. (2008a). Lacan réévalué par Lacan. In: *L'anthropologie structurale de Lévi-Strauss et la psychanalyse*. Paris: La Découverte.

Soler, C. (2008b). Le transfert, après. *Mensuel, École de Psychanalyse des Forums du Champ lacanien, France, 38*: 46–54.

Soler, C. (2008c). Lalangue, traumatique. *Revue des Collèges Cliniques du Champ lacanien, 7*: 195–205.

INDEX